GW01607395

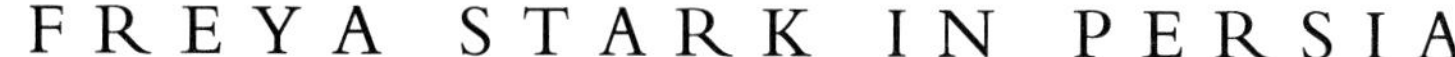

FREYA STARK IN PERSIA

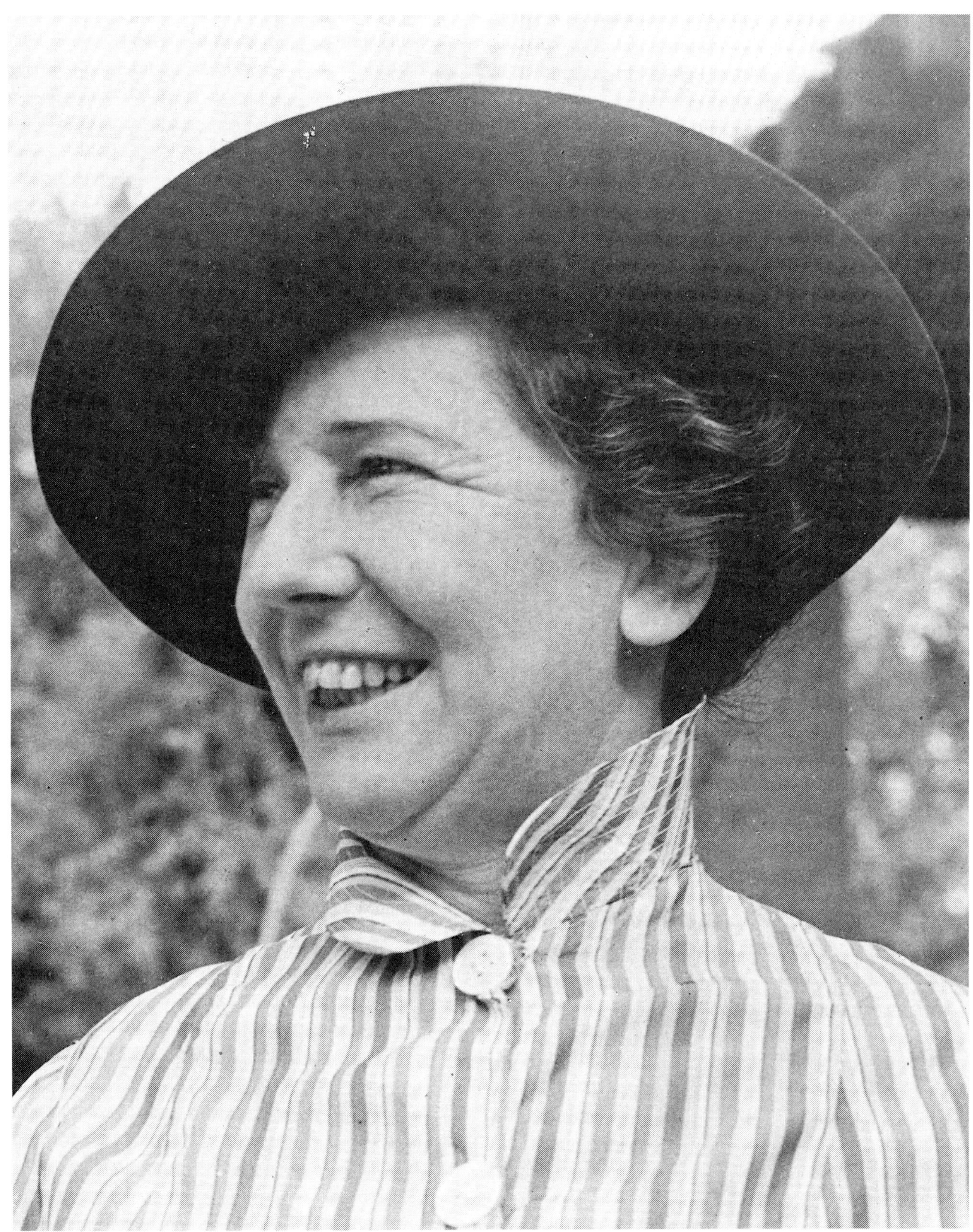

Freya Stark

THE ST ANTONY'S COLLEGE MIDDLE EAST ARCHIVES

MALISE RUTHVEN

FREYA STARK

IN PERSIA

GARNET PUBLISHING

First Edition

ISBN: 1 85964 011 7

British Library Cataloguing-in-Publication Data.
A catalogue record for this book is available from the British Library.

The photographs of Freya Stark on pages 2, 14 and 16 are reproduced courtesy of John Murray (Publishers) Ltd, with grateful thanks.

Design by Elizabeth van Amerongen.
Cover design by Arthur op den Brouw.
House editor Anna Watson
Typeset by Columns Ltd, Reading.
Reproduction by CCTS, London.
Printed in the Lebanon.

Published by Garnet Publishing Ltd,
8 Southern Court, South Street,
Reading RG1 4QS UK.

CONTENTS

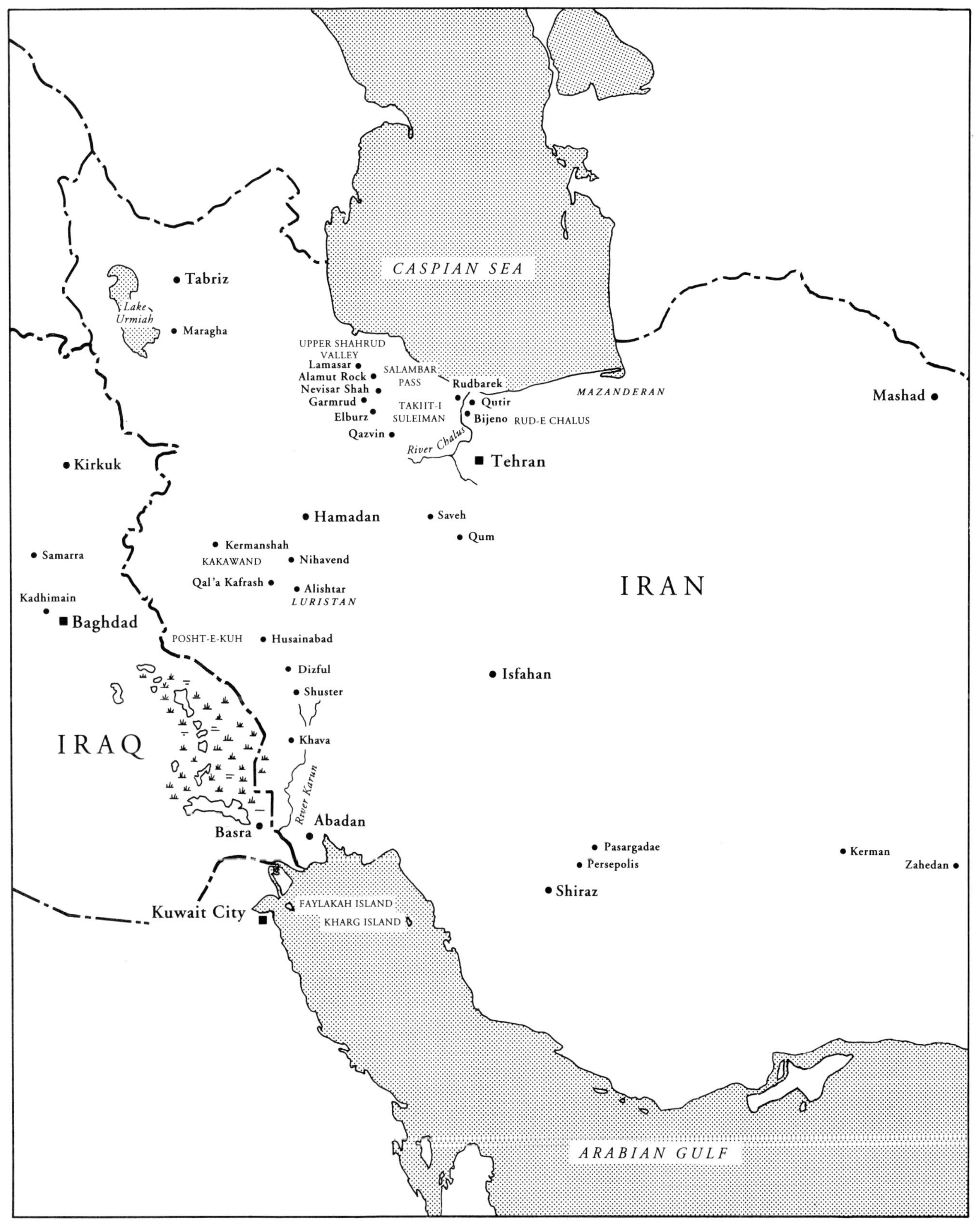

CASPIAN SEA
Tabriz
Lake Urmiah
Maragha
UPPER SHAHRUD VALLEY
Lamasar
Alamut Rock
Nevisar Shah
Garmrud
Elburz
Qazvin
SALAMBAR PASS
TAKHT-I SULEIMAN
Rudbarek
Qutir
Bijeno
RUD-E CHALUS
River Chalus
MAZANDERAN
Mashad
Tehran
Kirkuk
Hamadan
Saveh
Qum
Samarra
Kermanshah
KAKAWAND
Nihavend
Qal'a Kafrash
Alishtar
LURISTAN
IRAN
Kadhimain
Baghdad
POSHT-E-KUH
Husainabad
Dizful
Isfahan
Shuster
IRAQ
Khava
River Karun
Abadan
Basra
Pasargadae
Persepolis
Kerman
Zahedan
Shiraz
Kuwait City
FAYLAKAH ISLAND
KHARG ISLAND
ARABIAN GULF

INTRODUCTION

The idea of visiting Persia, to explore the ancient Ismaili castles in the Elburz mountains in Mazanderan, south of the Caspian Sea, had first taken shape in Freya Stark's mind in 1929, after the success of her expedition to the Jebel Druze in Syria. She wrote to her father in Canada: "I . . . have a good subject for the winter, if only it hasn't been exhaustively done already, and that is to combine a sort of history with travel notes to the fortresses of the Assassins, who were the followers of the Old Man of the Mountain and had a series of castles between Aleppo and the Persian borders. I am very vague about it all, but am trying to find out something more before going out. It seems to me rather promising, although it may all have been done by some thorough-going German already!"

During a visit to London she read the famous accounts by Marco Polo and von Hammer-Purgstall which described how the Assassins – an offshoot of the Ismaili branch of the Shi'a – adopted a secret agenda of world destruction, spreading terror throughout the Near East. Their leader was Hassan-i Sabbah, the legendary Old Man of the Mountain, who was supposed to have lured young devotees into his garden and drugged them with hashish before sending them out on missions of murder, providing the English language with the word 'assassin' (from the Arabic *hashshashin*, 'hashish-takers'). The story was always improbable. Terrorism, whether conducted with the knife or the bullet, demands a cool brain and a steady hand, and cannabis produces neither. Modern scholars, relying on newly discovered Ismaili manuscripts, have dismissed it as fabrication. Ironically, the scholarship which shows the Ismailis in a much more positive light, became available in the 1930s, just after Freya had completed her research for the journeys that would be recorded in *Valleys of the Assassins*.

It is doubtful, however, if Freya's desire to visit the Ismaili stronghold would have been dampened if she had studied the work of revisionist historians. The story appealed strongly to her romantic nature, and was interesting even without its narcotic embellishments. Alamut – until its destruction in 1256 by the armies of Hulagu, the grandson of Genghis Khan –

had been the headquarters of the Nizaris, a militant sect of the Ismailis who defended themselves against their enemies, the Crusaders and the Seljuk Turks, in a remarkably humane way. Knowing that medieval armies, particularly the Seljuk bands, were bound to their commanders by ties of personal allegiance, they concentrated their efforts on killing the leaders, causing the semi-nomadic groups to dissolve. Hassan-i Sabbah, who with his Syrian counterparts may have given rise to the legend of the Old Man of the Mountain, was really a philosopher-king whose enlightened version of Islam scandalized the pious. One of his successors even went so far as to proclaim the "Day of Resurrection", declaring the Divine Law of Islam to be suspended. The fast of Ramadan was abandoned, and wine is said to have flowed through the valley. Though the Nizaris later reverted to more orthodox practices, their reputation as dangerous radicals remained – at least until their latter-day Imams, the Aga Khans, established themselves in Europe and adopted the manners and customs of its aristocracy.

Unlike Syria and Iraq, where the Europeans were well protected, Persia in 1930 had come under a new government, only recently recovering from years of lawlessness. The new regime owed its toughness to Reza Shah Pahlavi, a former Cossack sergeant who seized the Peacock Throne in 1925. "Everyone speaks wonders of the Shah and the immense changes he has made to the safety of the country and its general prosperity," Freya wrote from Hamadan in April. Her own opinion, however, was more ambivalent: "I can't make out whether this new Persian regime is doing very well or very badly. The British business people here are very down on it. They are playing about with the currency and lowering the price of bread arbitrarily and so on, so that all business with the outside world seems at a standstill. The people on the other hand seem really enthusiastic, and there is perfect safety and a real look of national feeling."

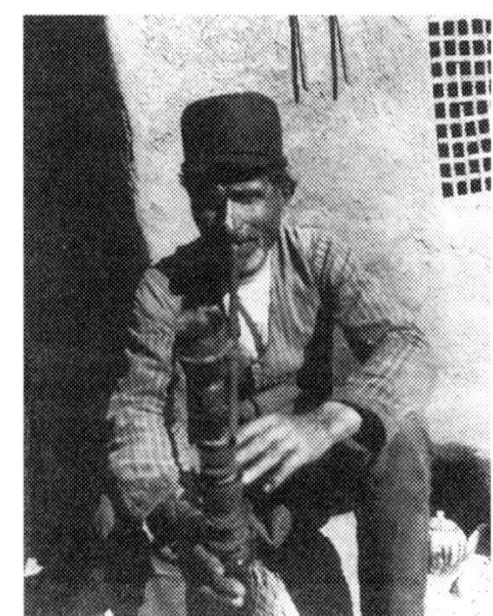
Tribesman with hookah and Pahlavi cap 1930

An illiterate autocrat, Reza Shah used strong-arm methods to force his people into adopting what he supposed were the indispensable practices of the twentieth century. His modernizing programme, however, failed to distinguish between the substance of modernity and its outward appearance. To weld his Kurdish, Turkish, Azeri, Lur, Baluchi, Arabic- and Farsi-speaking subjects into a unified homogeneous whole, he abolished local particularities of dress, requiring men to adopt

European clothes and the women to throw off the *chador*, the "veil" or nun-like habit worn by townswomen in public. Special attention was paid to headgear, traditional marks of ethnic or sectarian distinction in Islamic societies. Men from all backgrounds were required to adopt the round-peaked Pahlavi cap. The Shi'ite clergy, who were ordered to remove their distinctive cloaks and turbans, strongly resisted these changes, and developed a hostility to the Pahlavi dynasty's Westernizing agenda that would eventually bring it down. Half a century later, during the clergy-led revolution of Ayatollah Khomeini, the *chador* had its revenge when women were forced to readopt it.

In Persia, Freya's romantic soul found an affinity with people who seemed to prefer poverty with freedom to sub-colonial affluence. "In some subtle way", she told her father, "there was a pleasant sense of freedom after the efficient machinery" of British-run Iraq. "It makes one realise more than ever that people *prefer* their own muddles to other people's efficiency." Despite her admiration for Reza Shah, she had reservations about his sartorial reforms, which she observed at first hand. "The police show a government letter that says they must all take to European clothes in five days time," she wrote from Luristan. "Two handsome wild-looking Lurs come along, one hatless: his felt cap had been seized and torn to bits, to impress the fact that Pahlavi hats are now in fashion. I suppose it's all right to civilise people, but it is a horrid process."

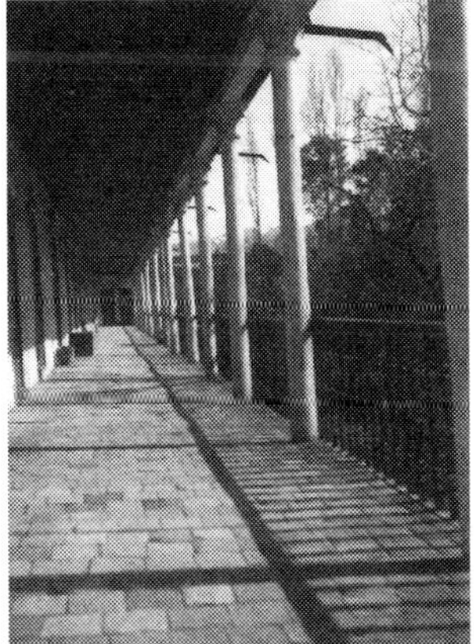

Hotel de France
Hamadan 1930

Before venturing into the mountains, Freya spent a month improving her Farsi in Hamadan, staying at the Hotel de France, "a lovely old Persian house in a walled garden full of blossoming trees." At 6000 feet the landscape, with its poplars and snowy ridges, reminded her of Northern Italy. The people obviously belonged "to our family, only wild because of the strange felt hats and black locks sticking out on either side." Her teacher, a mullah who had spent forty years teaching American missionaries, became very friendly when Freya explained that she preferred Muslim traditions to Christian evangelical piety. Texts from the Koran were interspersed with her lessons, along with "all sorts of odd bits of superstition: how the wives of Hamadan poison their husbands with wolf-fat; and the 121,000 [*sic*] prophets that have tried to improve the world since it began; and the wickedness of the present generation."

"Once again I was right and the experts who have been years out here wrong," she told her mother. "They told me the Koran was no use now for getting into touch with people. If I had not known the Koran and been able to talk to the old man from his own standpoint, he would never have started all these tales. The Koran has been their one source of inspiration for centuries: it is their background – and however Europeanised they may be, one is sure to get nearer to them really if one comes at them from behind as it were, through the things they knew as children, or that their parents and nurses knew, than if one comes through the medium of a new civilisation . . ."

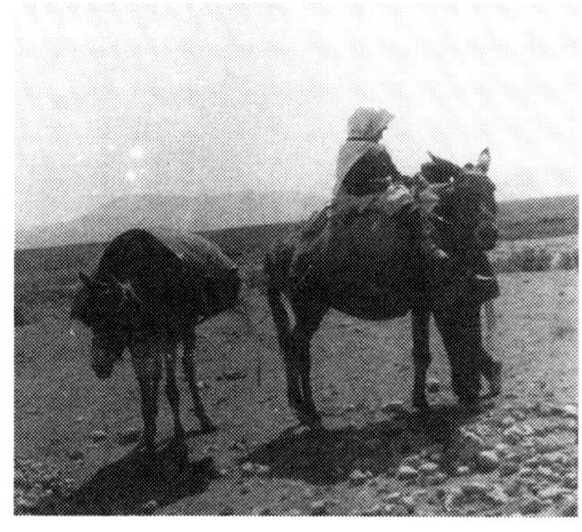
The Way to Alamut 1930

By the middle of May she felt confident enough in her language to set out with her muleteers for Alamut. The Persians, she reported, including the police, thought "nothing could be more natural and commendable that one should travel from London to visit the castle of Hassan-i Sabbah, and look upon me as a sort of religious pilgrim with great respect." With a characteristic rhetorical flourish she compared her experience to Xenophon reaching the Hellespont or Cortes the Pacific "and every adventurer and pilgrim, however humble, before them or after". "The thing which has been living in your imagination suddenly becomes a part of the tangible world. It matters not how many ranges, rivers or parching dusty ways may lie between you: it is yours now for ever." A certain breathless naïvety shines through her letters. When she inquired about the garden where Hassan-i Sabbah was supposed to have drugged his devotees, she allowed one of the locals to persuade her that he knew the exact location – some distance from the Rock, about 11,000 feet up near one of the passes. The place was still under snow, and would not be clear for another two months. "I got so excited I felt my fingers *trembling.* Ever since I went up to the castle and indeed came into the valley I have felt there must be a good deal in the old legend . . ."

Freya returned to the valleys the following year, in August 1931, to explore the castle of Lamasar, the last of the Ismaili strongholds to hold out against the armies of Hulagu. It was a bad season to travel. Her muleteer 'Aziz was held up by the illness of his son. Eventually, when Freya's message got to him, he sent the animals with a servant, Ismail, whom Freya found "simply hopeless for his stupidity". They found the castle, but the valleys were alive with mosquitoes. Freya succumbed, first to dysentery, then to malaria. The local people recommended a small *Imamzadeh* (a shrine dedicated to one of the Imams), and here, above the infested valley, she eventually recovered her strength.

The experience, however, shook her: not for the last time, she found herself far from medical help, and believed she was going to die. A doctor was summoned from five hours' ride away. He spent the afternoon with her, smoking opium and drinking spirits, and tried to reassure her by telling her the disease was nothing out of the ordinary. Serious illness, before antibiotics and vaccines were generally available, was one of the hazards of travelling in remote regions and on several occasions, according to her own account, Freya hovered at death's door. Yet living as she did to 100, she must have had an unusually robust constitution. Perhaps her exposure to illnesses toughened her. Perhaps she exaggerated their severity. I suspect that the qualities that made her such a fine travel writer – a vivid imagination, a sensitivity finely tuned to the spirit of people and places – also made her something of a hypochondriac. Whatever the case, part of the secret of her writing was the way she invited readers to share her vulnerability, the more to admire her courage for overcoming it.

On reaching Tehran in September 1931 she received the news of the death of her father in Canada. She had visited him the previous year, and though sad for herself, she was relieved that he had been spared a lengthy illness. A happy letter from him, written a month before his death, brought comfort. The financial news that Britain had left the gold standard was also bad, knowing as she must that her income would fall. Never one to dwell on adversity, she immediately set about trying to turn her luck. Instead of moping, she let the prospect of buried treasure draw her to Luristan.

Freya's travels in Mazanderan and Luristan provided her with her first public recognition. Impressed by her maps and an article she had written in its *Journal* the Royal Geographical Society awarded her the Back Memorial Prize in June 1933. The following year she became the first woman to receive the Royal Asiatic Society's Burton Memorial Medal. More significantly, these successes led to a commission for a book with the prestigious house of Murray in London, one of the oldest names in British publishing. *The Valleys of the Assassins,* the account of her Persian travels, was an instant success. Reprinted three times within six months of its publication in May 1934, it is still in print, having earned its place in the canon of travel literature. In the 1980s, when Freya was in her nineties, the Italian translation won the Alberto Moravia award. Only Vladimir Ivanow, doyen of modern Ismaili studies, sounded a slightly jarring note. In his book on Alamut and Lamasar, published in Tehran 1960 he remarks: "I hope I shall not be impolite to 'Madmasel', as she is still remembered in Alamut, if I express genuine regret that her eminently readable and entertaining book . . . when so many times reprinted, was never revised, and errors corrected. Surely, this would not take much time, especially to delete her rather outrageous excursions into the history of the Isma'ilis."

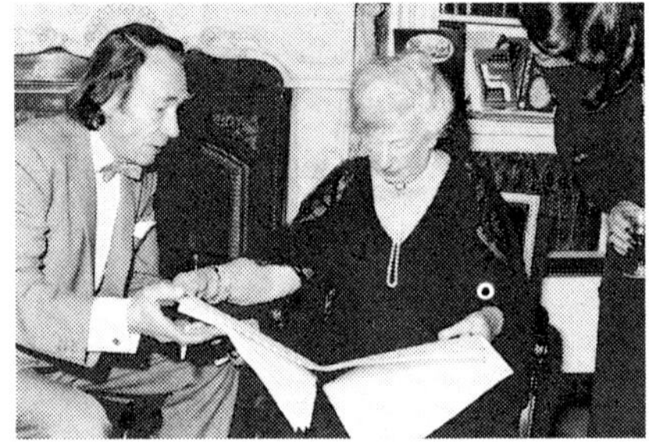
Freya Stark with Jock Murray in London c 1980

The book not only established Freya as a travel writer, it inaugurated a partnership with Jock Murray that would last until her death at the age of 100 in May 1993. Eighteen years her junior, Jock became her literary adviser and intimate friend. Murray's elegant office in Mayfair, with its portraits of Lord Byron, epitomized the respectable end of British publishing. It became her headquarters in England, the launching pad for numerous expeditions and the centre of her social network. At the age of forty, Freya Stark had finally "arrived".

It would be nine years before she would return to Iran after her trip to Luristan. Her travels from 1935 until the outbreak of war were mainly in Southern Arabia. Her work as a propagandist for the Ministry of Information took her to Cairo in 1940 and then to Baghdad. A visit to Isfahan in the spring of 1941 had to be abandoned when the Iraqi crisis erupted [see *Freya Stark in Iraq and Kuwait*]. She had gone to Tehran for consultations with Sir Reader Bullard, the British Minister. Persia, like Turkey, had remained neutral after the outbreak of hostilities. But the British, mindful of the importance of Iraqi oil supplies for their military effort in North Africa, were becoming increasingly nervous of Axis influence. With Greece being evacuated and the Germans advancing towards Egypt, there seemed every likelihood that Reza Shah would throw in his lot with the Axis. "The general feeling of the country", Freya confided to her diary on 28 April, "is that of a rabbit hypnotised by a snake – we are not masters of events and things have gone beyond ordinary methods. None of the two thousand or more technicians of the Axis here are over thirty-five."

On 22 June Hitler invaded Russia and the Soviet Union entered the war. Iranian neutrality, and the presence of German technicians, were now major obstacles between the British and their new allies in the East. The Allies demanded a reduction in the number of Germans; when the Shah failed to comply, the British and Russians invaded his country forcing him to abdicate in favour of his twenty-two-year-old son Muhammad Reza. Under the Tripartite Treaty of Alliance signed in January 1942 Britain and the USSR undertook to "respect the territorial integrity, sovereignty and political independence of Persia" and to defend it from aggression. The Persian government for its part granted the Allies unrestricted means of communications.

Freya's second journey through Persia during the war was the occasion of an episode that appears to have earned her some black marks with her employers in the British government. In March 1943 she was invited to spend her leave with Lord Wavell, former Commander-in-Chief of the British forces in Egypt, who had become Viceroy of India. At that time transport and petrol were in very short supply. However, she managed to obtain from Wavell a special permit to purchase a car and drive it from Delhi to Baghdad – on the clear understanding that when the vehicle arrived at its destination it would enter the Embassy car pool. Johnny Hawtrey, a former Inspector of the Iraqi Air Force now attached to the RAF, used up his leave to act as her driver. Setting off from Quetta, they reached Mashad after driving for several days across Baluchistan over gravel roads protected by the Indian Army and kept going by constant infusions of gravel, while teams of "bearded men with rakes and flowing rag garments keep the spiky stones fresh and lively for the cars that deal with Russia in the North." At Mashad, where they spent a few days as guests of the British Consul, they discovered the road to Tehran was blocked by floods that would take several days to subside. Instead of waiting, as they had been advised, Freya insisted on returning to Zahedan, on the borders of India, taking the southern route to Tehran by way of Kerman. It was a detour of some 1200 miles, but it allowed her at last to visit Isfahan.

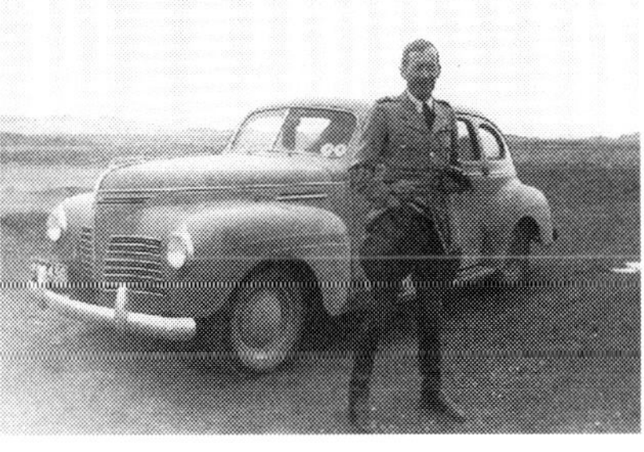

Johnny Hawtrey with the official car Freya sold in 1943

When they eventually arrived in Tehran she lost no time in selling the car at a 500 per cent profit through a private deal arranged by the chauffeur of her diplomatic hosts. The latter were understandably surprised, but to their astonished inquiries she gave no answer, disclaiming any awareness of transgression. When tackled later by her chief at the Ministry of Information in Cairo, she simply smiled her quizzical little-girl smile: "But I put all the money into War Loan!"

Freya Stark's biographer, Molly Izzard, suggests that the incident may have cost her a career in the Foreign Office after the war. Sir Reader Bullard "let it be known quietly that he did not want to see Freya about his Embassy again". During her wartime employment she had learned to appreciate the advantages of earning a regular salary, and given her distinguished record of employment in the Ministry of Information during the war, and for a period afterwards by the Foreign Office in Italy, she had reason to suppose that a permanent post might be found for her. In the event, her contract with the Foreign Office was not to be renewed. The unofficial explanation was that she was "too old" (in 1947, she was fifty-four). But Sir Reader Bullard's comments cannot have helped.

If Molly Izzard's inference is correct, Bullard did Freya a service. Despite her success in wartime, Freya was not made for the official life. She loathed the petty snobberies of the British expatriates she met in Iraq and Aden. During her brief marriage to Stewart Perowne she champed at the duties of an official wife. At times of emergency, improvisers like Freya tend to thrive; in normal times their very qualities disrupt the flow of ordinary routine. Her talents were too eclectic and her sympathies too broad to be comfortably merged with the interests of a disintegrating empire. It was better for her, and far better for her readers, that her imperial imagination was allowed to range over times and spaces untrammelled by the shabby, mundane facts of imperial business. At the Foreign Office she would have been, at best, a middle-sized cog in a large, rather antiquated machine. Mounted on a mule, or poised above the beautifully crafted circular desk made for her in Asolo, she had the world at her feet.

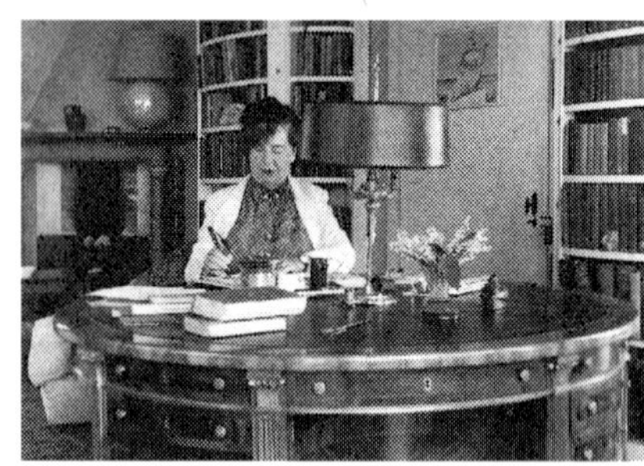

Freya at her desk in Asolo c 1960

JOURNEY TO ALAMUT

Freya set out for the ancient Ismaili fortress of Alamut, "the Place of Eagles", in May 1930, with two muleteers, 'Aziz and Elias. Starting from Qazvin, the party climed the 10,000-foot Chala pass through hills of flowering thorns, and followed the Alamut River into the almost impregnable valley. "The whole place gives one the feeling that, walking down into it, you are in a closed place shut off from all the world". Arriving at the head of the valley, where they stayed with a doctor's family, they saw the castle rock standing out from the mountain "like a ship broadside on". As they approached it, walking up the Alamut valley from the south, the great rock continued to dominate the view. "The castle rock is always in sight," she wrote, "and as you come near you see what a magnificent position it was: romantic isn't the word. It holds the enormous fortified valley, overlooking it from one end to the other over the lower ranges, across the tilted pasture-desert to the snowy range of Elburz and his brother peaks."

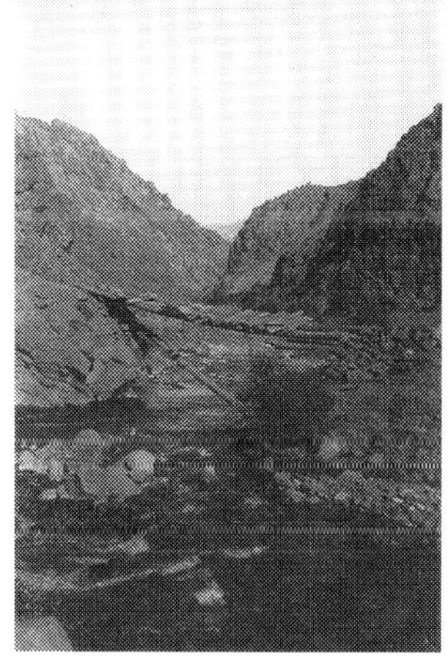

Collapsed bridge near Garmrud 1930

Freya inspected what was left of the castle – fragments of buttresses, walls and tunnels, evidently just a completion of the magnificent natural defences. There were shards of blue-glazed pottery dating from the Mongul period, but otherwise few signs of human habitation after more than six centuries. Freya and her guides retraced their path to the entrance of the valley, and then headed south-east along the Alamut river to Garmrud, where they climbed to the Assassin castle of Nevisar Shah. The whole region had an idyllic, medieval quality – "village touching village with dark green fields of corn and little terraced lakes where the baby rice is growing". The peasants in their round felt caps and tight waistcoats reminded her of the figures from Italian frescoes. "I can *see* how the story of the Assassins really was," she told her mother. "I can see the life here in the valley and the devotion of their people, and the remoteness from all the world." From Nevisar Shah they turned north and proceeded down through narrow wooded valleys of tall trees and rushing streams that reminded her of the Pyrenees; until they reached the Caspian Sea, lying quiet and grey beyond a brightly coloured belt of paddy fields, oranges and flowering pomegranates whose colours resembled the lacquer on a Japanese tray.

On her second visit to Mazanderan the following year, in August 1931, Freya made some maps of the region, having received instruction from the Royal Geographical Society in London. She visited a third Assassin castle, Lamiasar, or Lamasar, known but hitherto unidentified. This castle, perched above a high ravine, was inaccesssible to mules, and Freya had to scramble up to the summit in her stockinged feet. At the village of Garmrud, which she had visited the previous year, she attended three weddings, and watched as the brides were fetched by the young men on their horses. "The thing is to show reluctance, the bride only appears the fourth time or so, and then the little procession goes out round the cornfields across the river, the bride completely hidden in her blue chadur and held on her horse by her brother." Shaken by a bout of dysentery, she abandoned plans to climb the 15,000-foot Takht-i Suleiman (the Throne of Solomon), the third highest summit in Persia. Instead she contemplated the peaks from the 11,000-foot Salambar pass, before descending through densely forested valleys where chalet-like houses, with balconies and jutting eaves designed for ornament as well as comfort, suggested "an old prosperity". The "Jungalis" who dwelt near the coast wore thick felt capes or *shaulars* with dummy sleeves to keep off the Caspian rain.

Freya reported that she lost many of her pictures on this journey: "A terrible fate pursues my photos – my three best films all spoilt: I nearly wept."

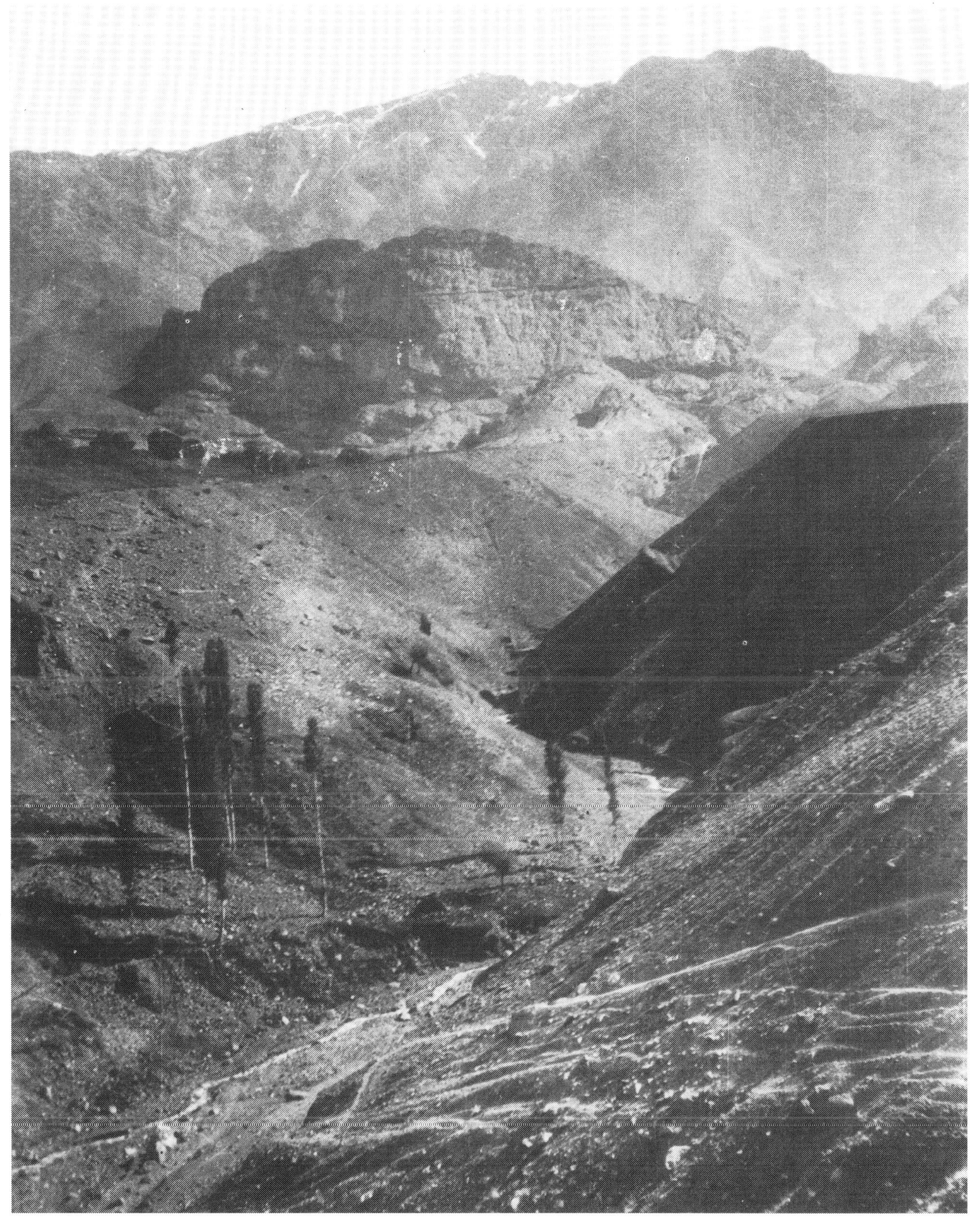

The Alamut Rock (Qal'a'i Gazur-khan) from the south 1930

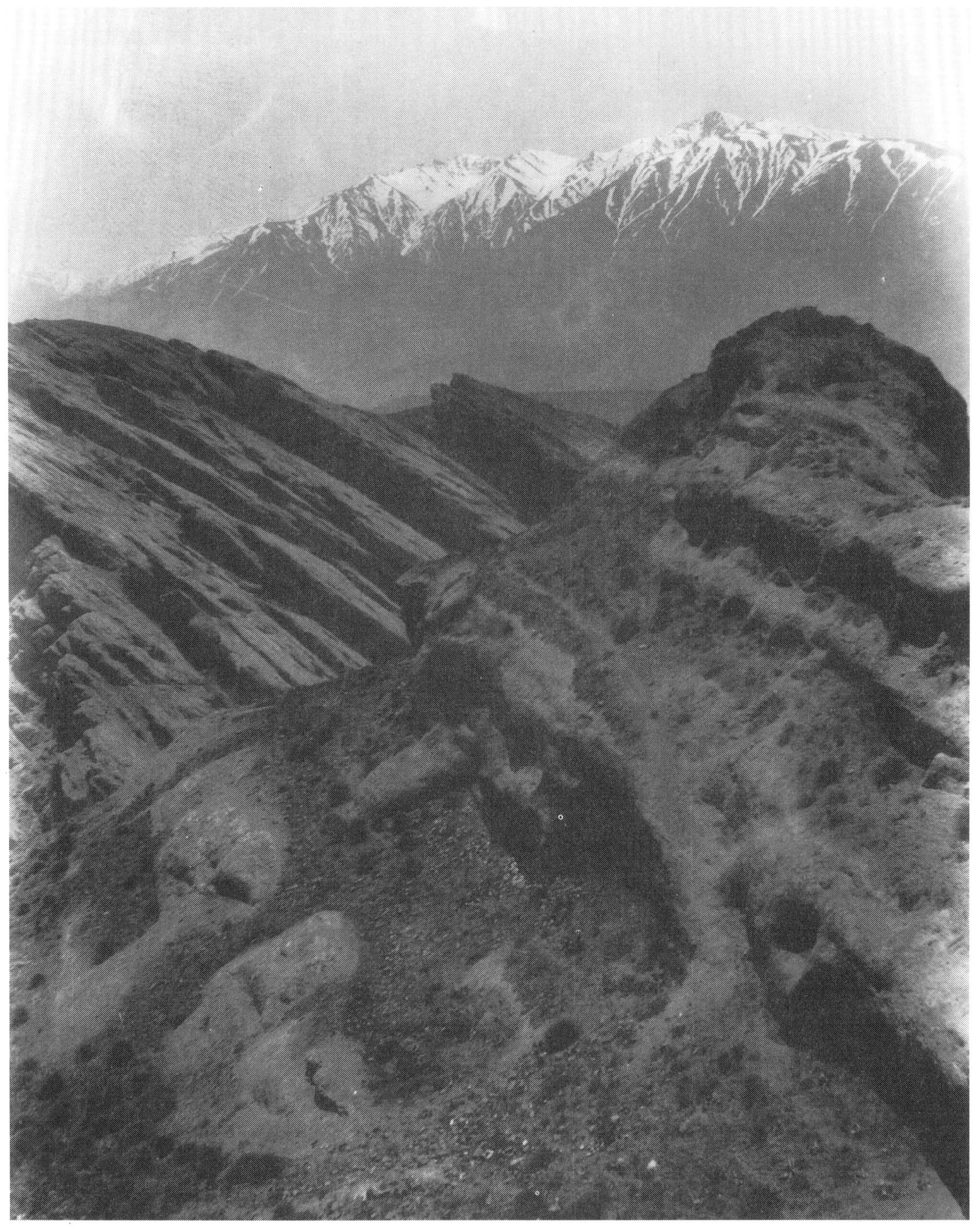

Alamut: eastern side of the Rock 1930

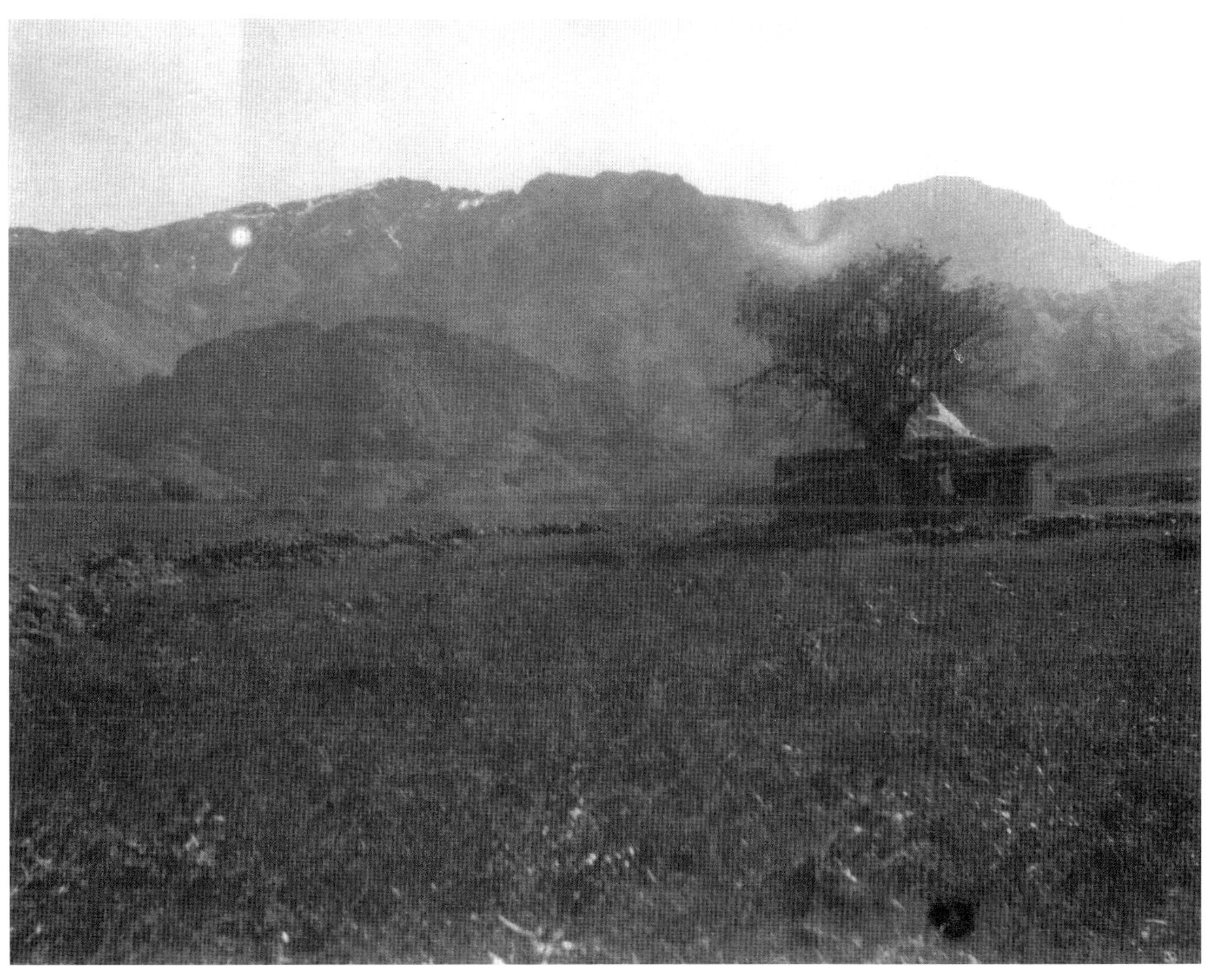

Alamut Rock and *Imamzadeh* 1930

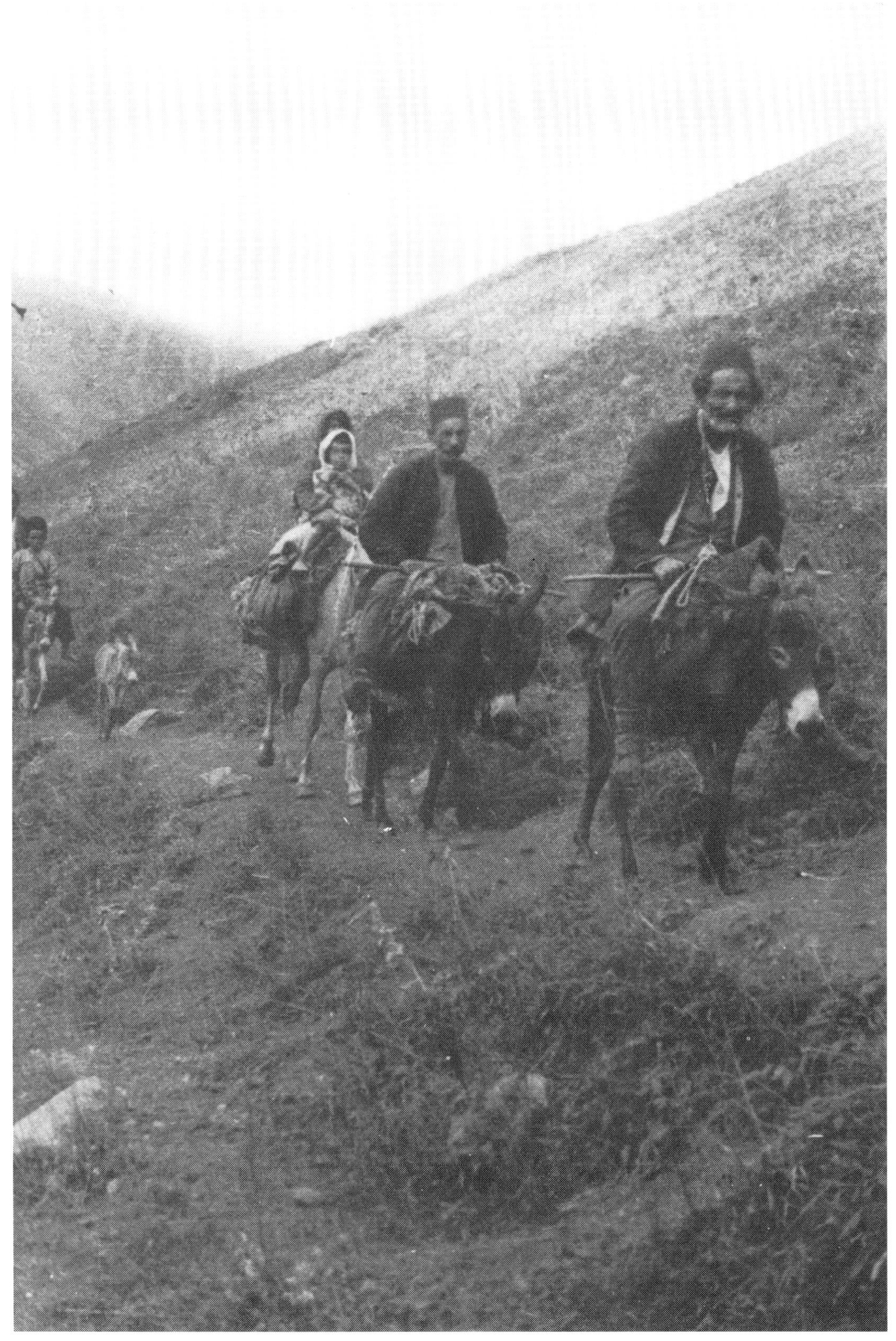

Pilgrims, Upper Sardabrud 1931

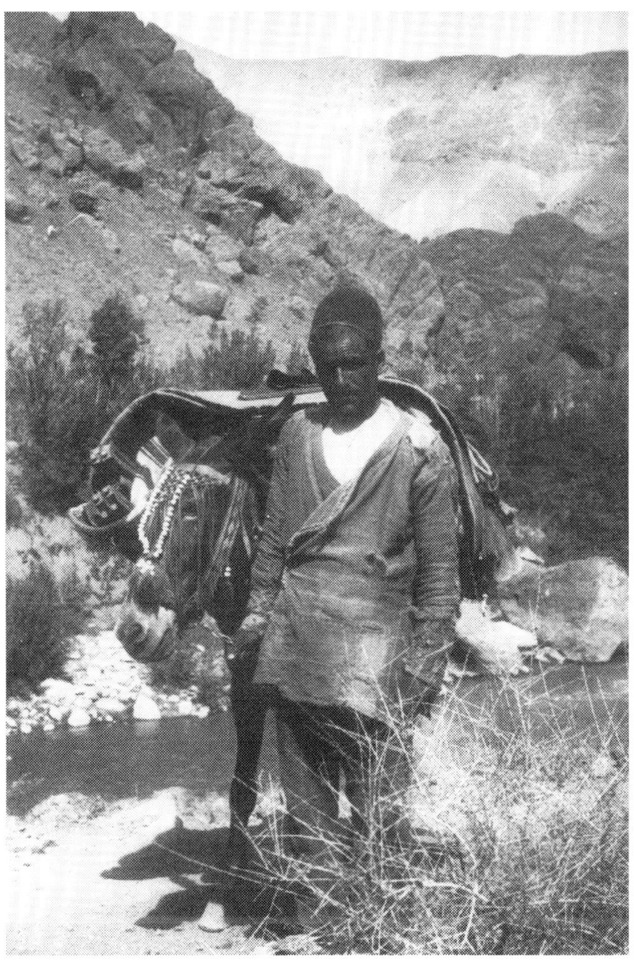

Ismail, Freya's muleteer 1931

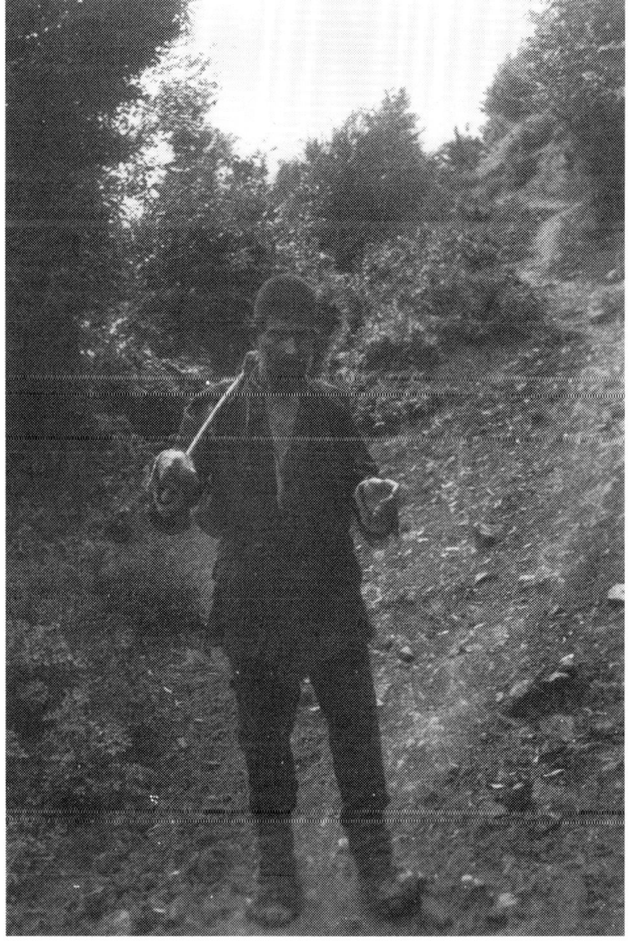

Chalus woodman 1931

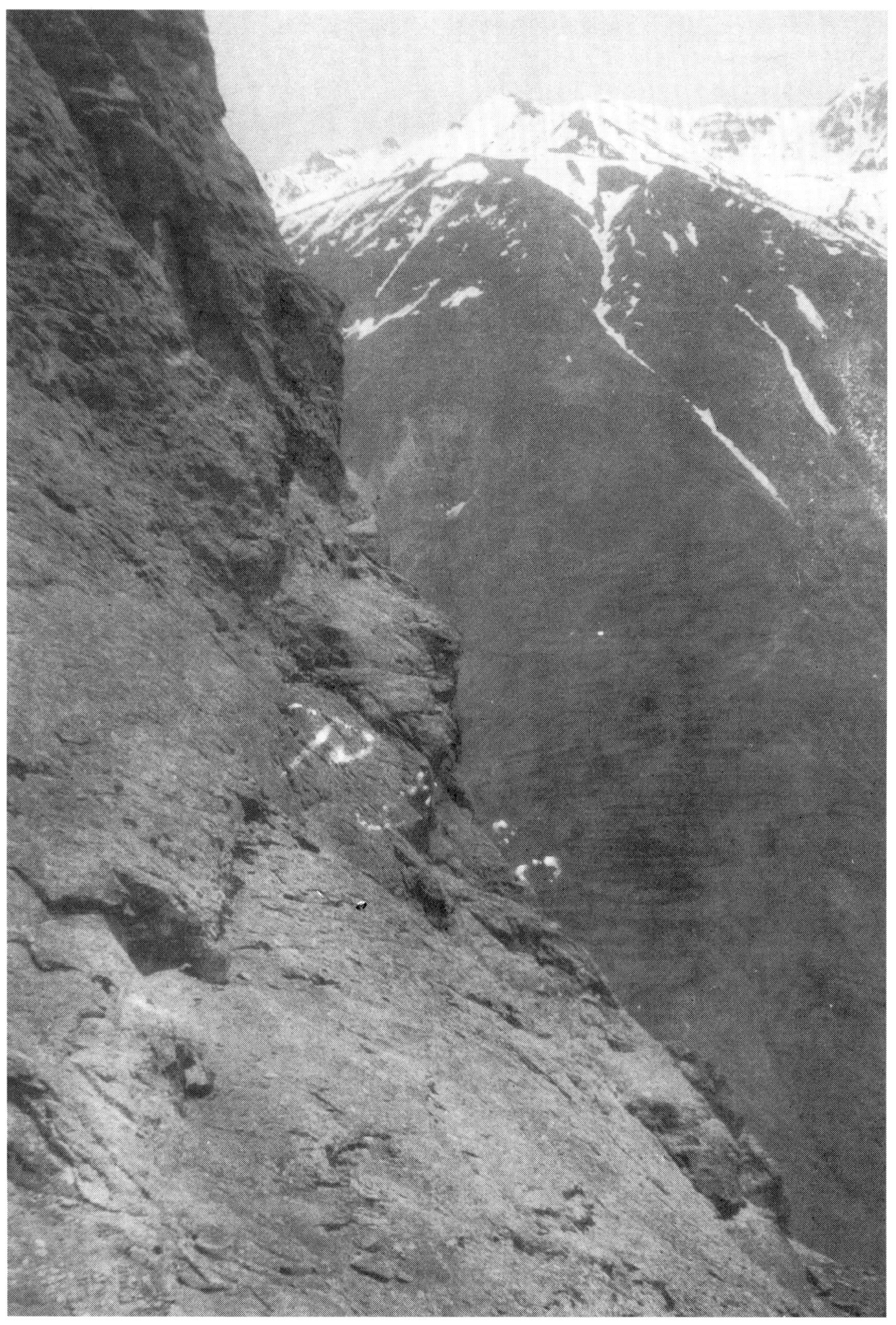

Descent from Nevisar Shah 1930

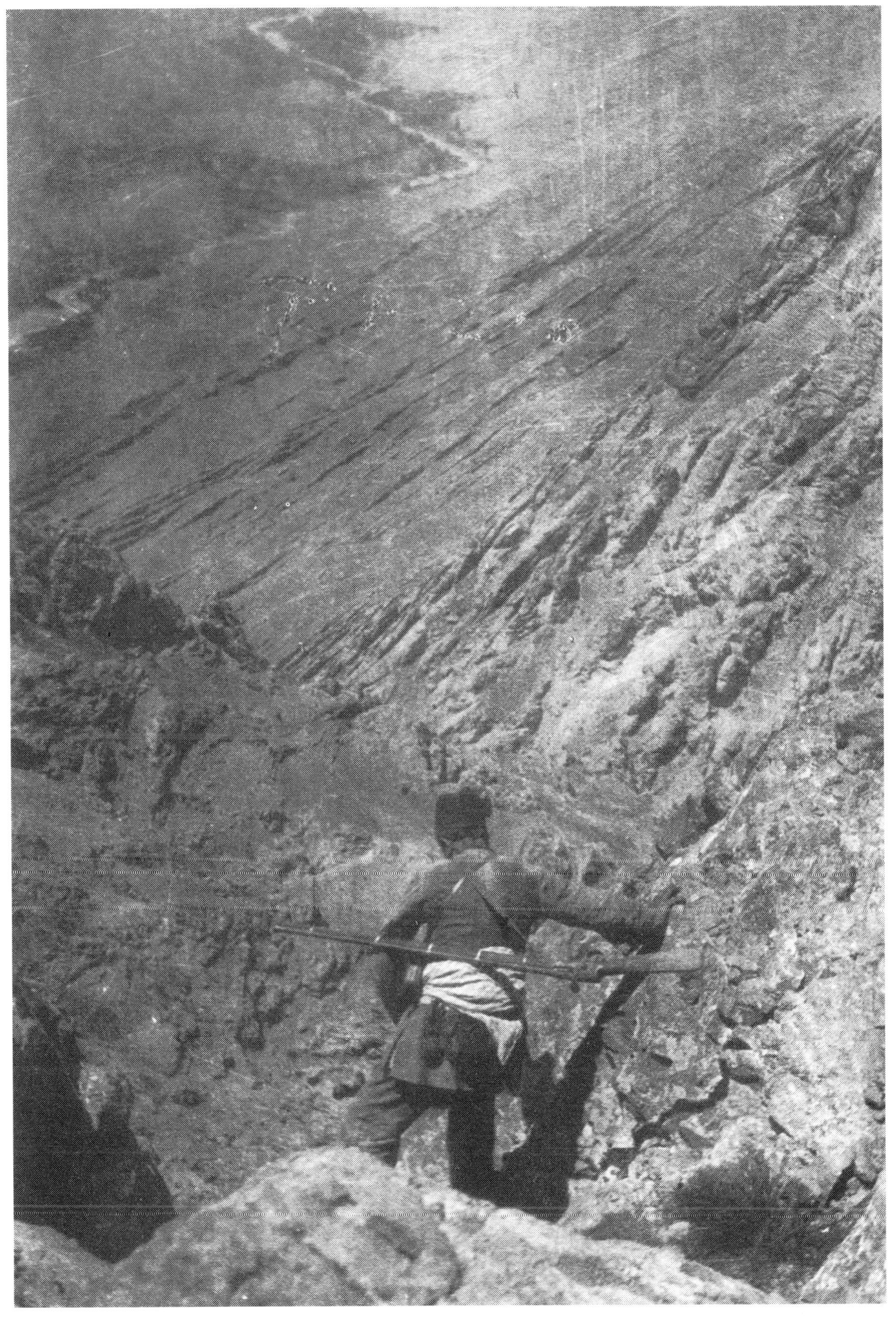

Descent from Nevisar Shah 1930

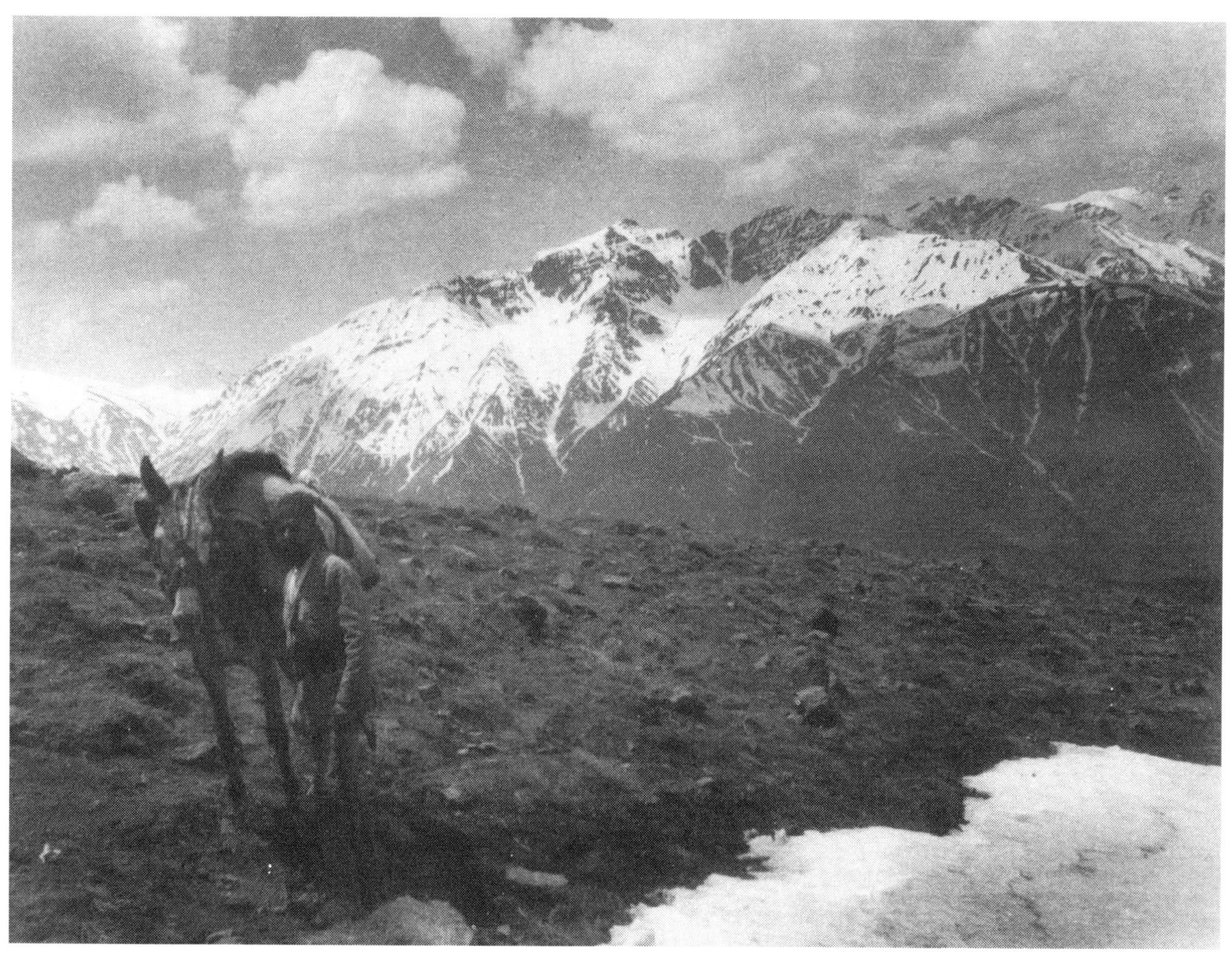

Elburz from Salambar 1931

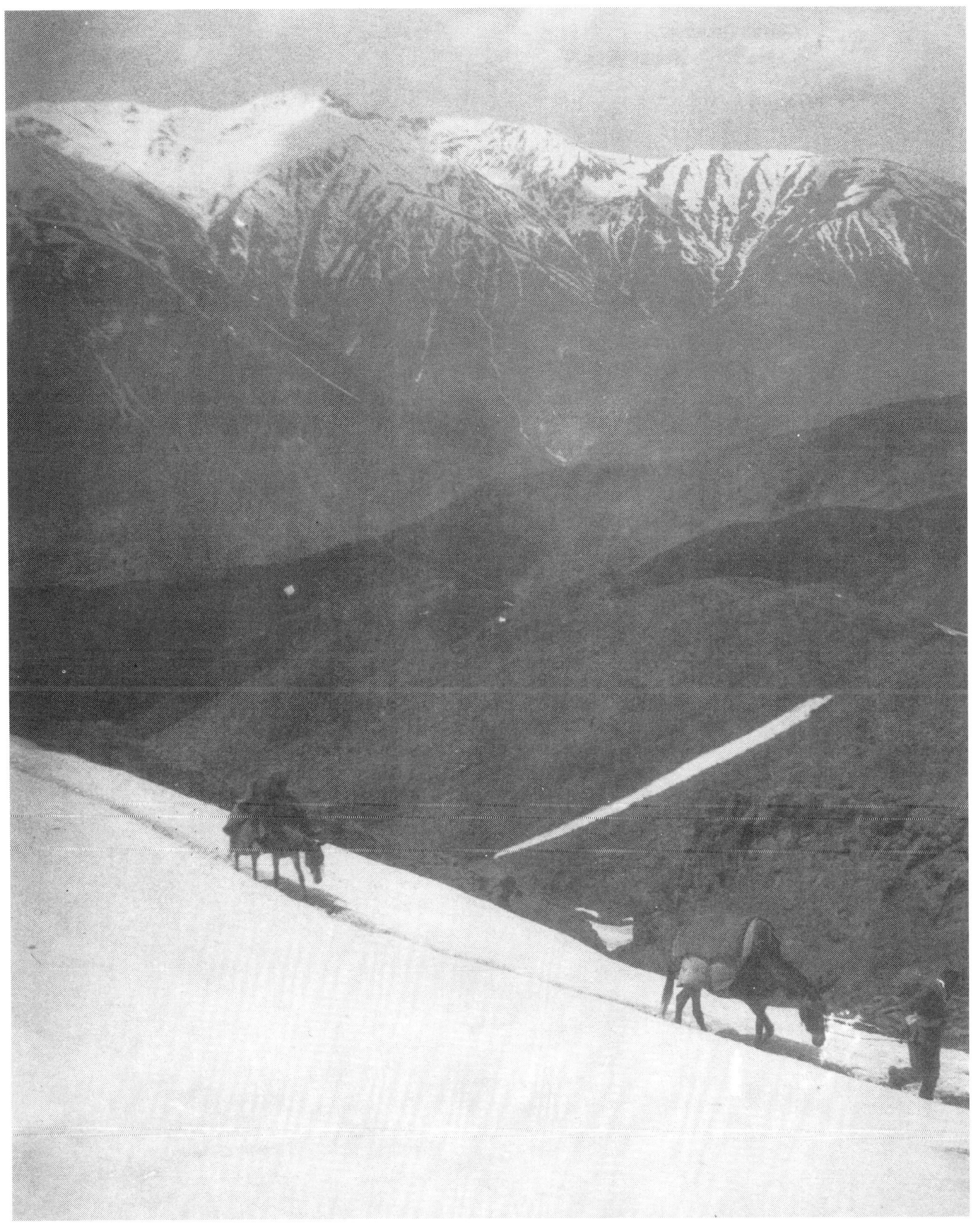

Salambar Pass 1931

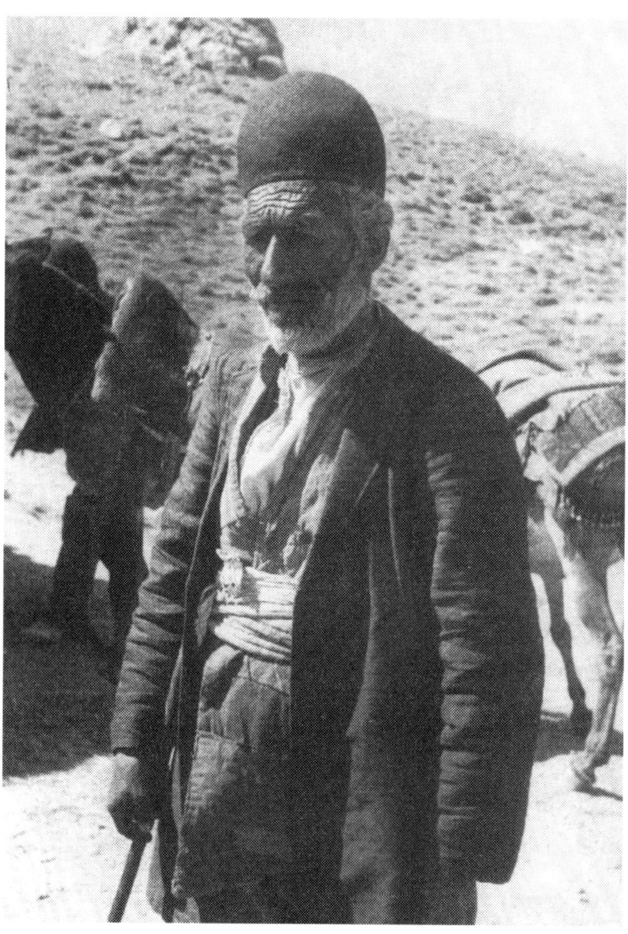

"Keeper of the Pass: owner of a small hut where muleteers stop to drink on the Shirabash Pass over the Elburz" 1930

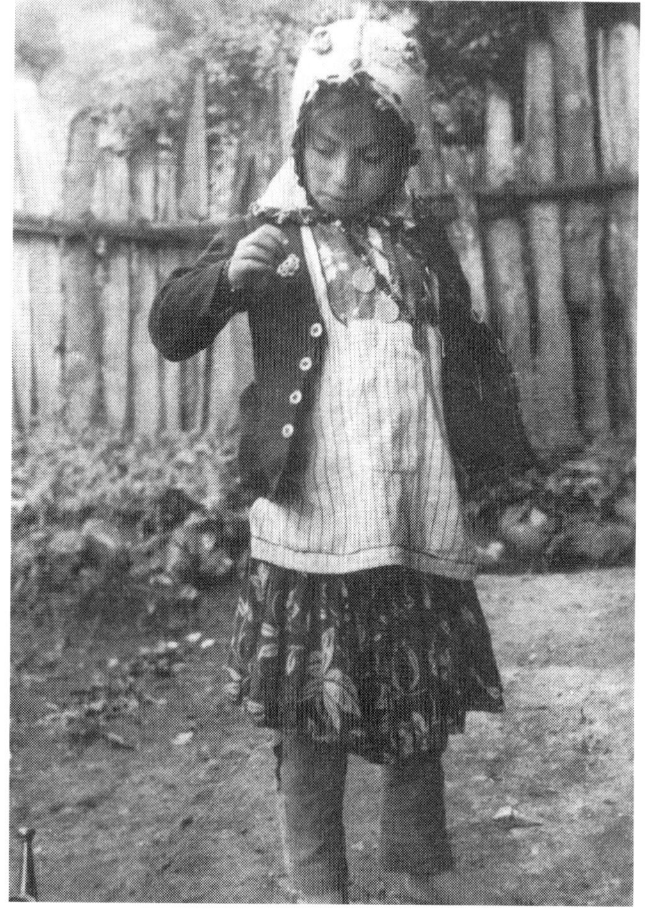

Girl, Bijeno, Kalar Dasht 1931

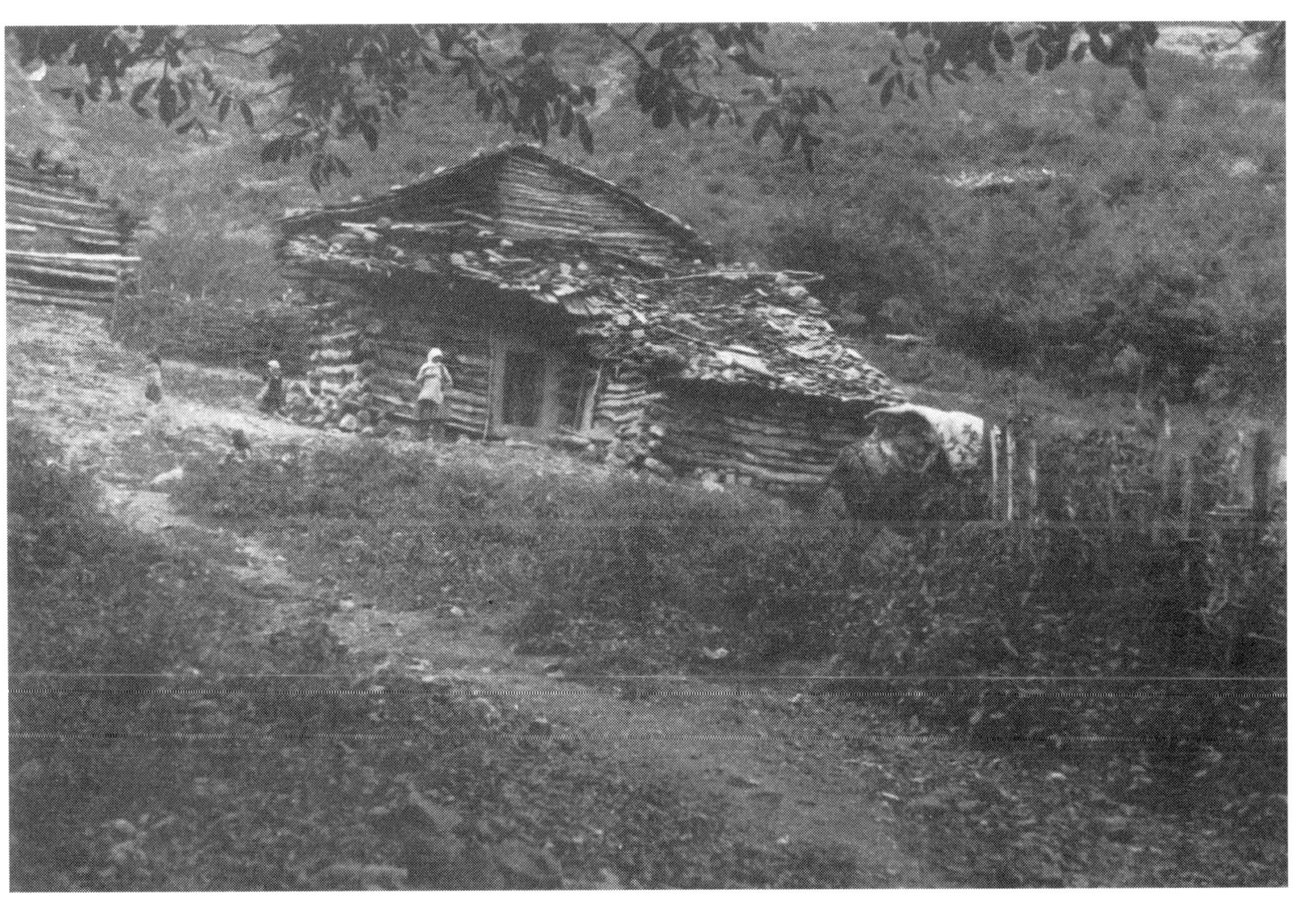

"They winter in wooden houses." Qutir, Chalus Valley 1931

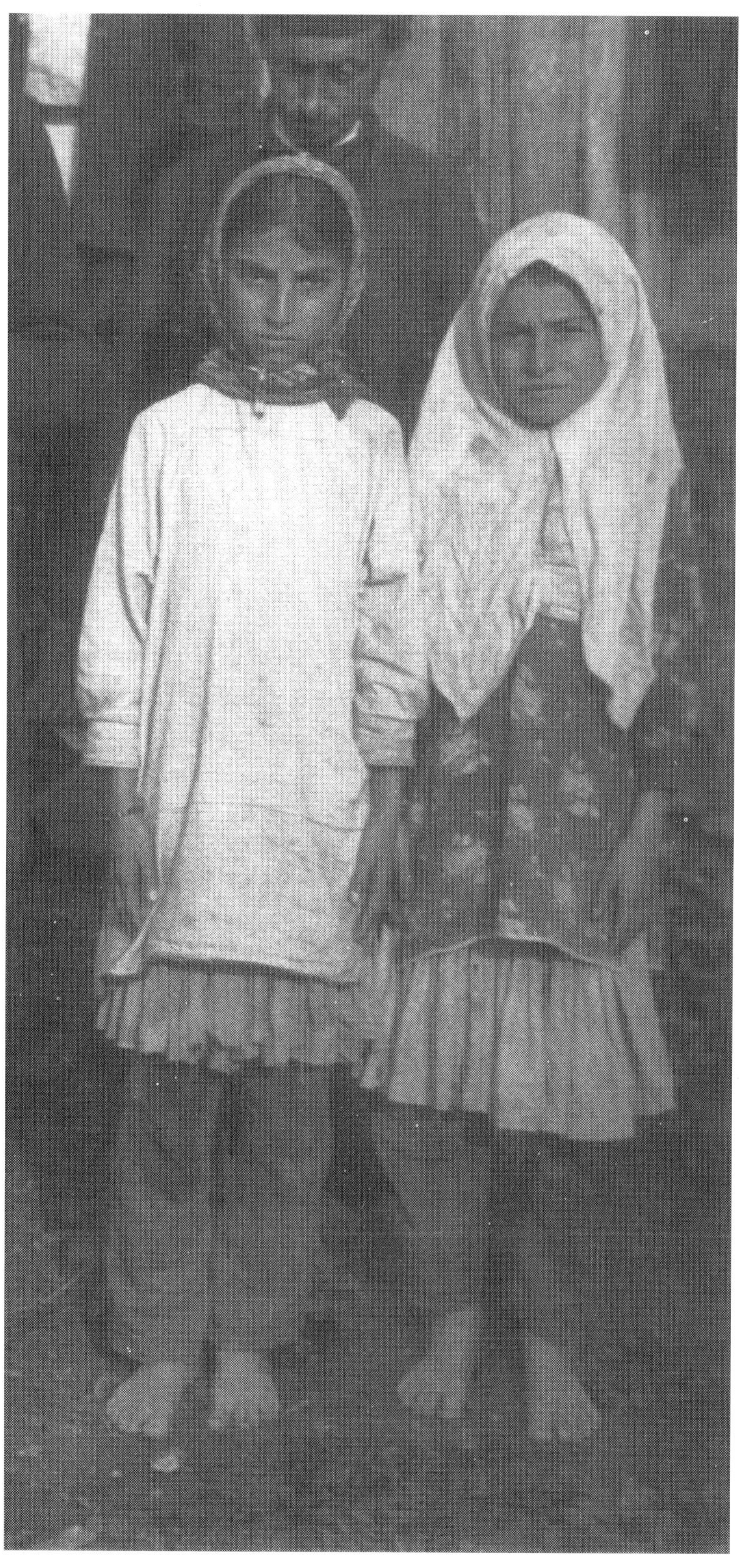

Unidentified girls, probably Kurds from Rudbarek 1931

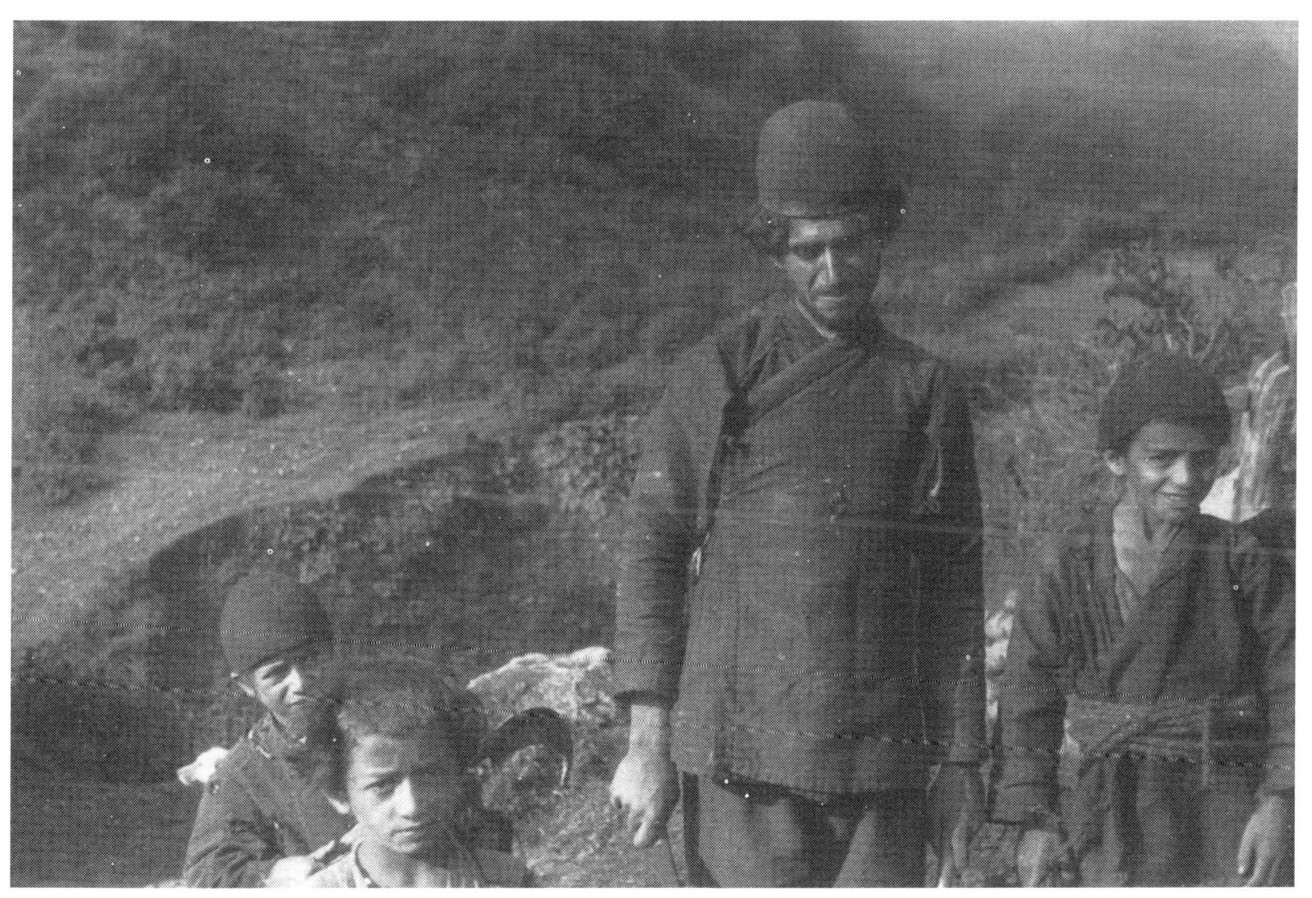

Bijeno man and boys 1931

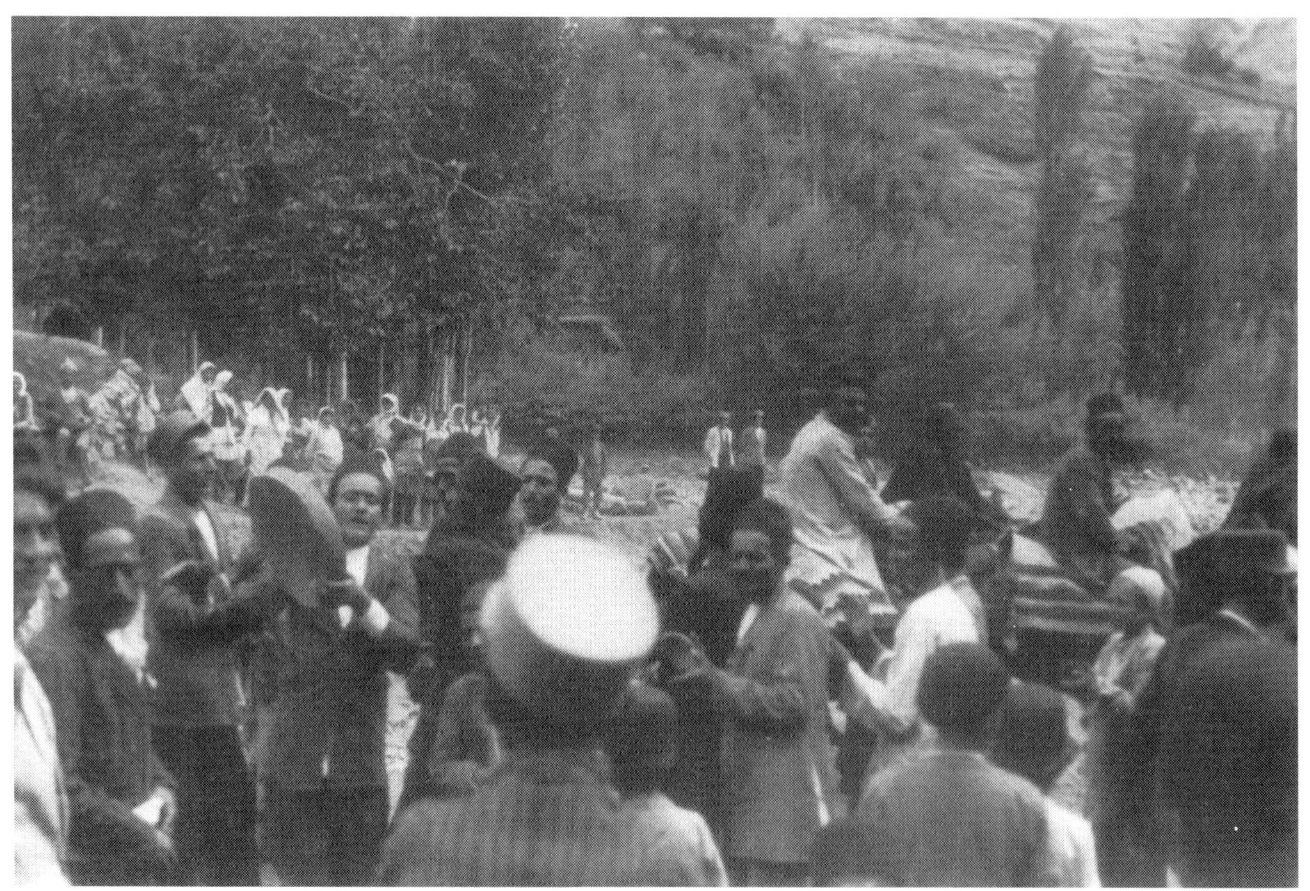

Wedding, Garmrud 1931

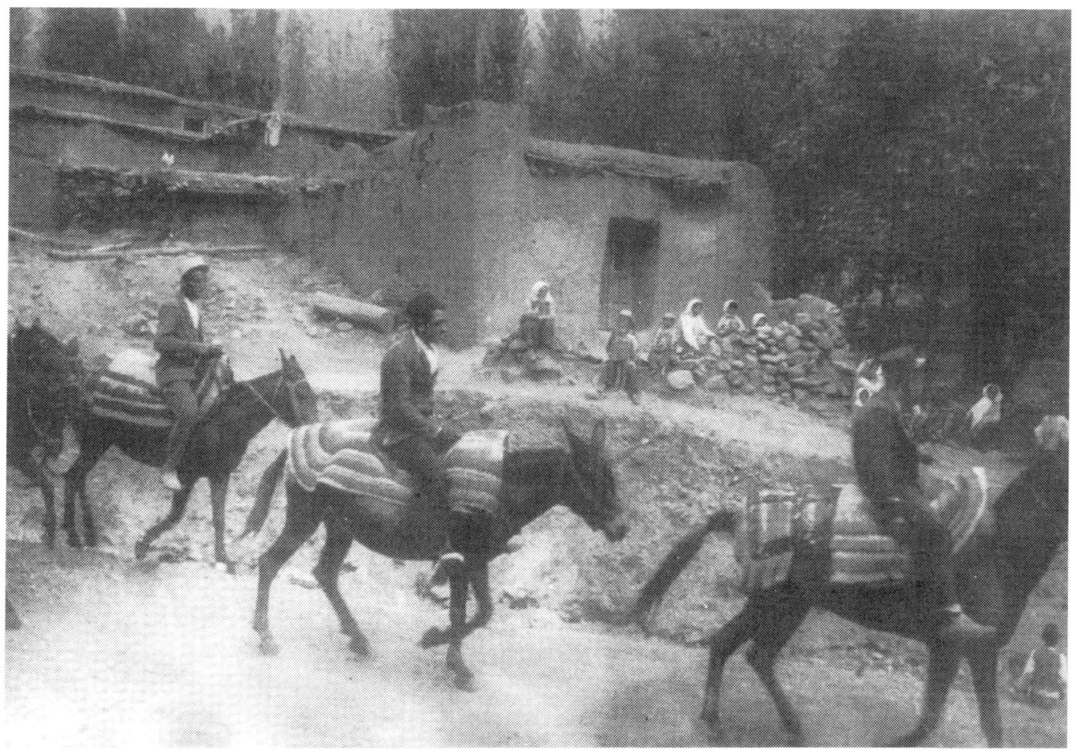

Wedding, Garmrud 1931

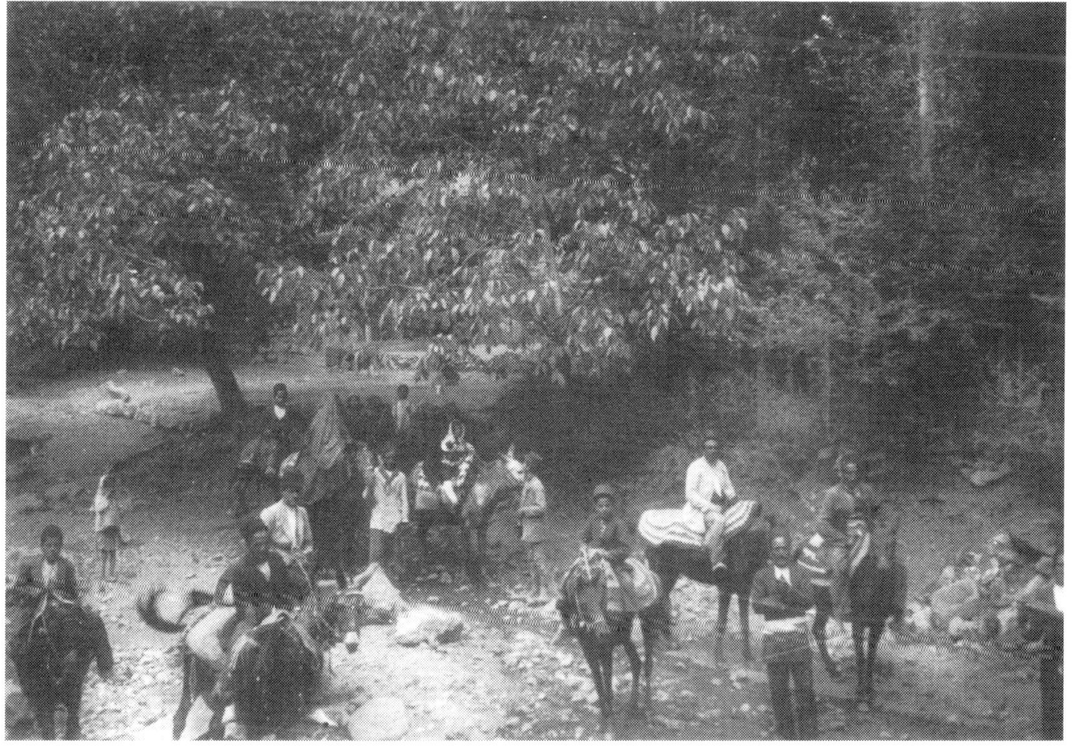

Wedding, Garmrud 1931

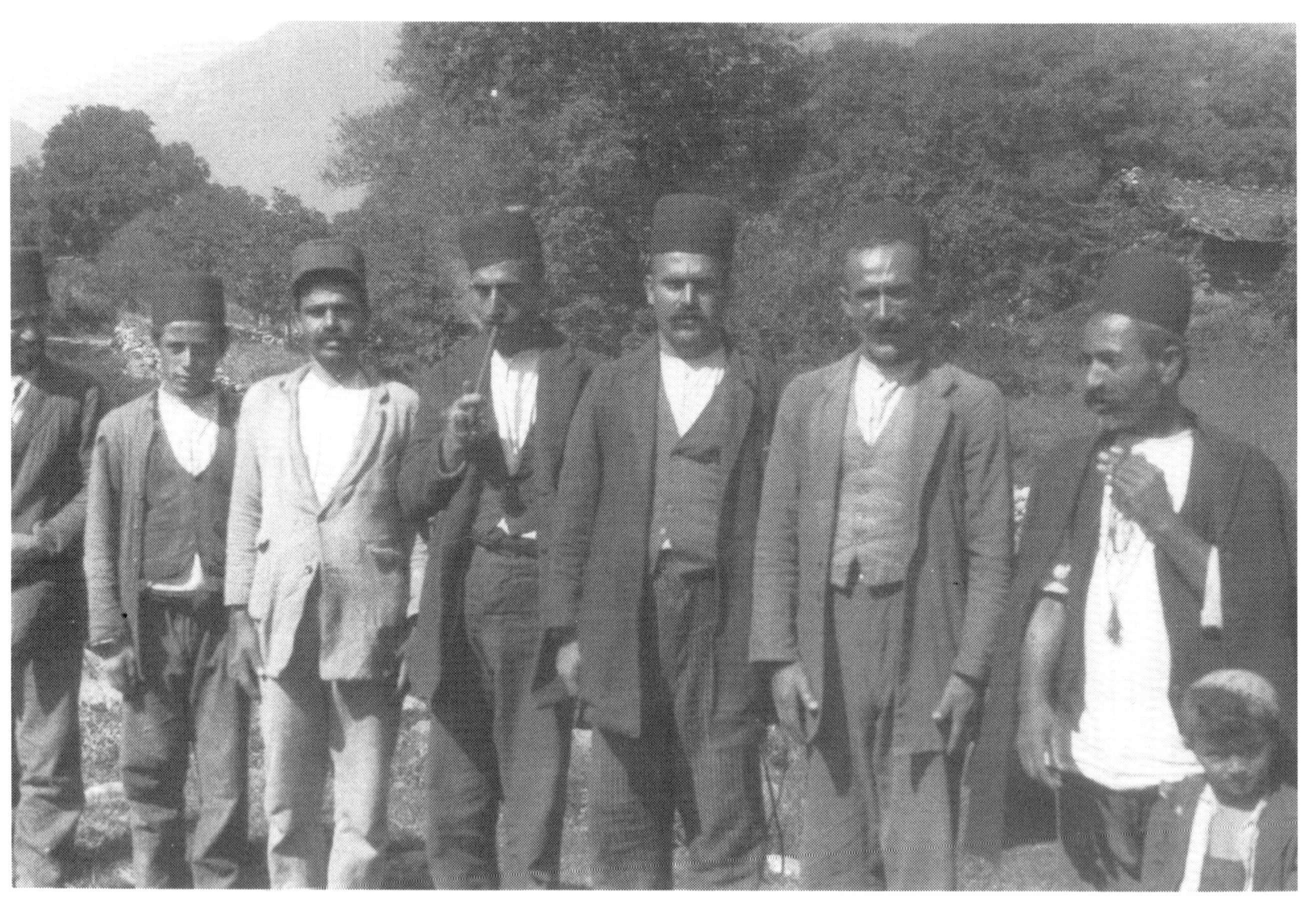

Kurdish men of Rudbarek 1931

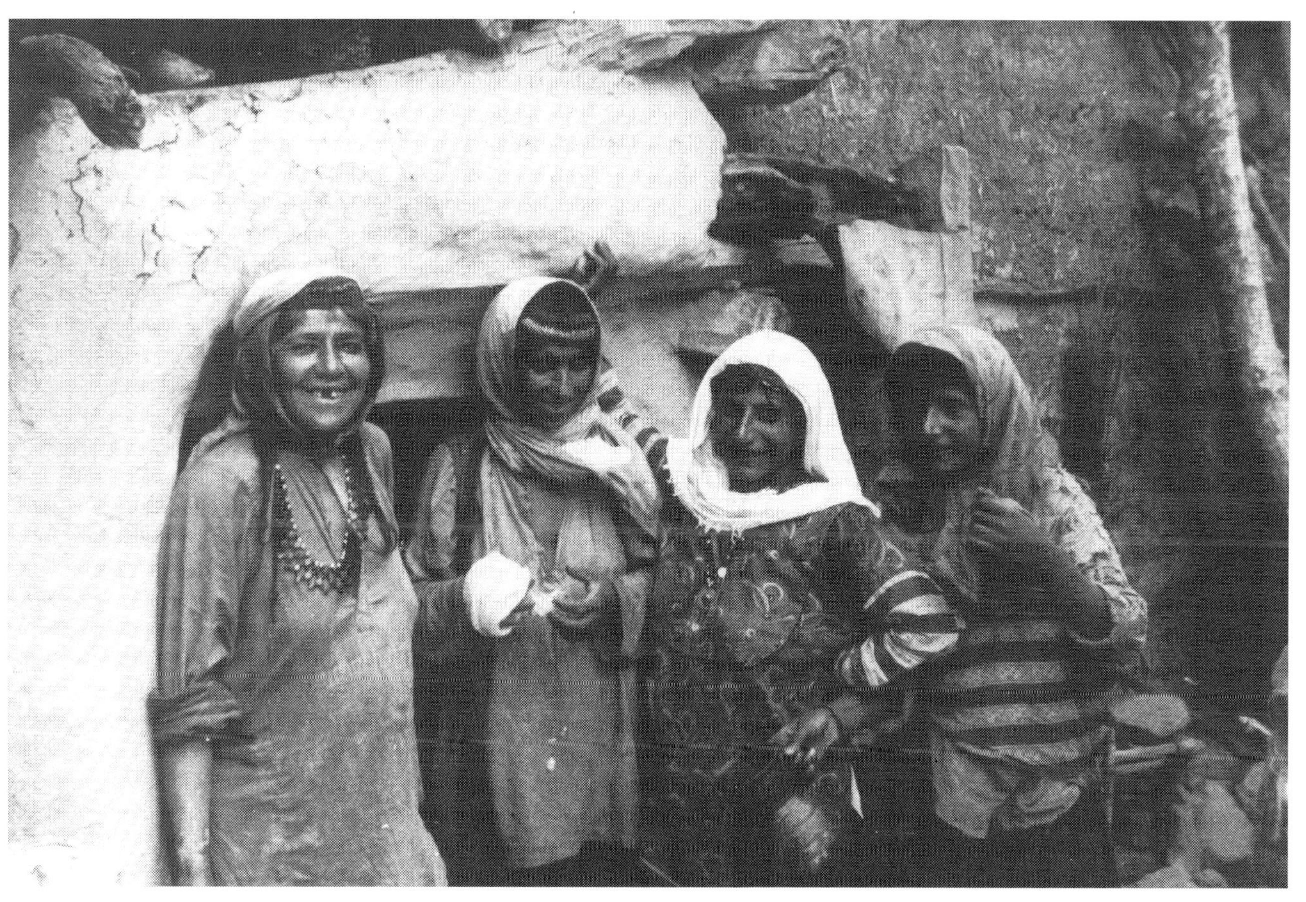

Women of Meres, Chalus Valley 1931

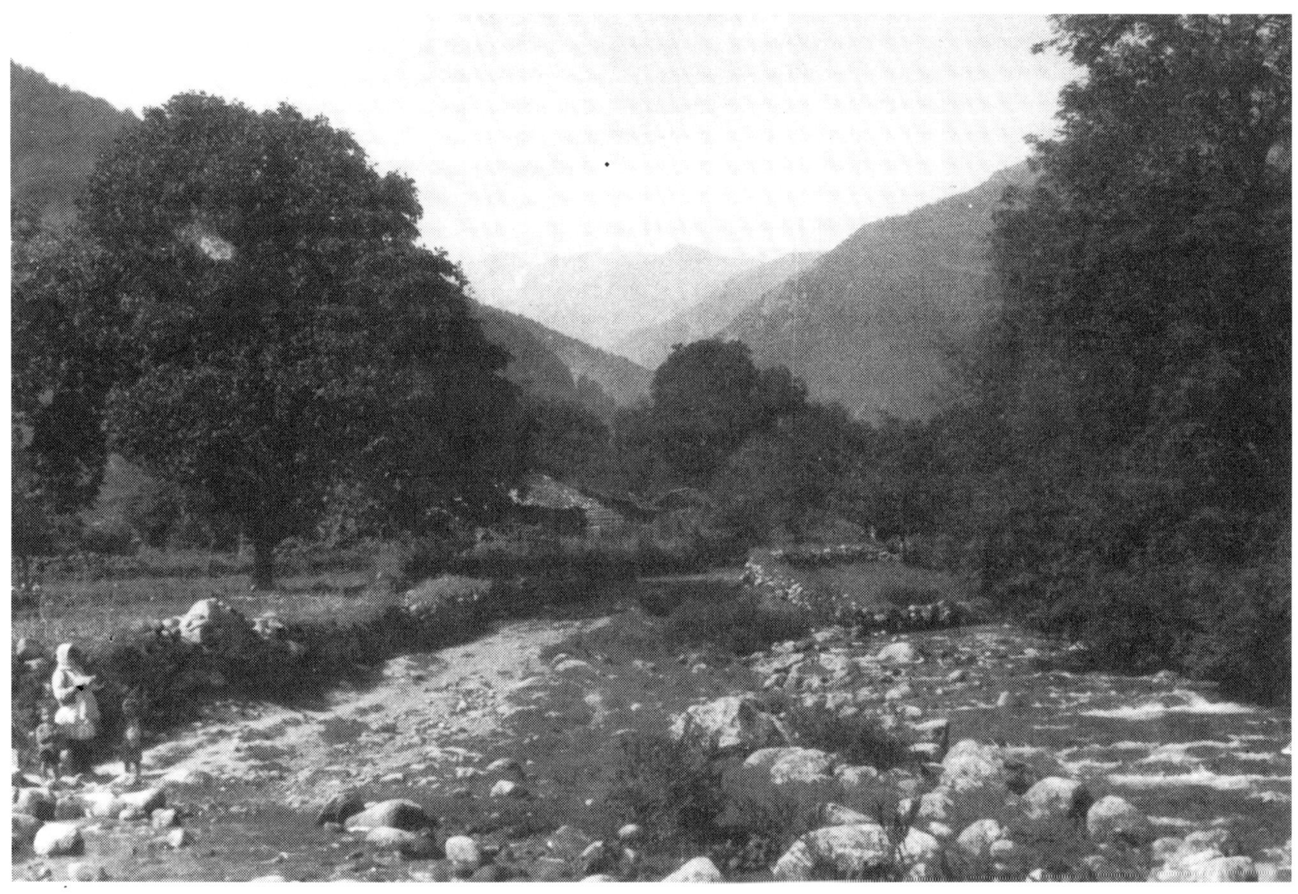

Rudbarek in Kalar Dasht 1931. "The most beautiful of the villages, inhabited by a Kurdish tribe."

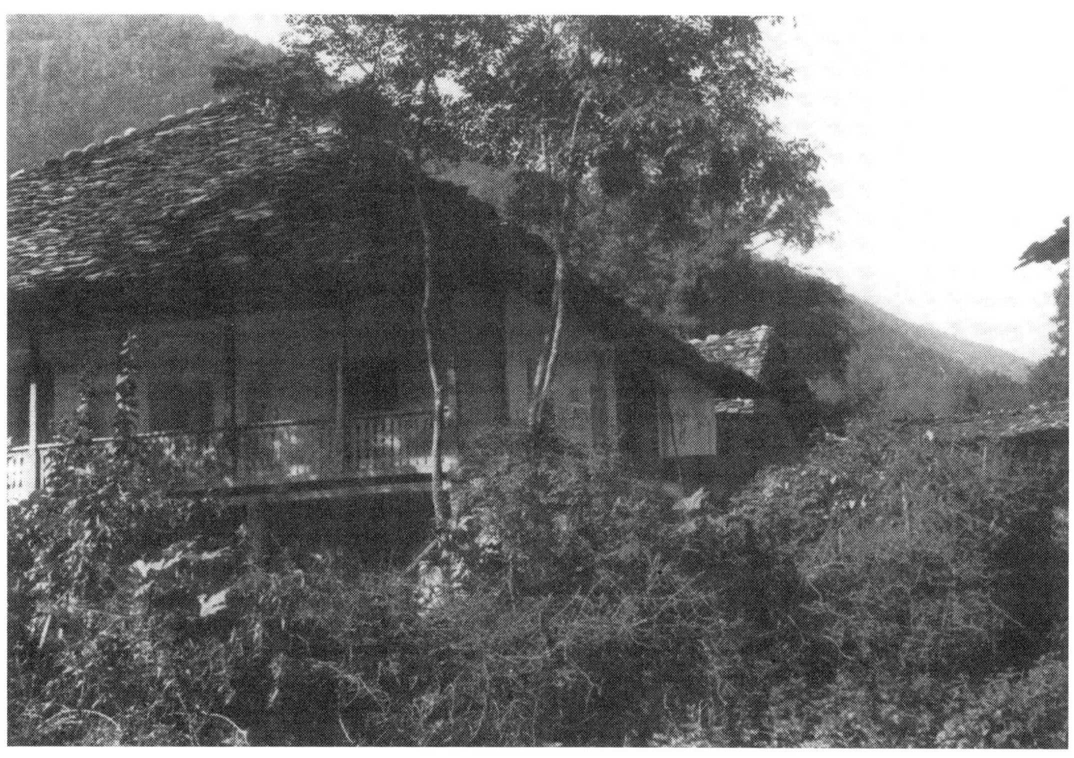

House, Rudbarek 1931

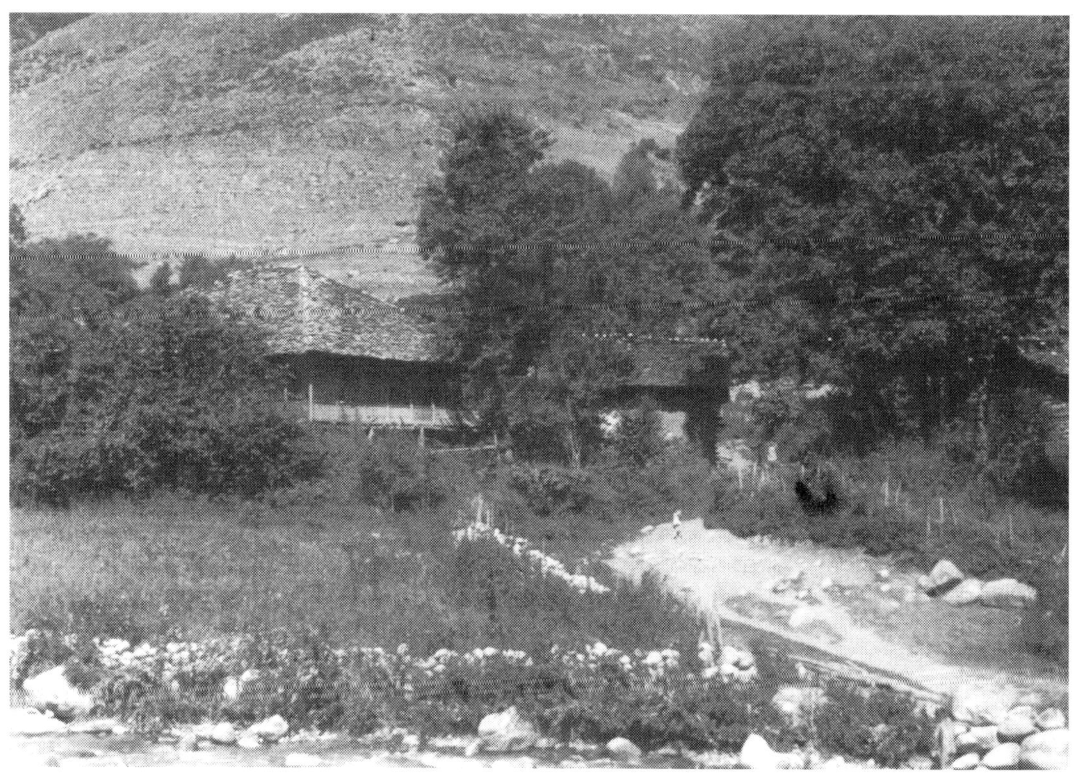

Rudbarek 1931

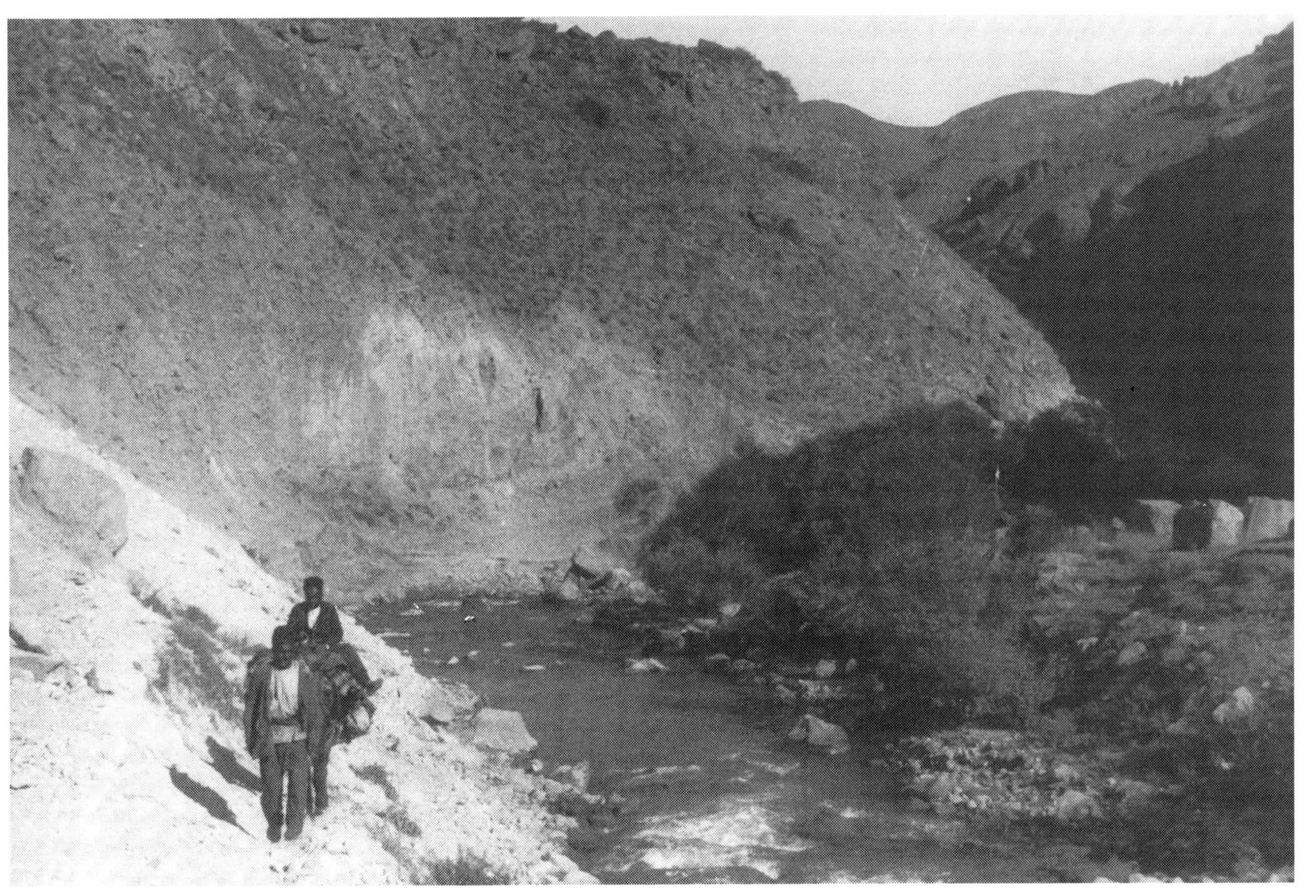

Main road along Upper Shahrud Valley 1930

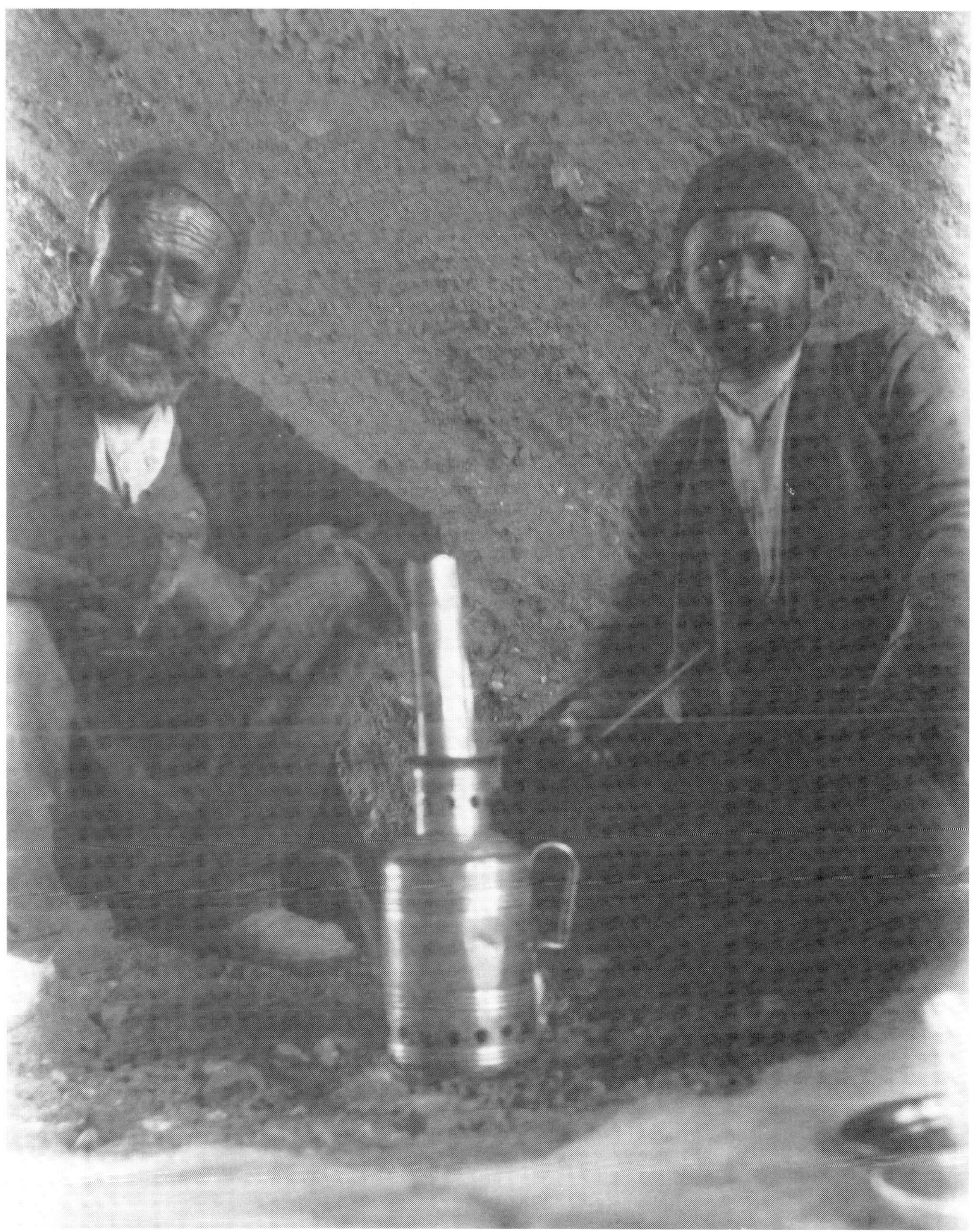

Men of Gazur-khan, Alamut 1931

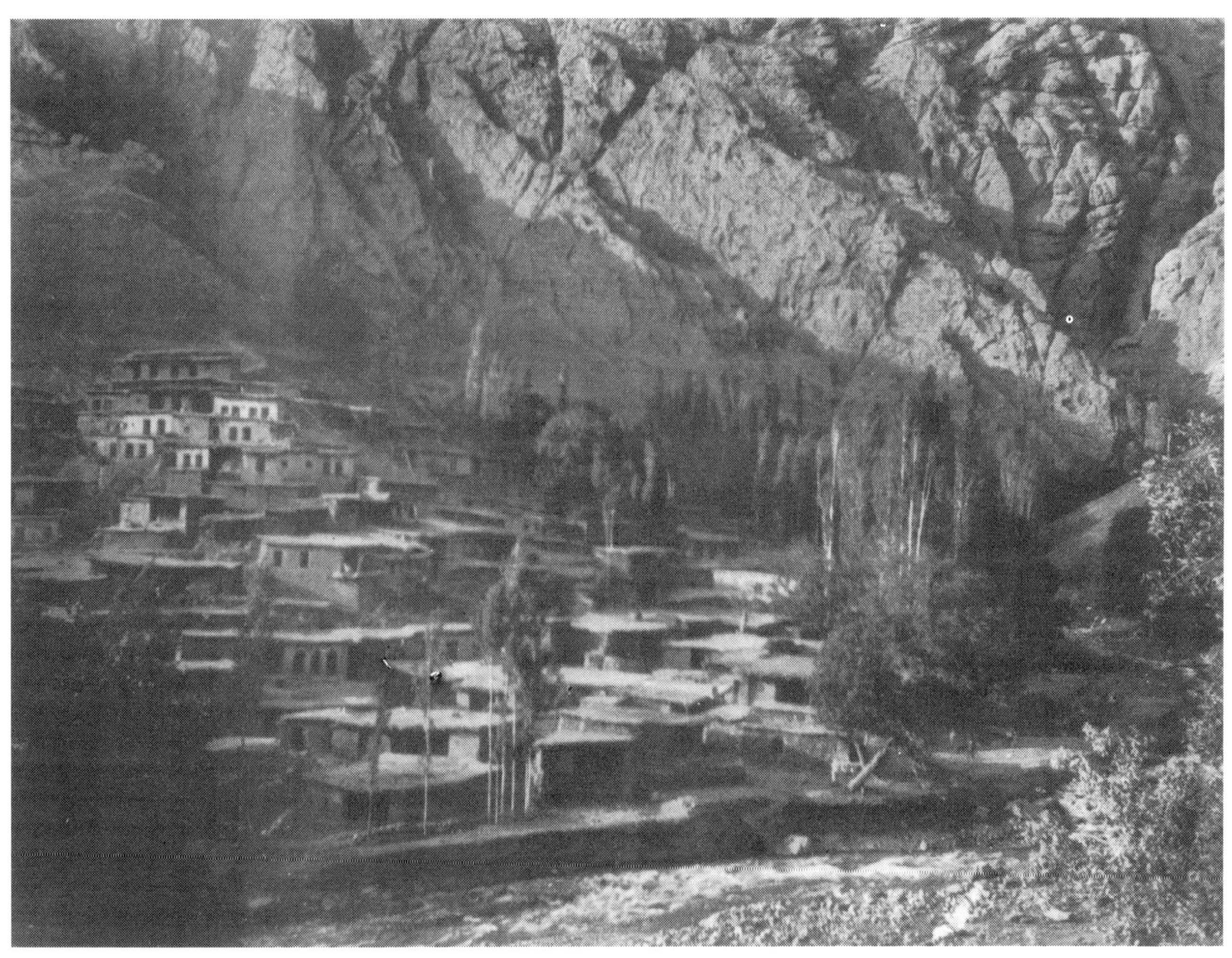

Garmrud 1930

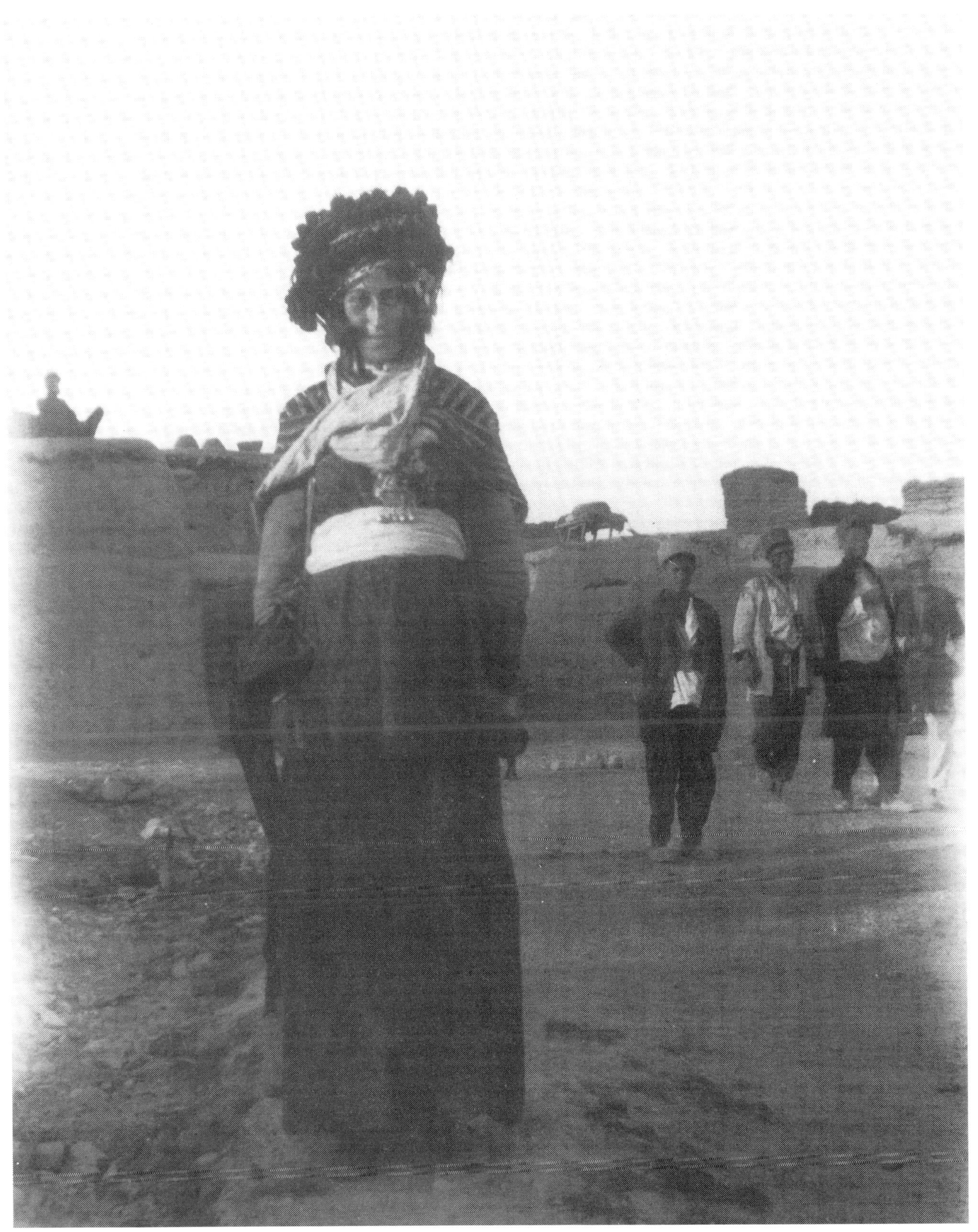

Kurdish Woman, Senna 1932

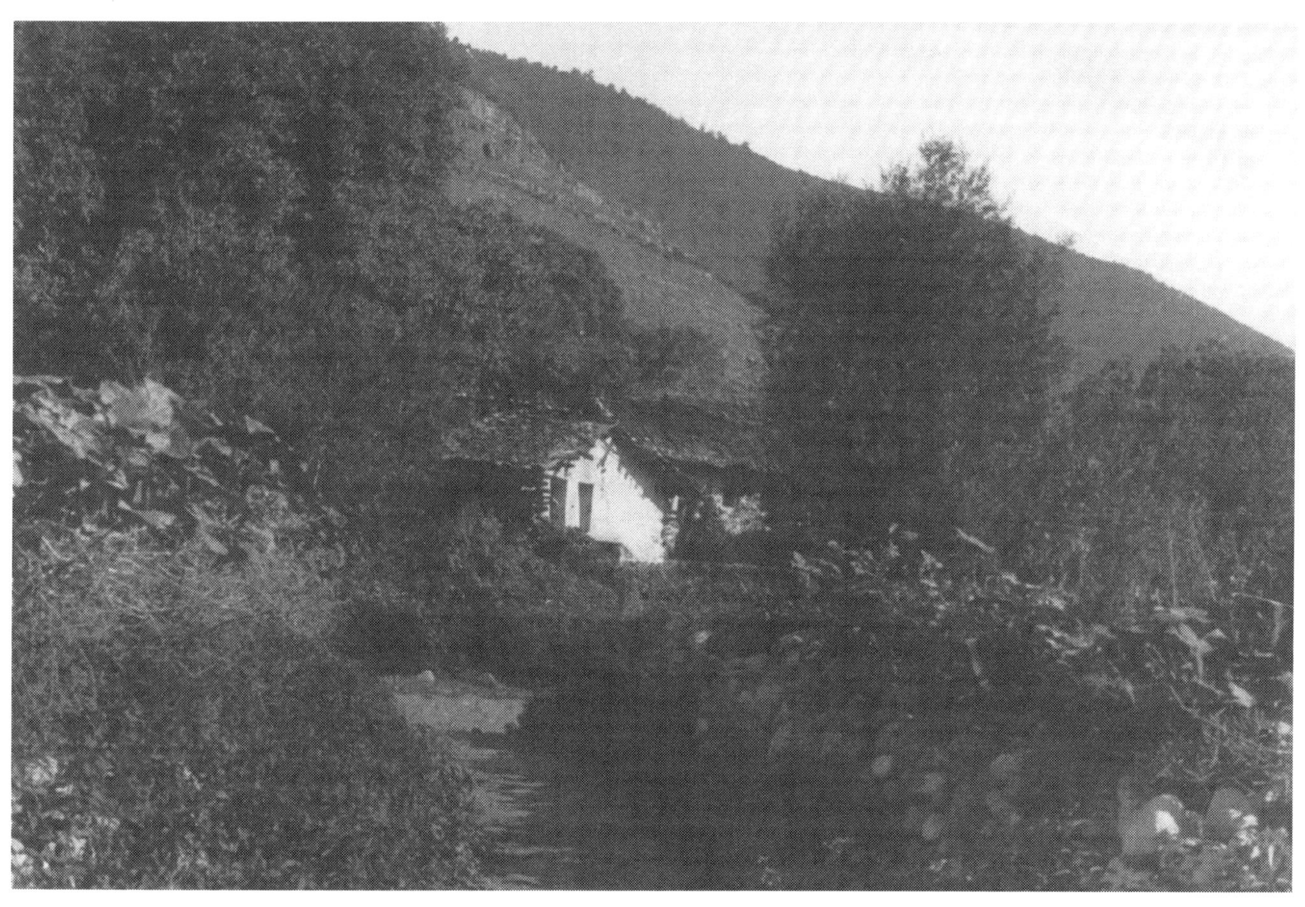

Rudbarek 1931

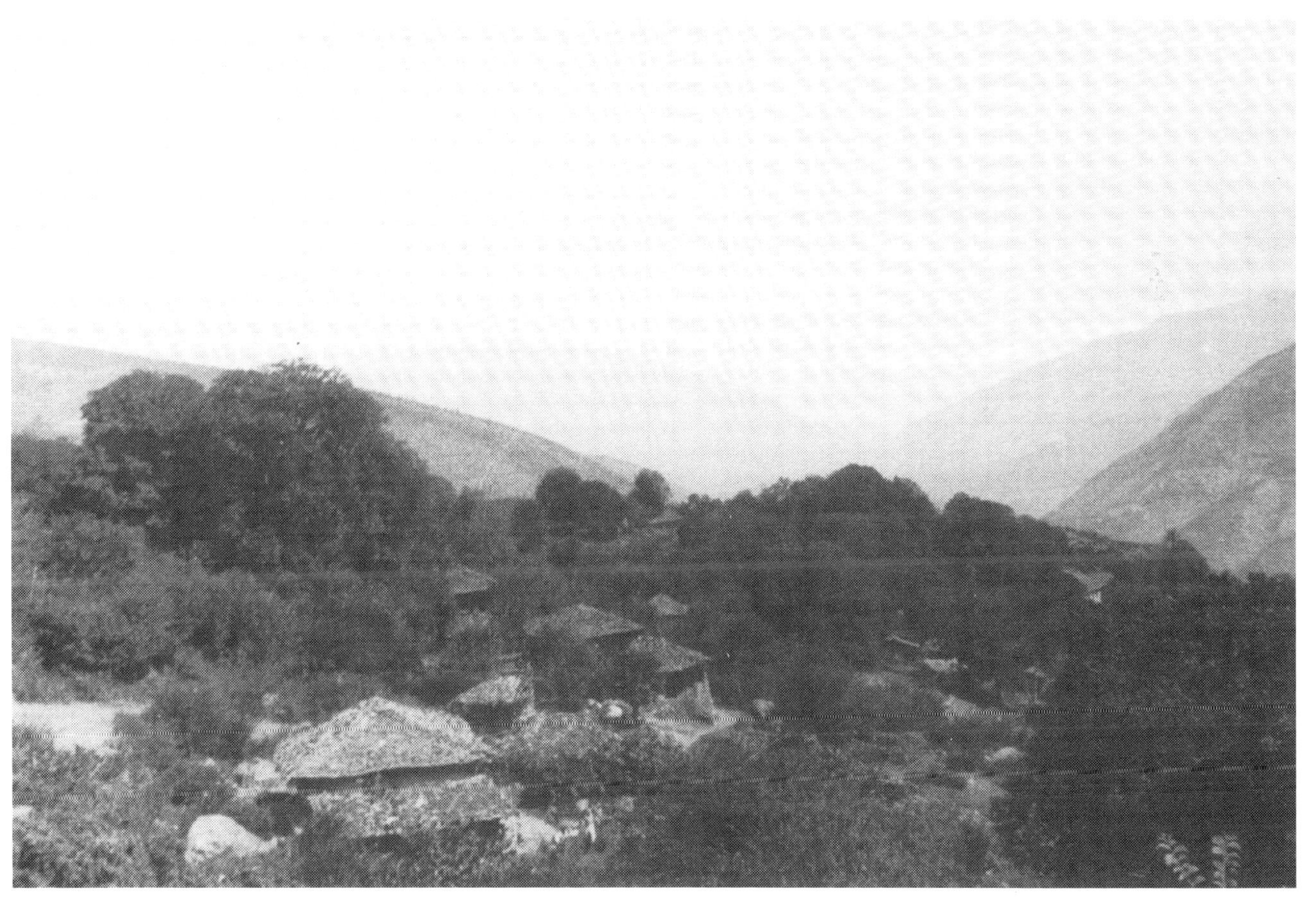

Chalus Valley from Qutir 1931

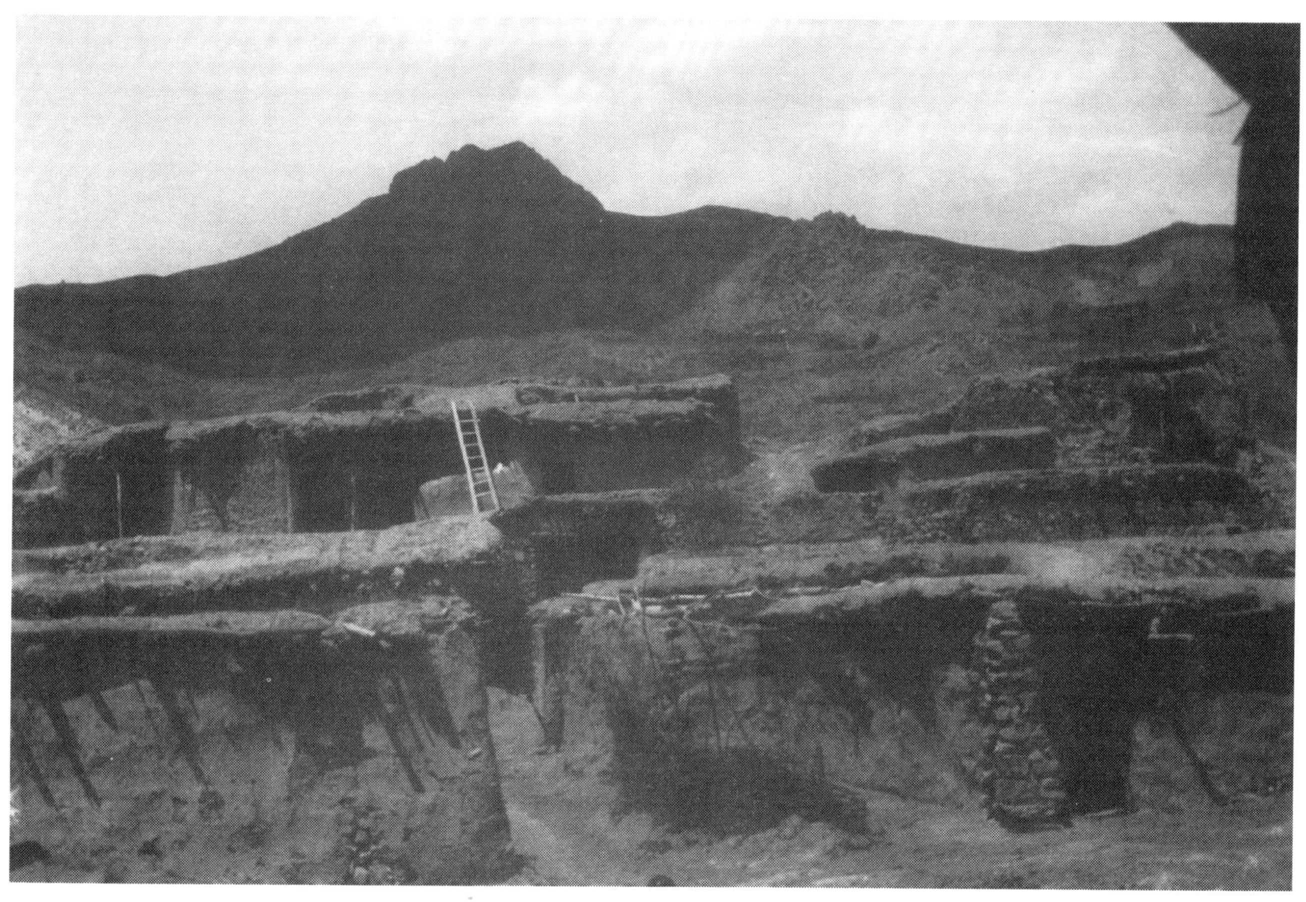

Chalus Valley 1930

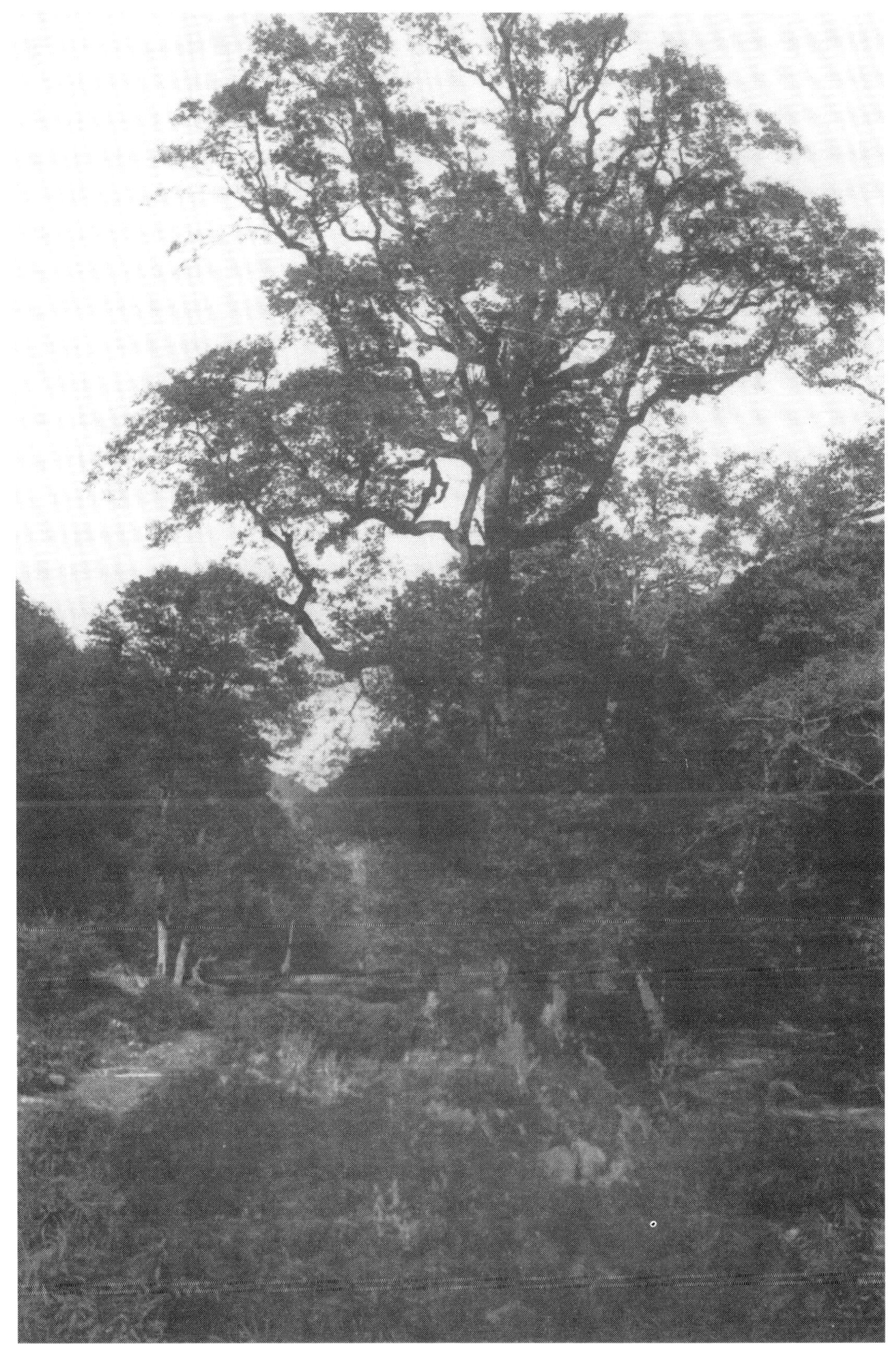

Sardabrud Jungle 1931

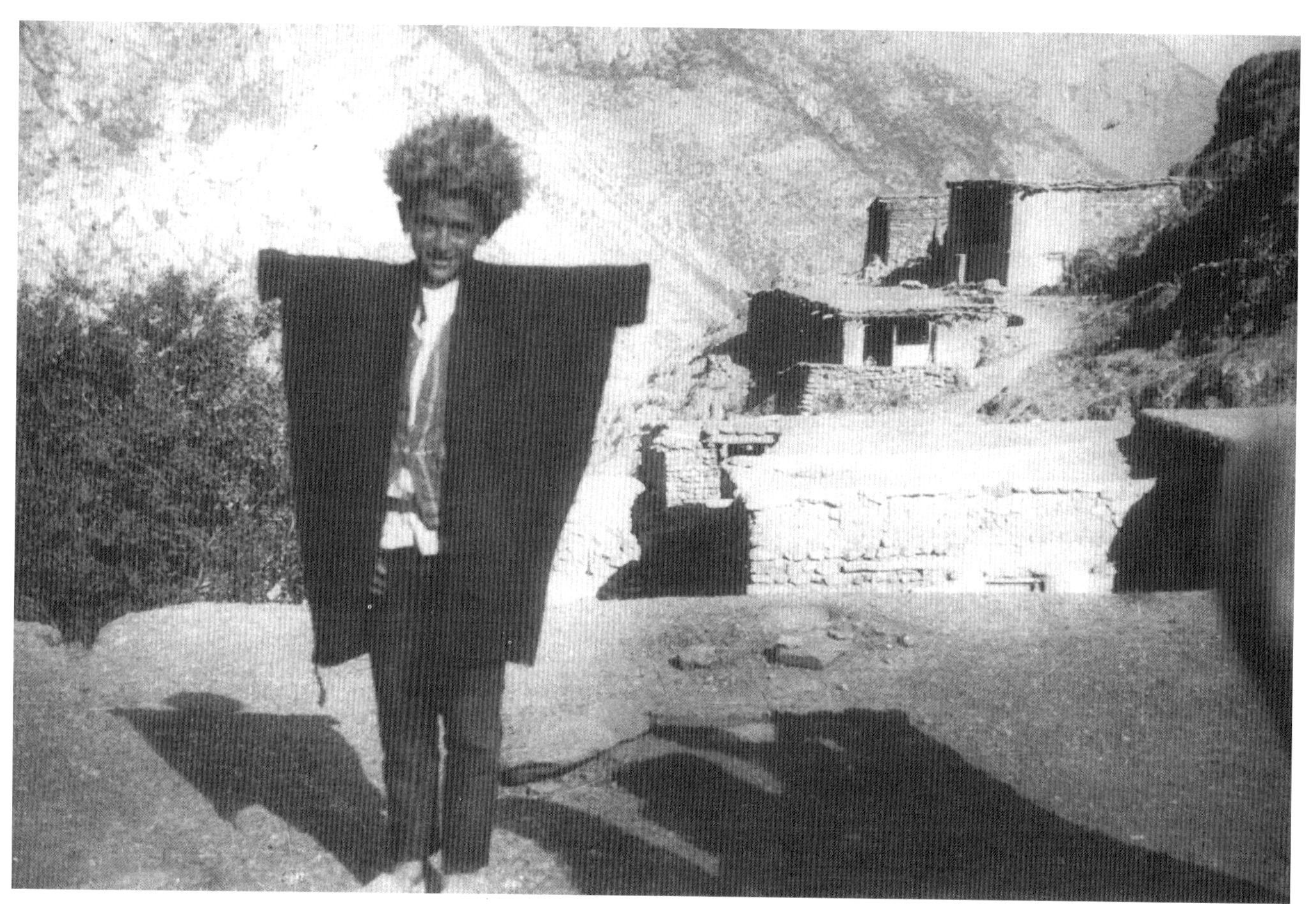

Felt coat and sheepskin cap of Jungali boy 1931

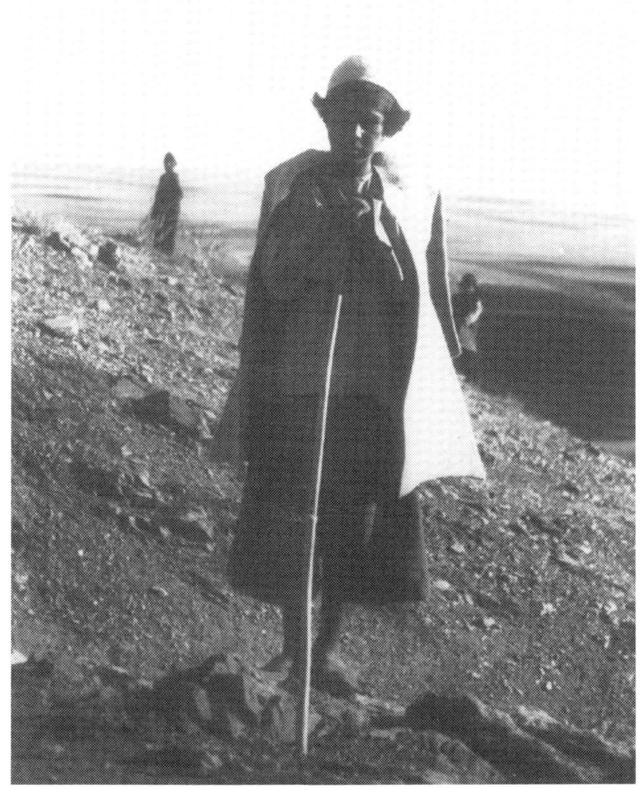

Jungali shepherd 1931

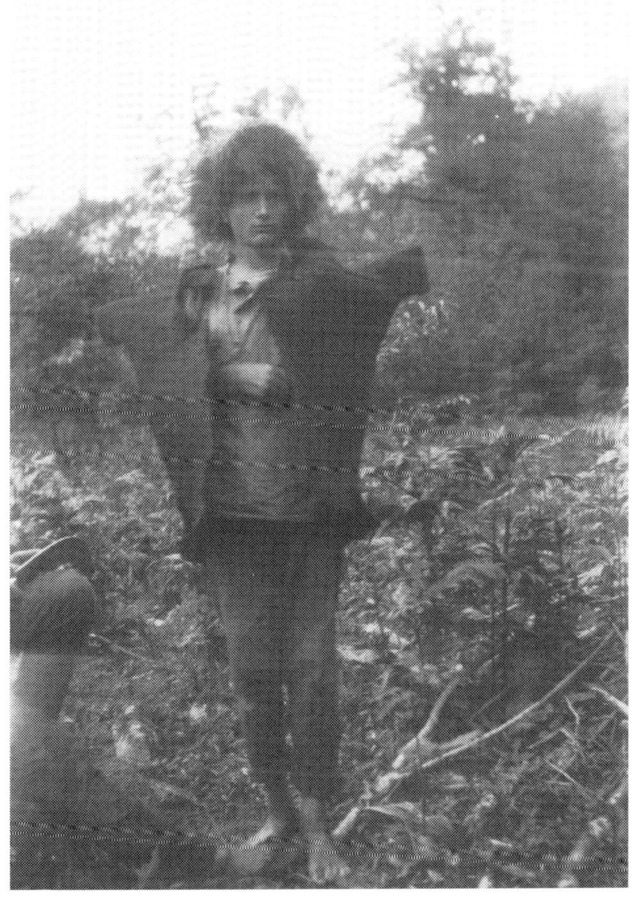

Jungali wood-cutter 1931

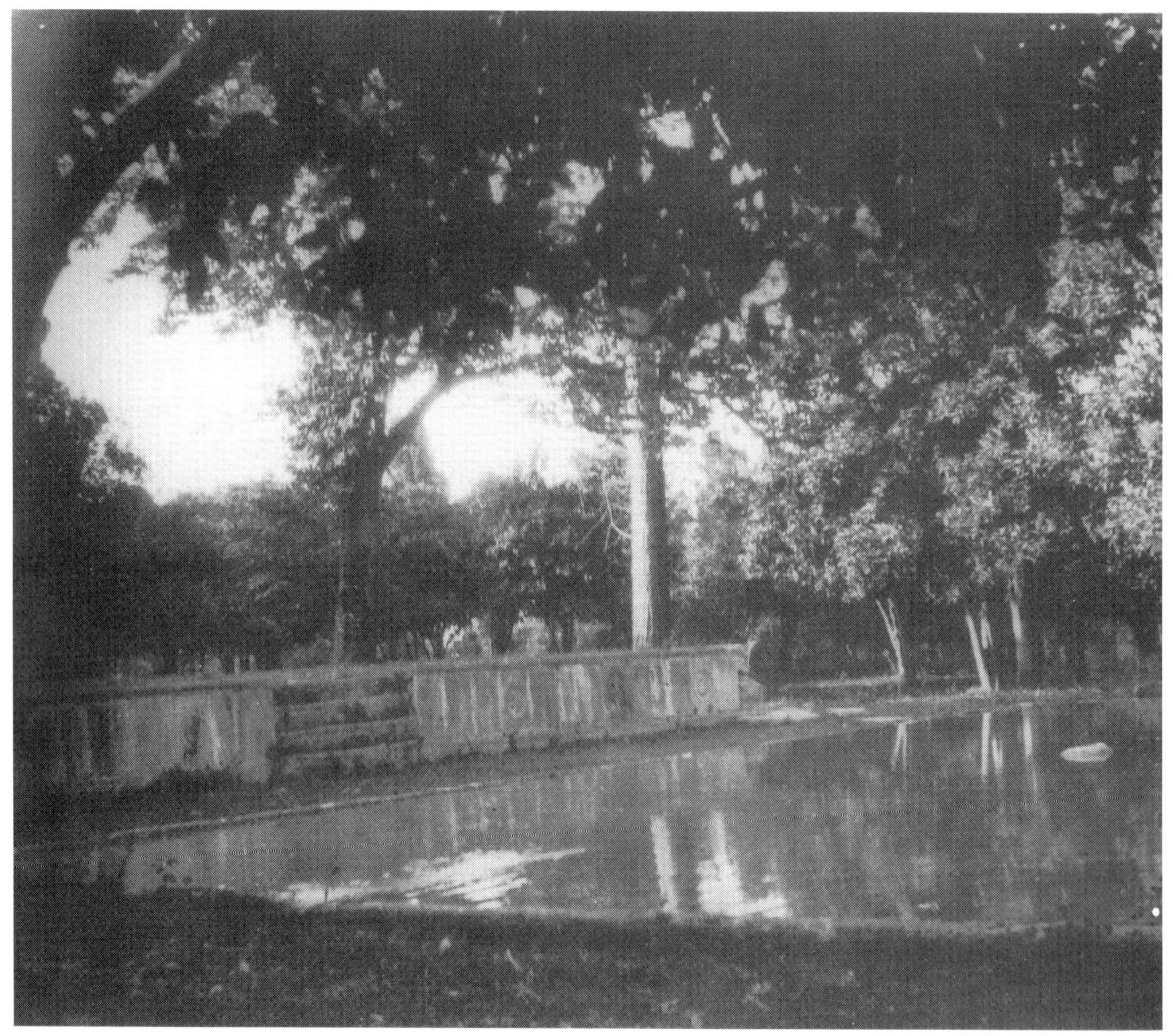

Tanakabun on the Caspian 1930

TABRIZ

After the famous expeditions to Mazanderan there is no record in her published letters that Freya ever returned to the area. It is possible that she may have hired a jeep in Tehran and driven into the mountains. Several photographs in the albums she bequeathed to St Antony's College are captioned in her hand "Way to Takht-i Suleiman 1960". The places, however, are not identified and there is no sign of any Elburz peak in the background. When she assembled the albums she was already in her eighties, and memory was fading. In 1984, when I drove her into the Monte Grappa near her home in Italy she was convinced we were in the Himalayas. Nothing I said to the contrary would persuade her otherwise.

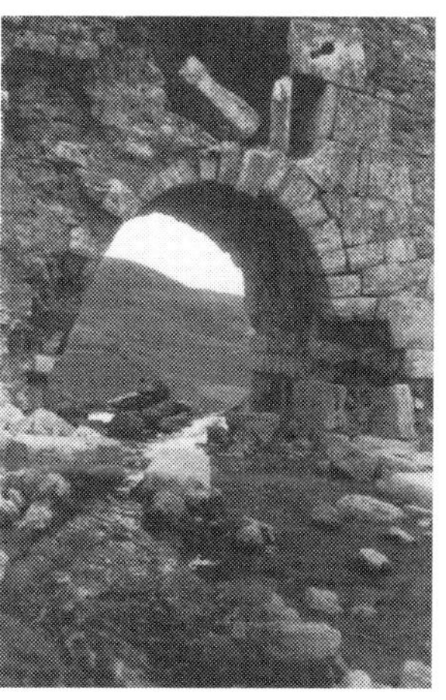

Parthian gate at Phraaspa 1959

Her visit to the mountainous area south of Tabriz in May 1959, however, is well documented. In a long letter to Jock Murray she describes a trip to the ancient Parthian city of Phraaspa "a ten-hour jeep ride from anywhere" where Mark Antony was defeated in the Roman civil wars and "had to march back through the wild mountain land losing his men at every river crossing". Persia, she found, had not changed greatly since her previous visits during the Second World War. Two good things had happened: DDT had killed off the malaria and the Government had stopped the growing of opium. "Also the hideous peaked cap has reverted to the felt skull-cap of the peasants. But they are so poor, and the rich so rich."

She spent two days in Tabriz where "the Blue Mosque was all it should be and, with the ruined feeling added to the sunlight, making a different sort of beauty among its broken piers and vanished domes." Then she took the train to the little town of Maragha where the governor and his young wife sent for a huge brass bedstead so she could sleep in his office.

At 5.30 the next morning her jeep collected her, and after skirting Lake Urmiah they turned eastwards, passing the Afshar Kurds driving their sheep to the high pastures. The next night, spent in the village near Phraaspa, was a good deal less comfortable. There was only one guest room in the headman's house which she had to share with her driver, two of his relatives and an extra man. Hoping that the privilege of being female might lead to something better, Freya inspected the harem. The headman's Kurdish wife, however, "lived in absolute squalor, draughts and darkness, cooking and washing, with six daughters and only one son – but with one splendid carpet six by five yards on a loom, its colours shining like some cathedral window in all that squalor."

The carpets reminded her of the tapestries of medieval times – prompting her to observe that Persia was still living in the feudal age; "if this were not an airmail letter and quite a long one already I would tell you what I think of the danger of ignoring this feudal element." Her thoughts on the Ayatollah Khomeini who overthrew the Shah in 1979 when she was 86 are not on record. She might not have approved, but one can imagine her pursing her lips and saying of the Shah and his extravagantly modernizing and corrupt régime 'I told them, but they wouldn't listen'.

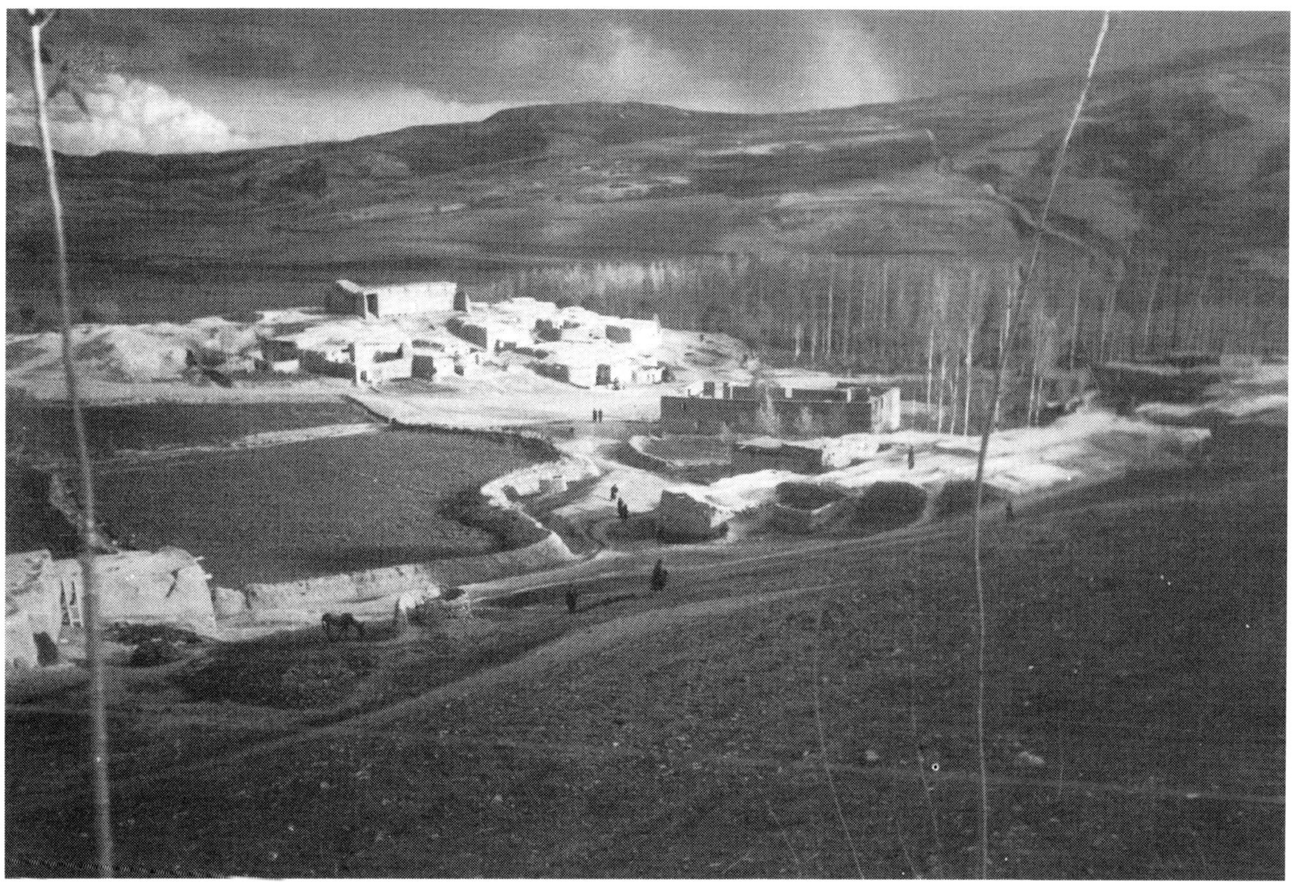

Unidentified village, probably near Maragha 1959

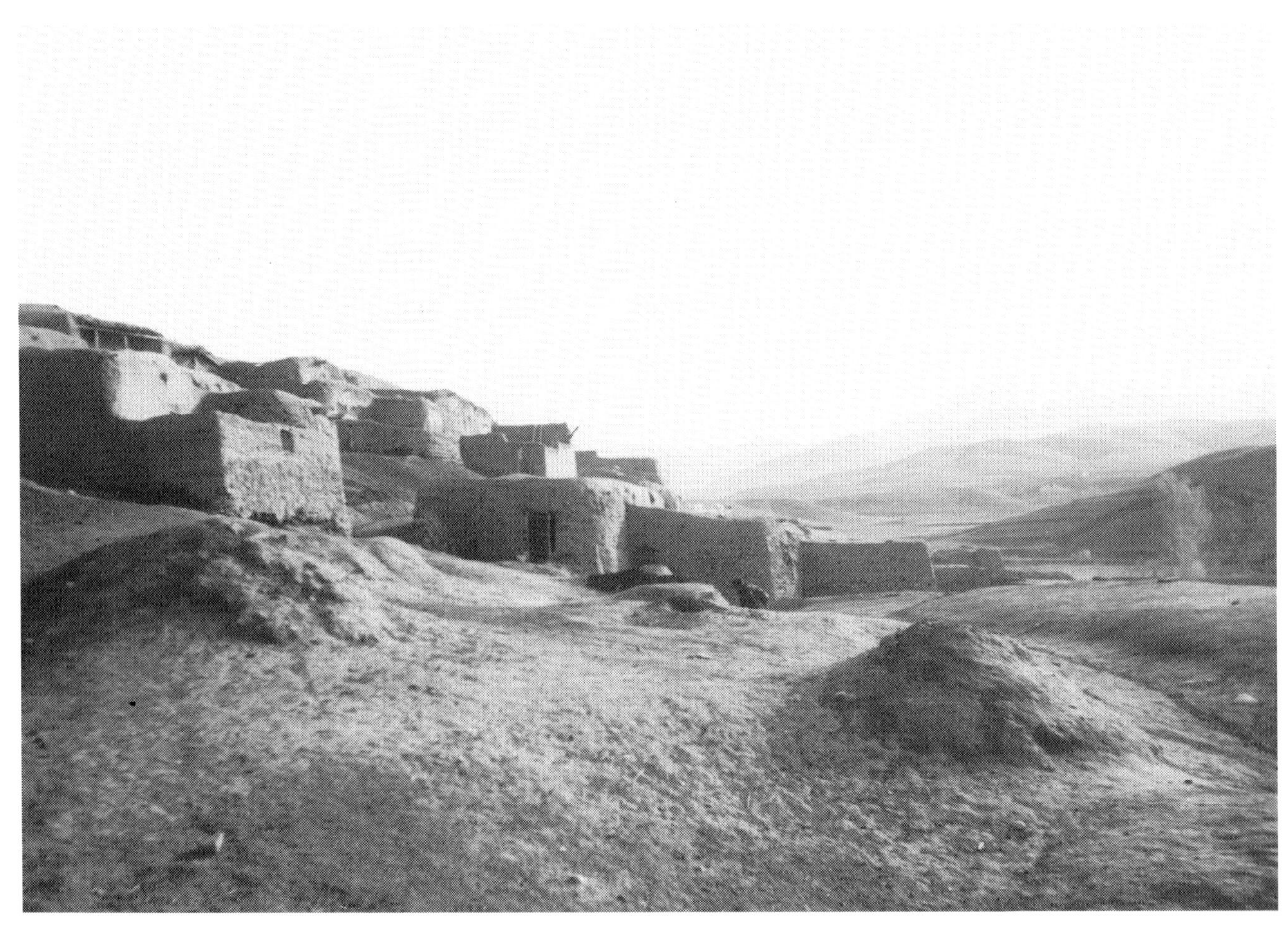

Unidentified village, probably near Maragha 1959

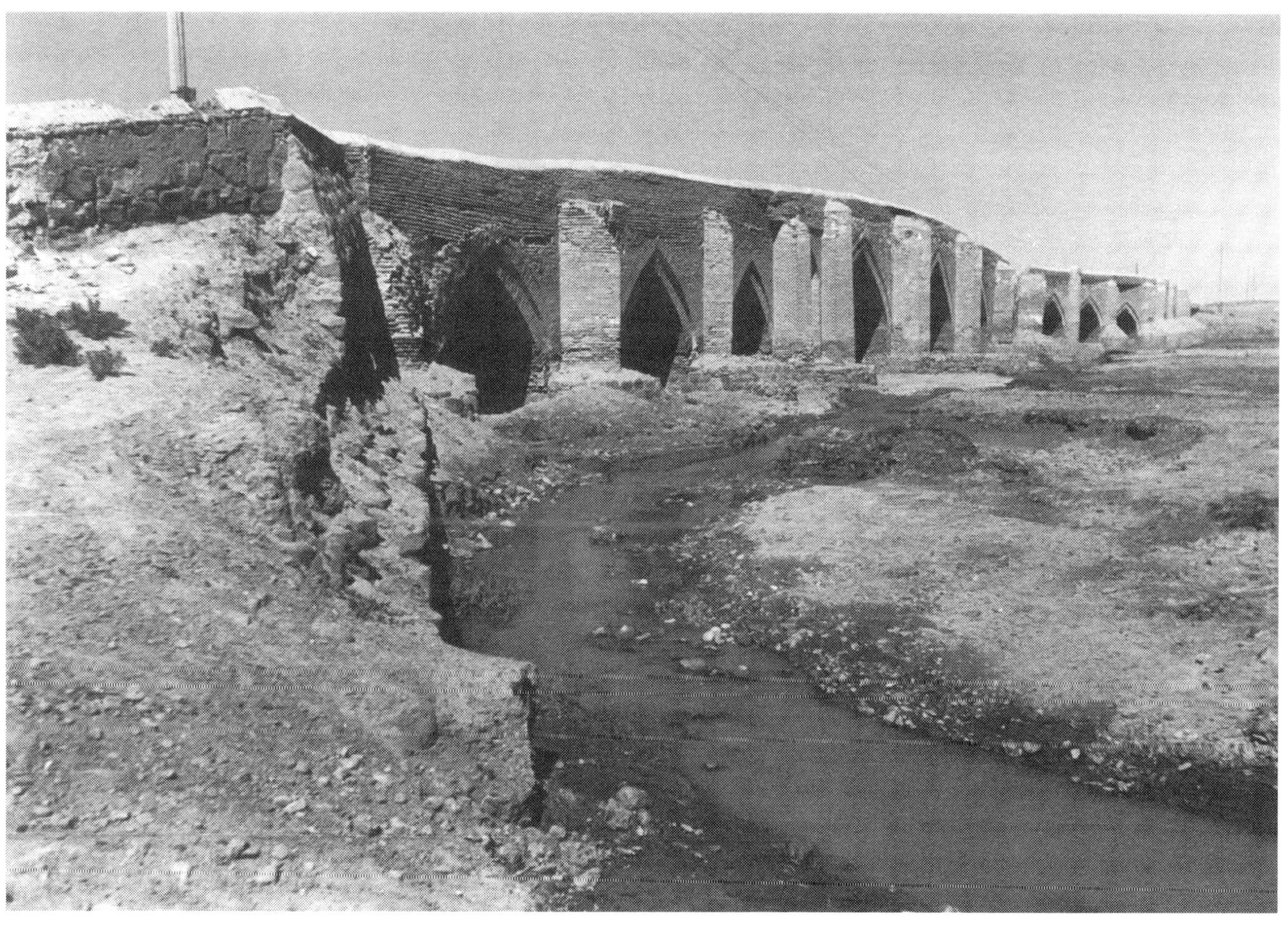

Bridge, Tabriz 1959. "Great bridges carry future and past."

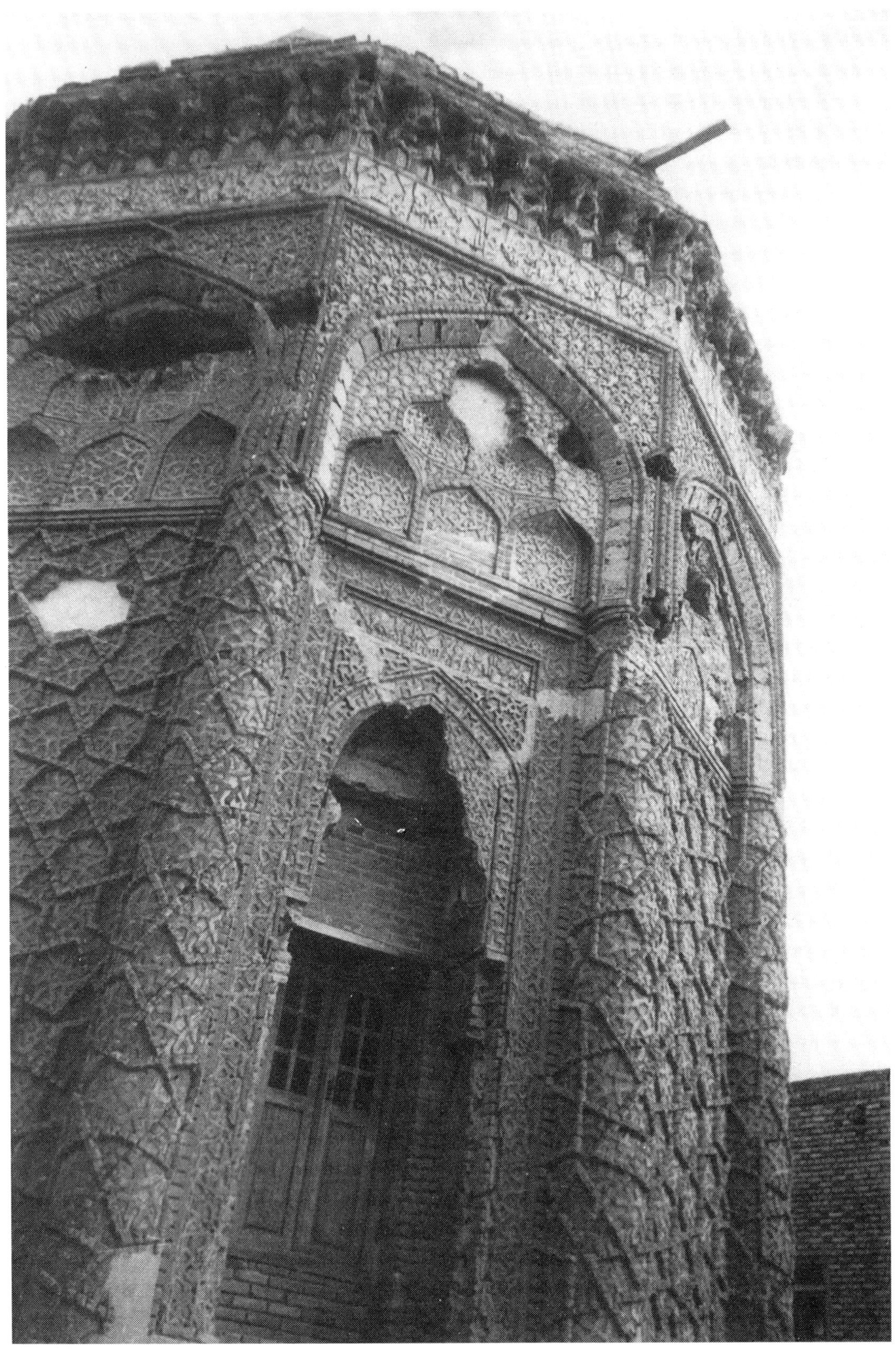

Seljuk Tomb, Maragha 1951

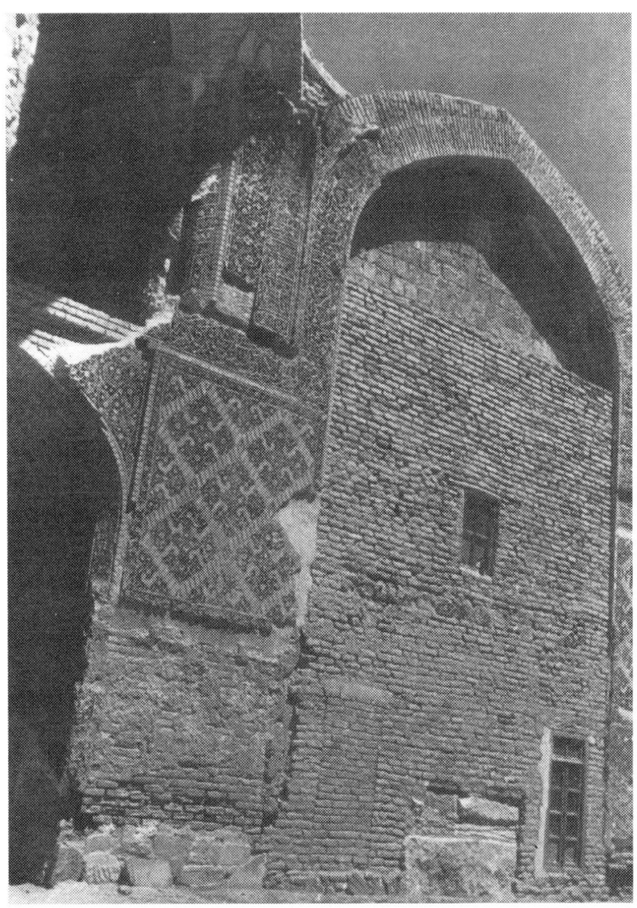

Tabriz Blue Mosque 1959

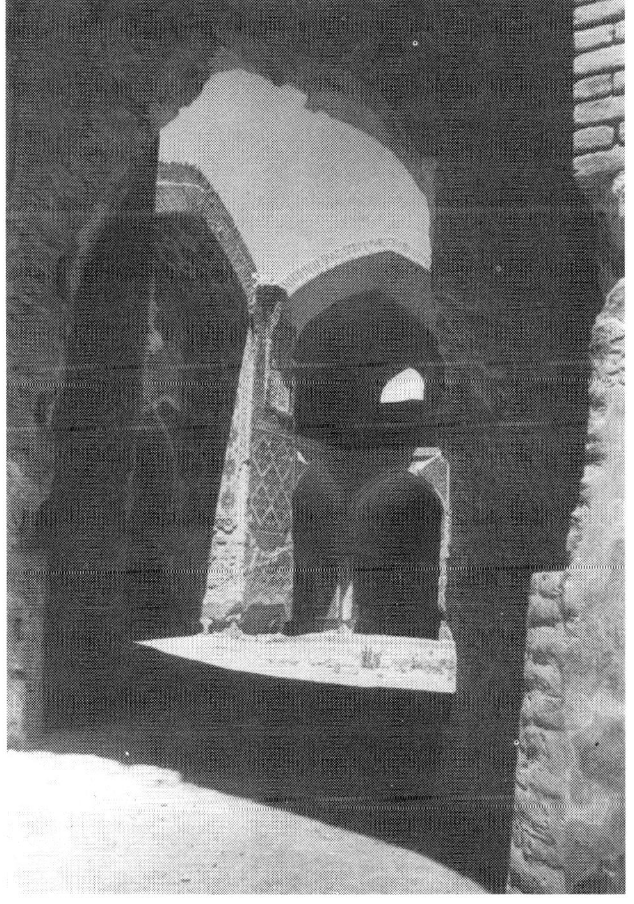

Tabriz Blue Mosque 1959

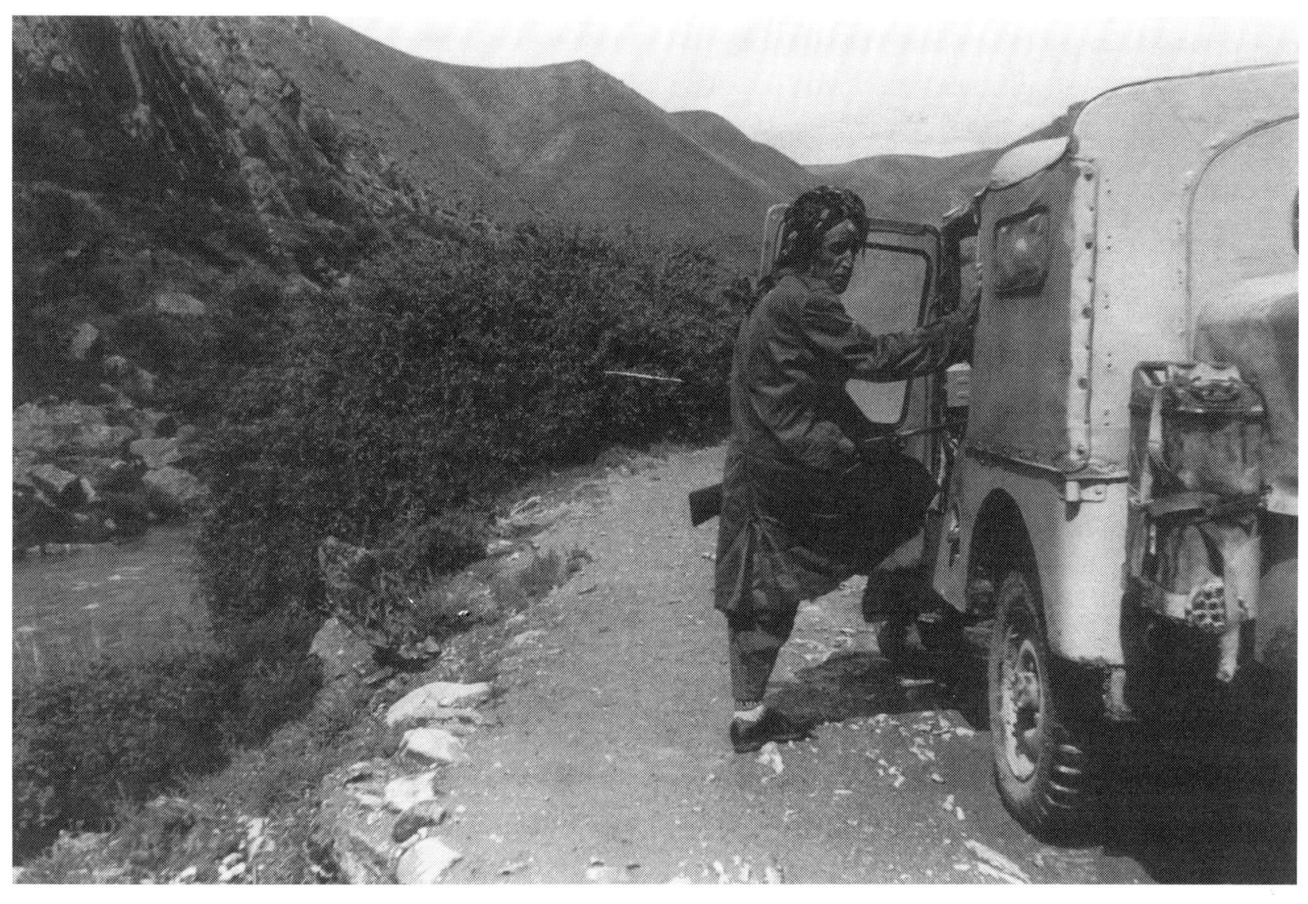

Way to Phraaspa 1959

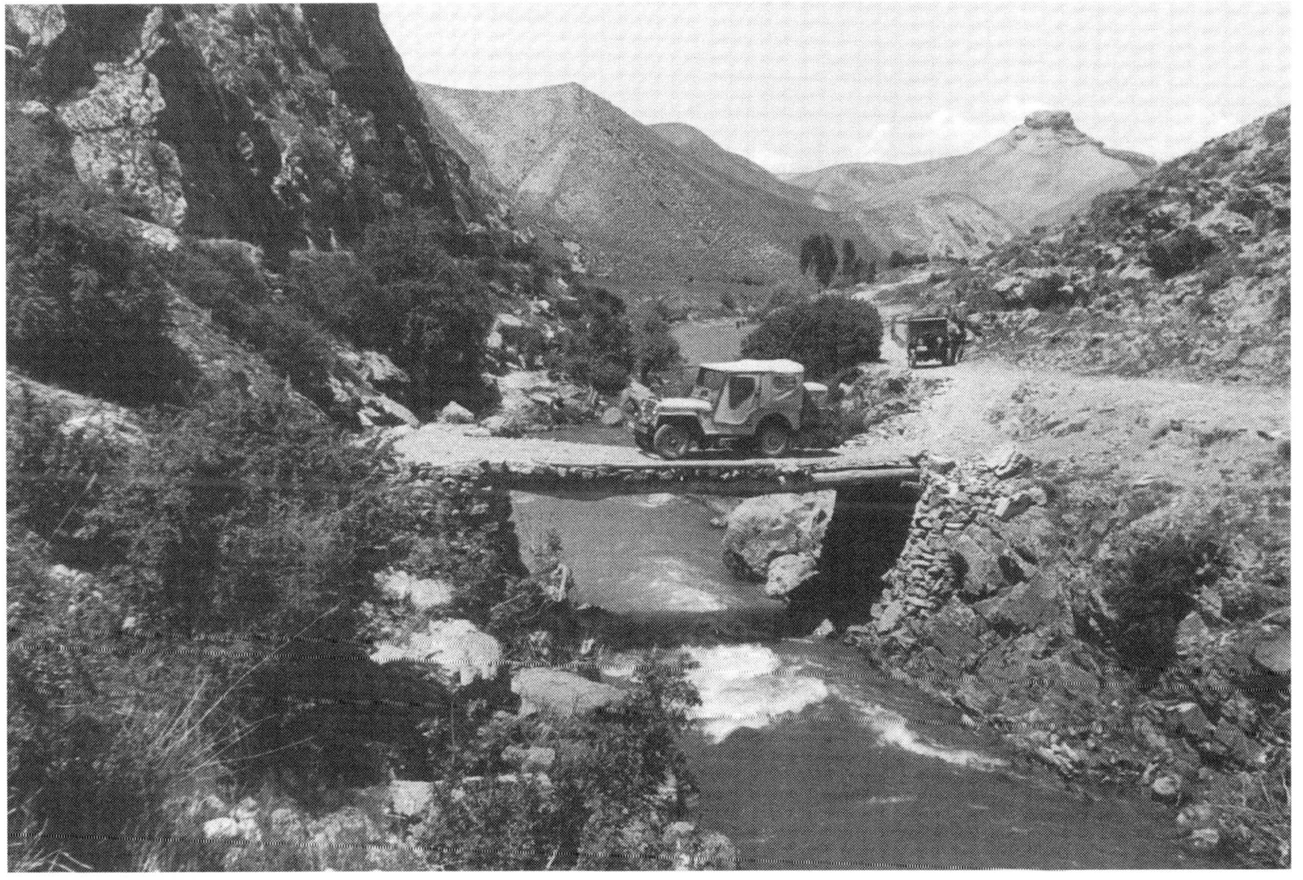

Saman Dag from Maragha 1959

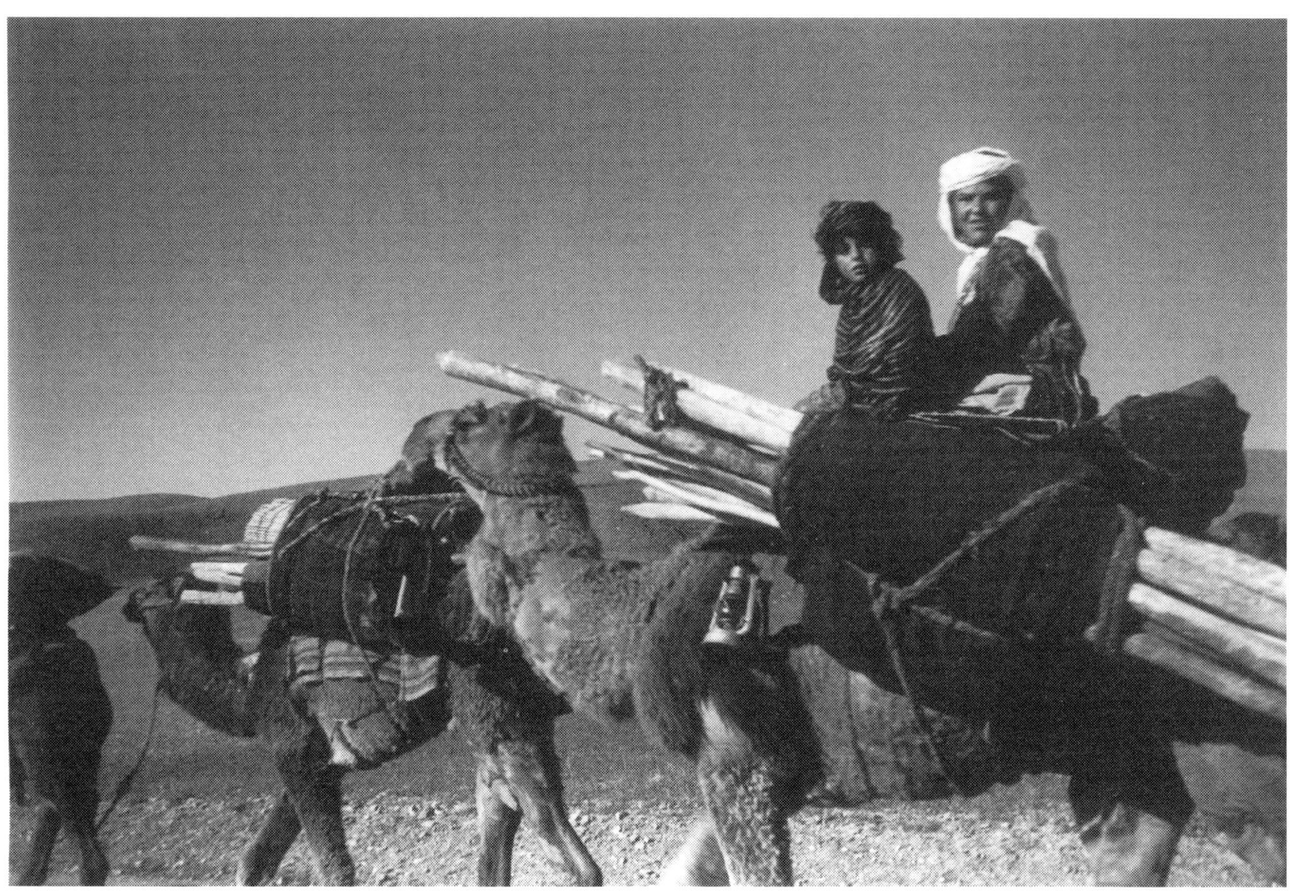

Nomads near Tabriz 1959

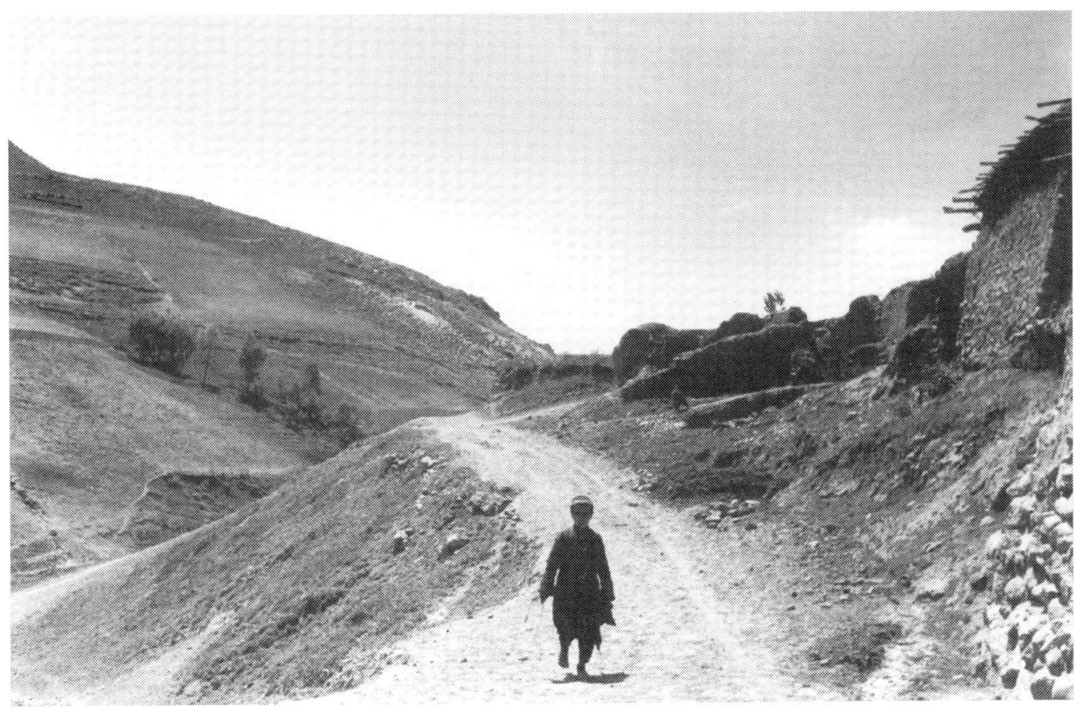

Road to Phraaspa 1959

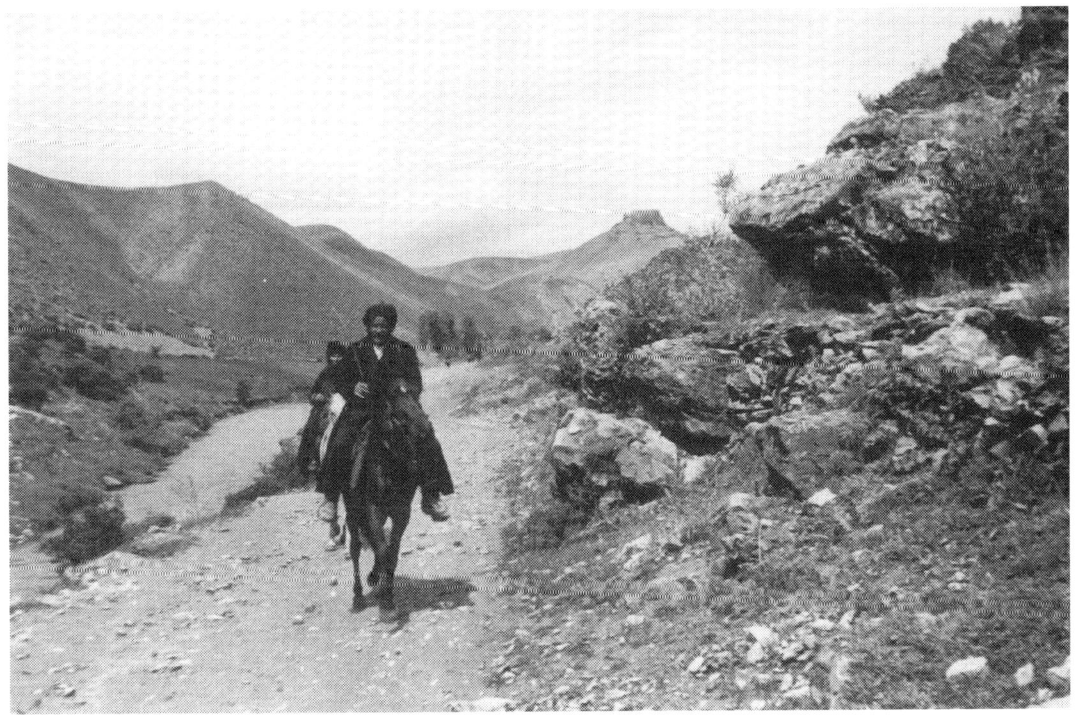

Road to Phraaspa 1959

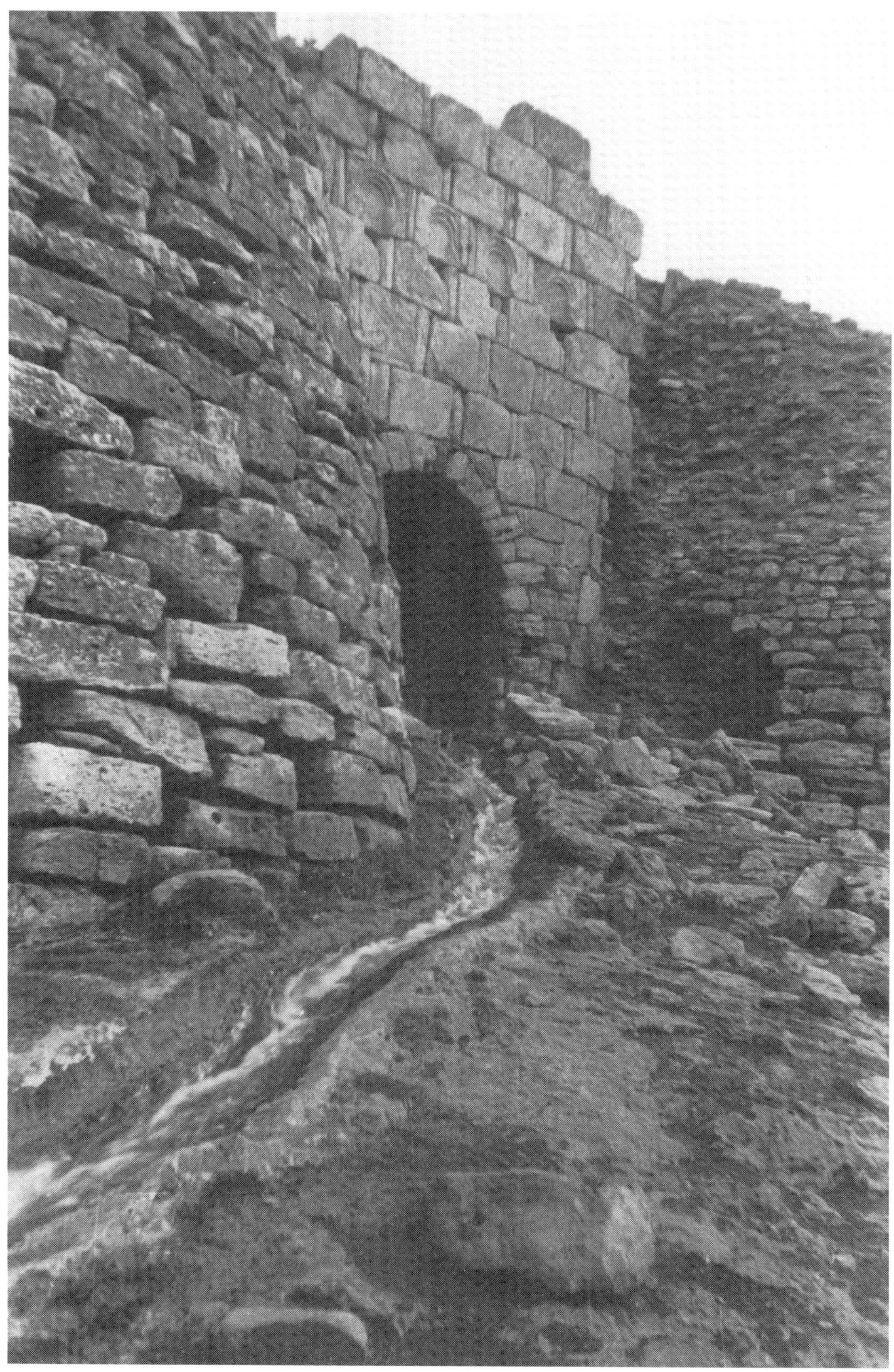

Parthian arch with calcareous brook Phraaspa 1959

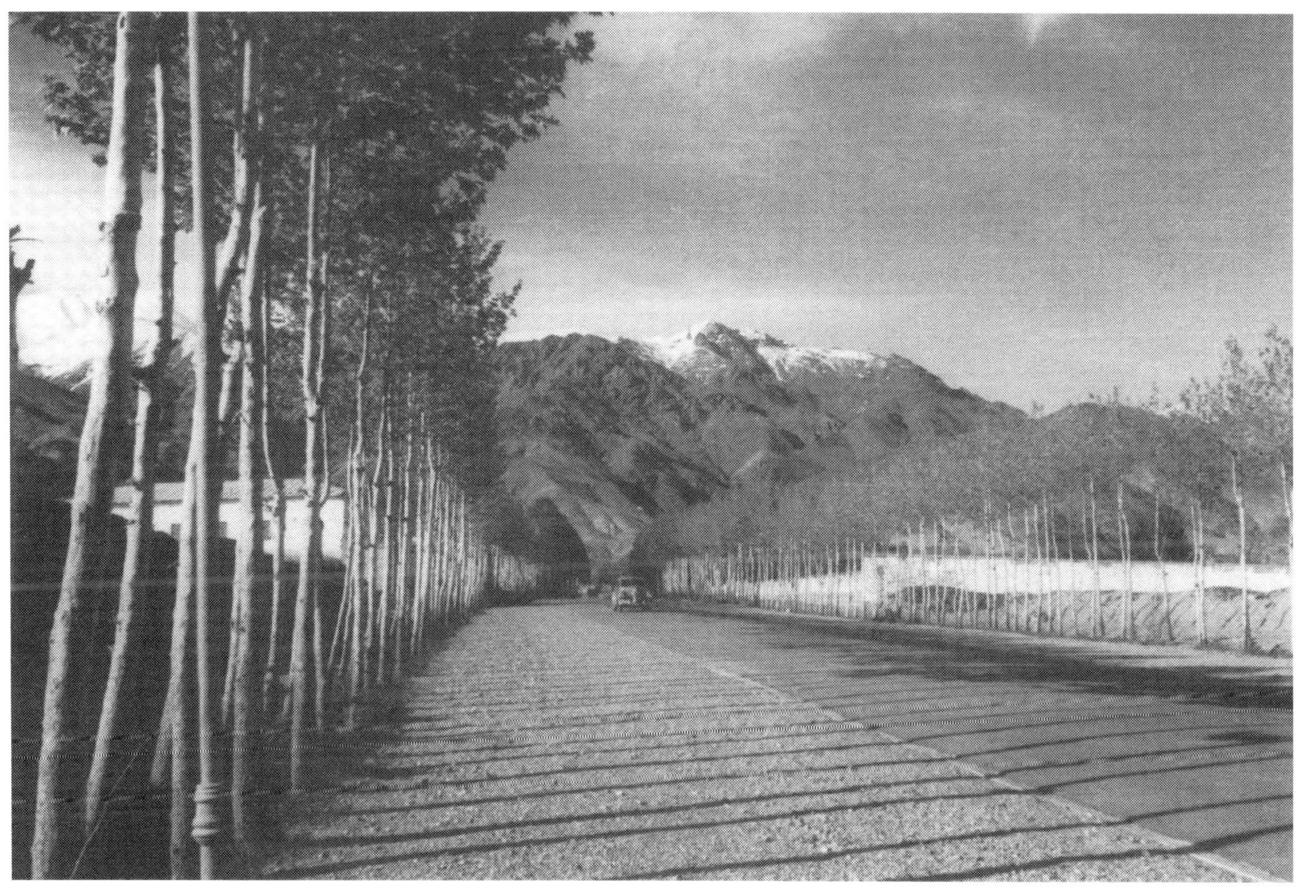

"Modern Teheran" 1959

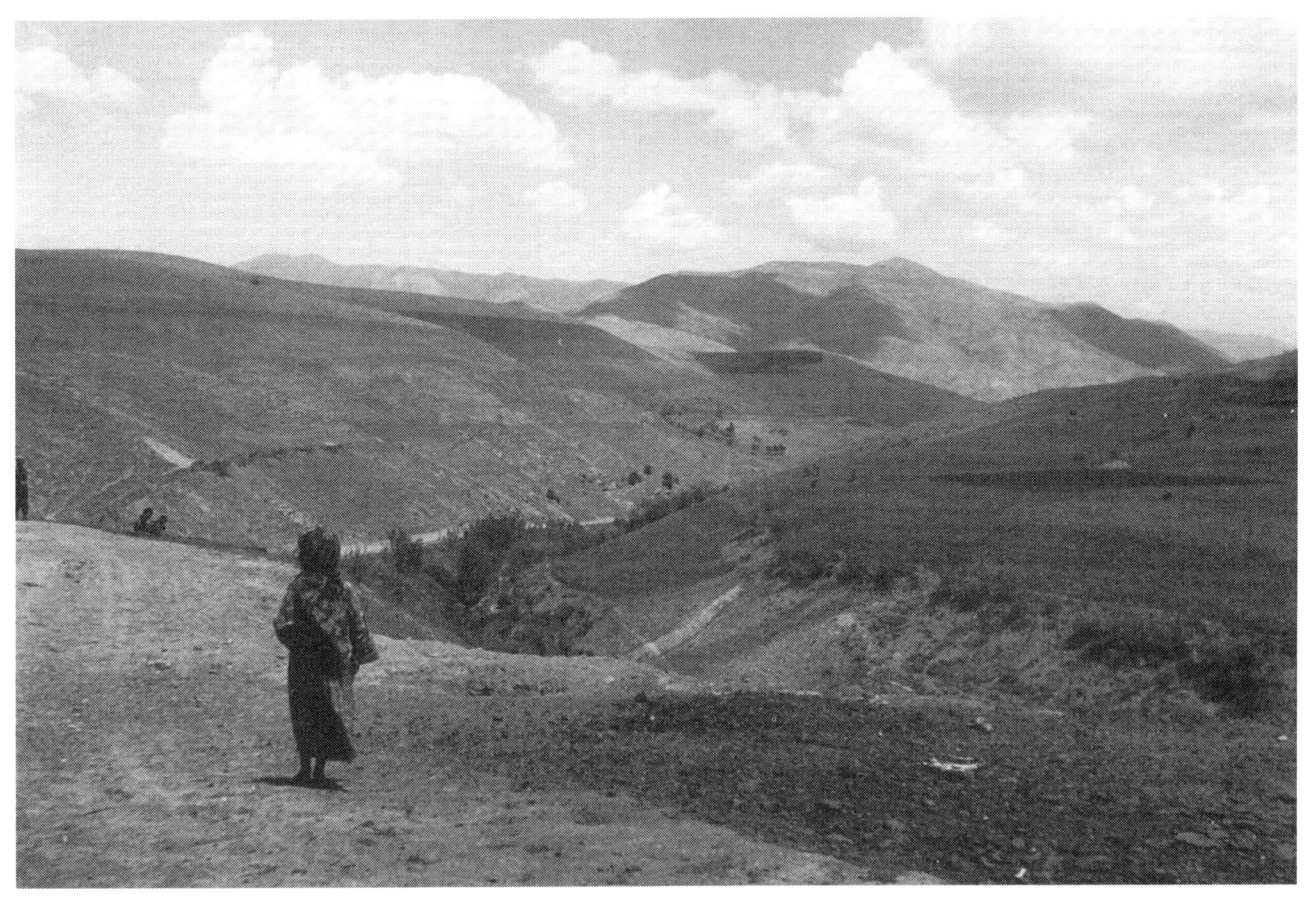

"Kurdish Country" probably in Tabriz area 1959

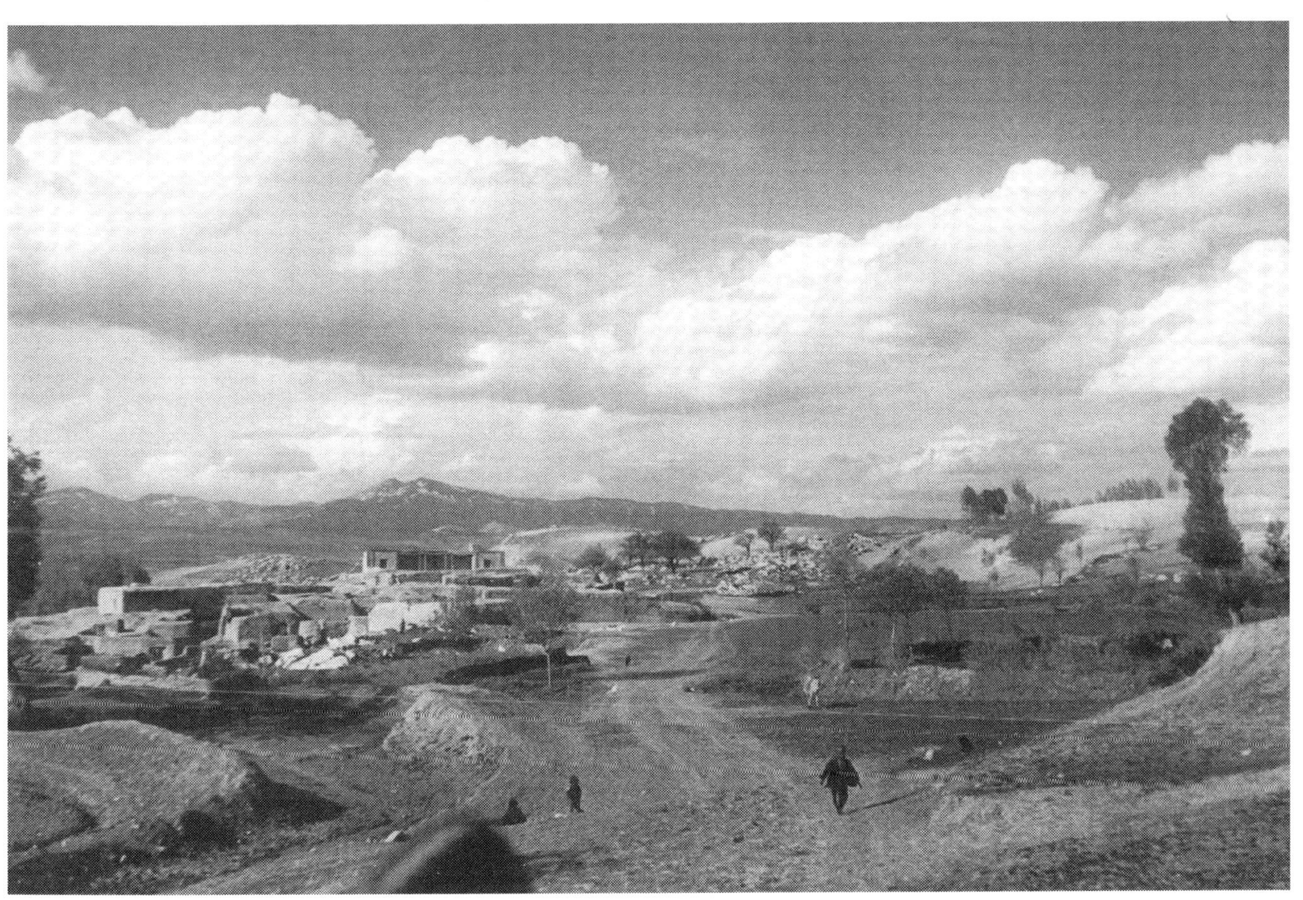

"Above Tokab" Tabriz area 1959

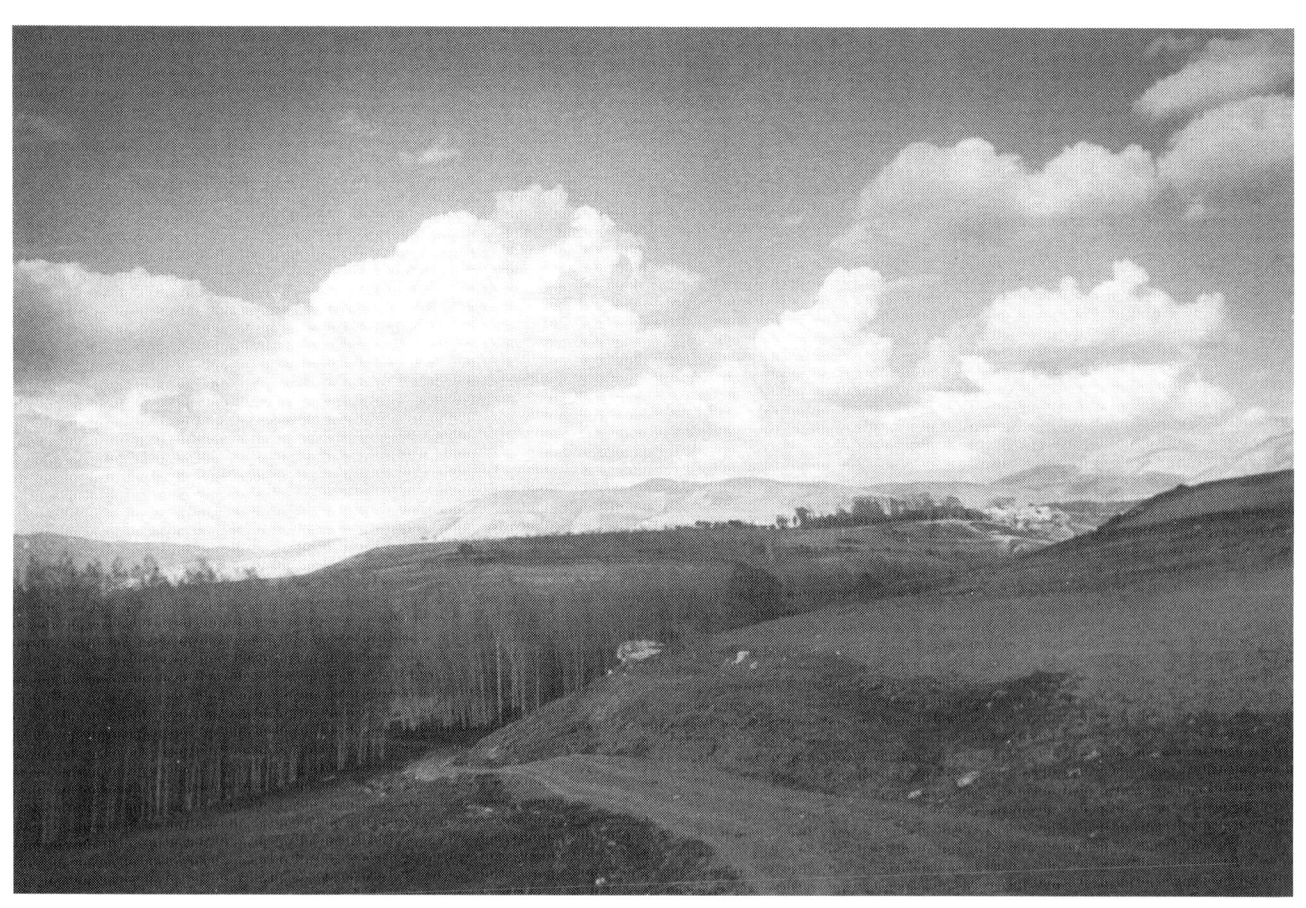

Tabriz area 1959

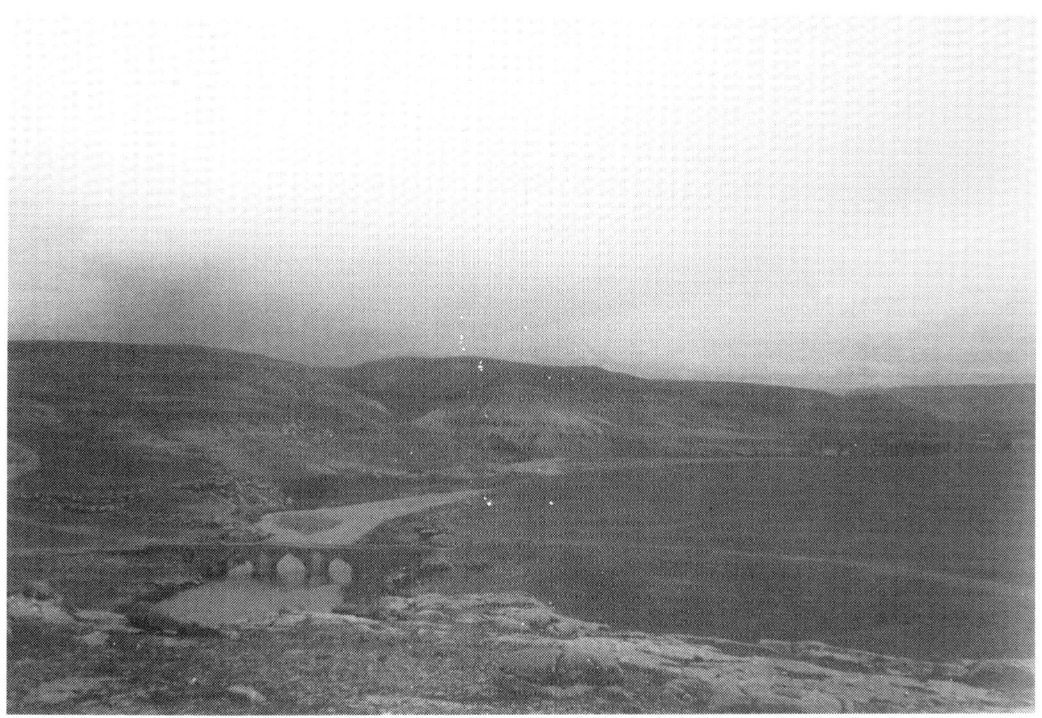

"Sarrinerud" Tabriz area 1959

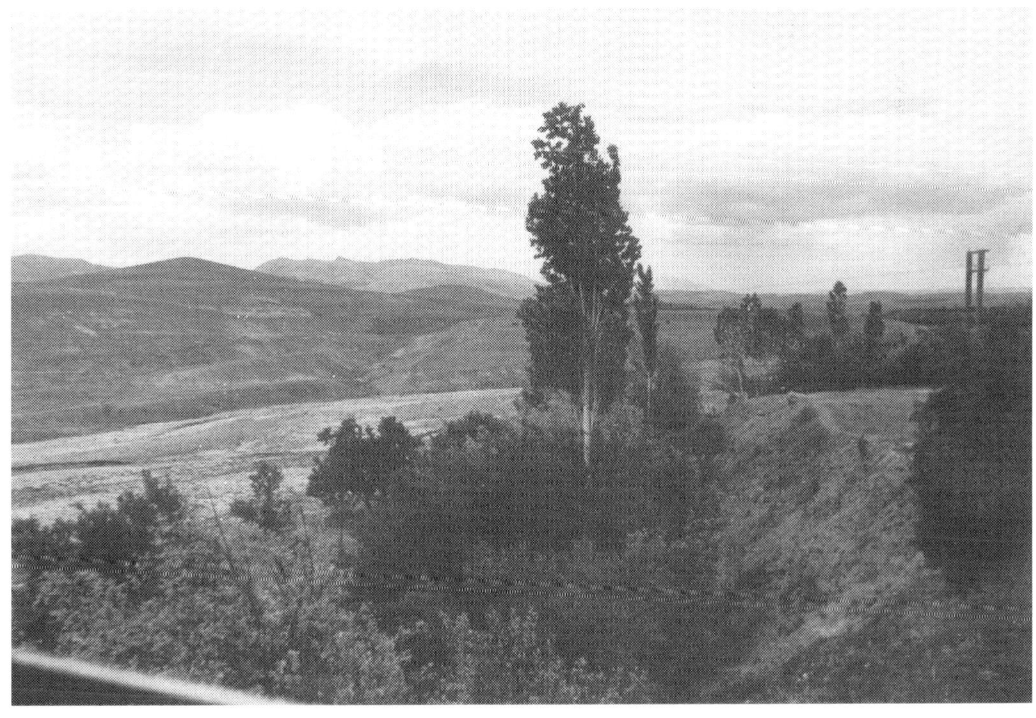

"Tabriz by train" 1960

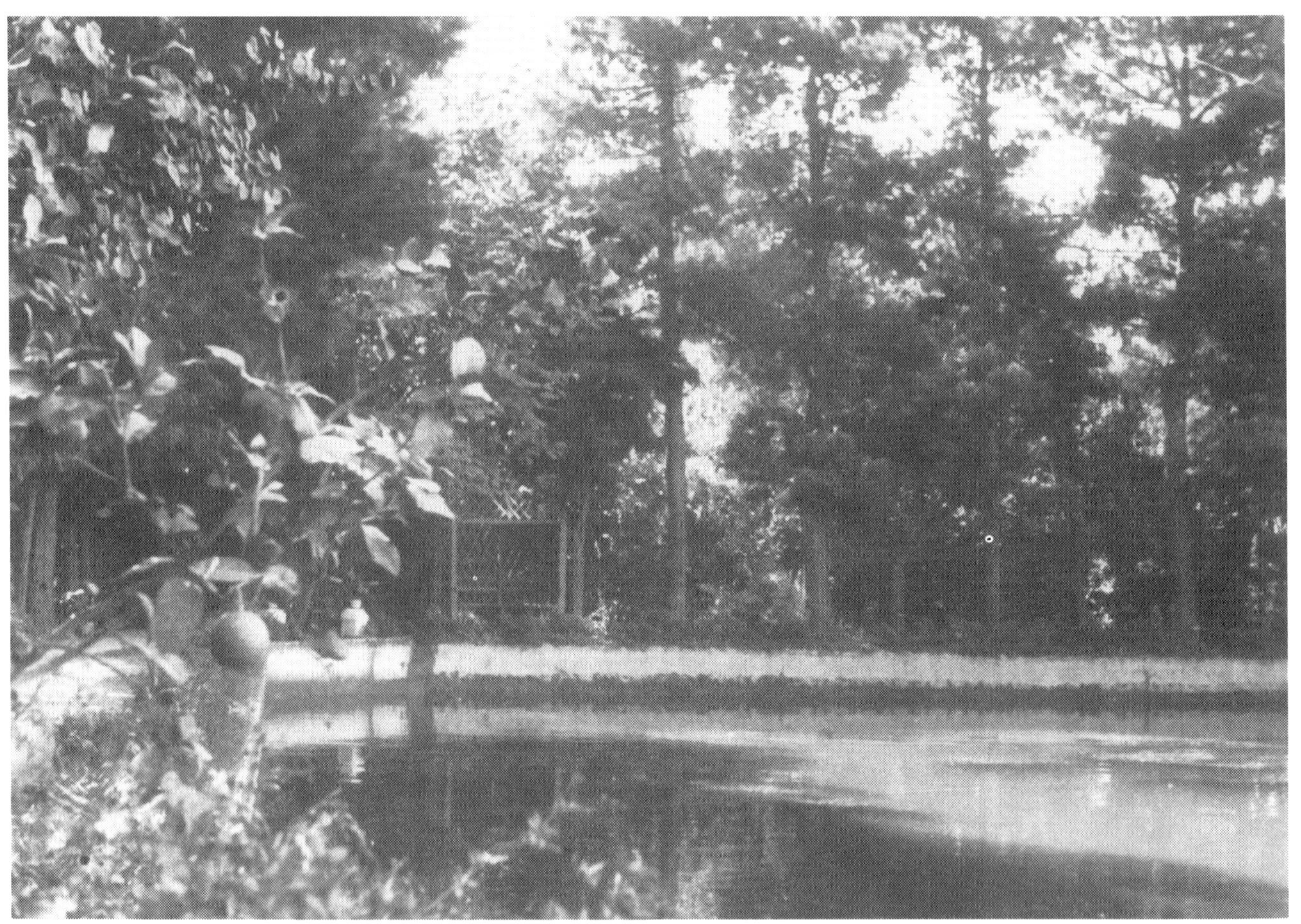

Tehran 1931

TREASURE HUNT IN LURISTAN

Arriving in Tehran after her second visit to the Elburz Mountains in the summer of 1931 Freya Stark saw some bronze-age figurines which, she learned, came from an unexplored part of Luristan, near the Iraqi border. This was a wild and dangerous place where, until its pacification by Reza Shah, "one was murdered for half a toman". Unable to resist the challenge, she decided to return to Baghdad by way of Luristan in the hope of finding some ancient graves and more statuettes. A letter to the governor got her safely to Alishtar, in north-west Luristan; but it turned out that the bronzes were in a different part of the country. Freya returned to Baghdad and arranged a new expedition the following year. Shortly before setting out she met a young man from the area, a nephew of the chief, who had been educated in Europe. He promised to show her a hoard of gold ornaments, coins and idols hidden in a cave, and they arranged a secret rendezvous, planning to enter Luristan separately in order to avoid arousing suspicion. Freya slipped across the Persian border illegally, as her guide was without a passport. They reached an area of low hills and scrubby oaks where the Lurs tended to their flocks.

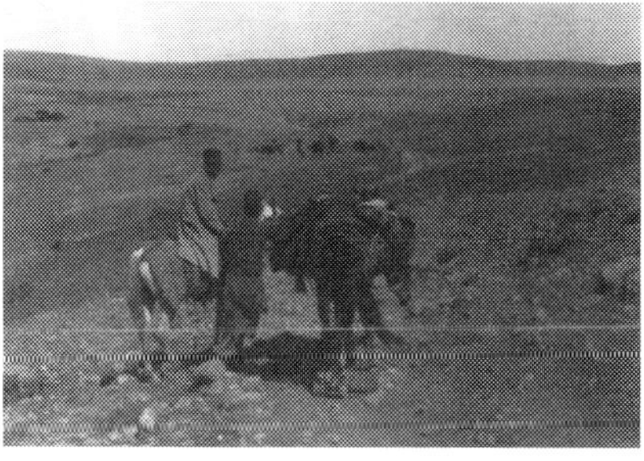

Lur guides wearing Pahlavi caps 1931

Freya found some graves, probably early Muslim ones, but discovered nothing of value. She took a skull, for identification, which she placed in her saddlebag. Soon afterwards she ran into a posse of mounted police, who insisted on taking her to the district governor. For a time, however, she eluded them, and hunted for the secret cave among the oaks and ravines. She found neither the treasure nor her Lurish accomplice. When she was brought before the governor at the district capital of Husainabad, he expressed his amazement that she had survived in so notorious a region. "No wonder", he said, "that yours is a powerful nation. Your women do what our men are afraid to attempt."

Instructions arrived from Tehran ordering Freya's immediate deportation to Iraq. On arriving at Baghdad, she found that her Lurish accomplice had been arrested on a trumped-up charge, due to the machinations of a rival treasure hunter. The same man had bribed six Lurish porters from Baghdad to intercept her. She could easily have been murdered without the culprits ever being discovered. In the event, the Persian police may have been responsible for saving her life. They had heard rumours about a strange foreign woman wandering about Luristan opening graves containing golden skulls. They had acted before her would-be murderers caught up with her.

The treasure hunt was a fiasco, but Freya had experienced the excitement of being in unexplored country among nomads and semi-nomads untainted by civilization. Like the Druzes she had visited in Syria and the Kurds and Shammar Arabs in Iraq, the Lurs and the other nomadic peoples she met on this journey appealed to the romantic side of her nature. "It is not the turbulence of the tribesman that one admires," she would write, the excitement recollected in tranquillity, "but the virtues that go with his turbulence, so that the two are associated together. His treasure is the freedom of his spirit: when he loses that, he loses everything . . . In many cases he will refuse the greater comfort of the settled life because he definitely prefers his spiritual heritage to more material things. He is an aristocrat."

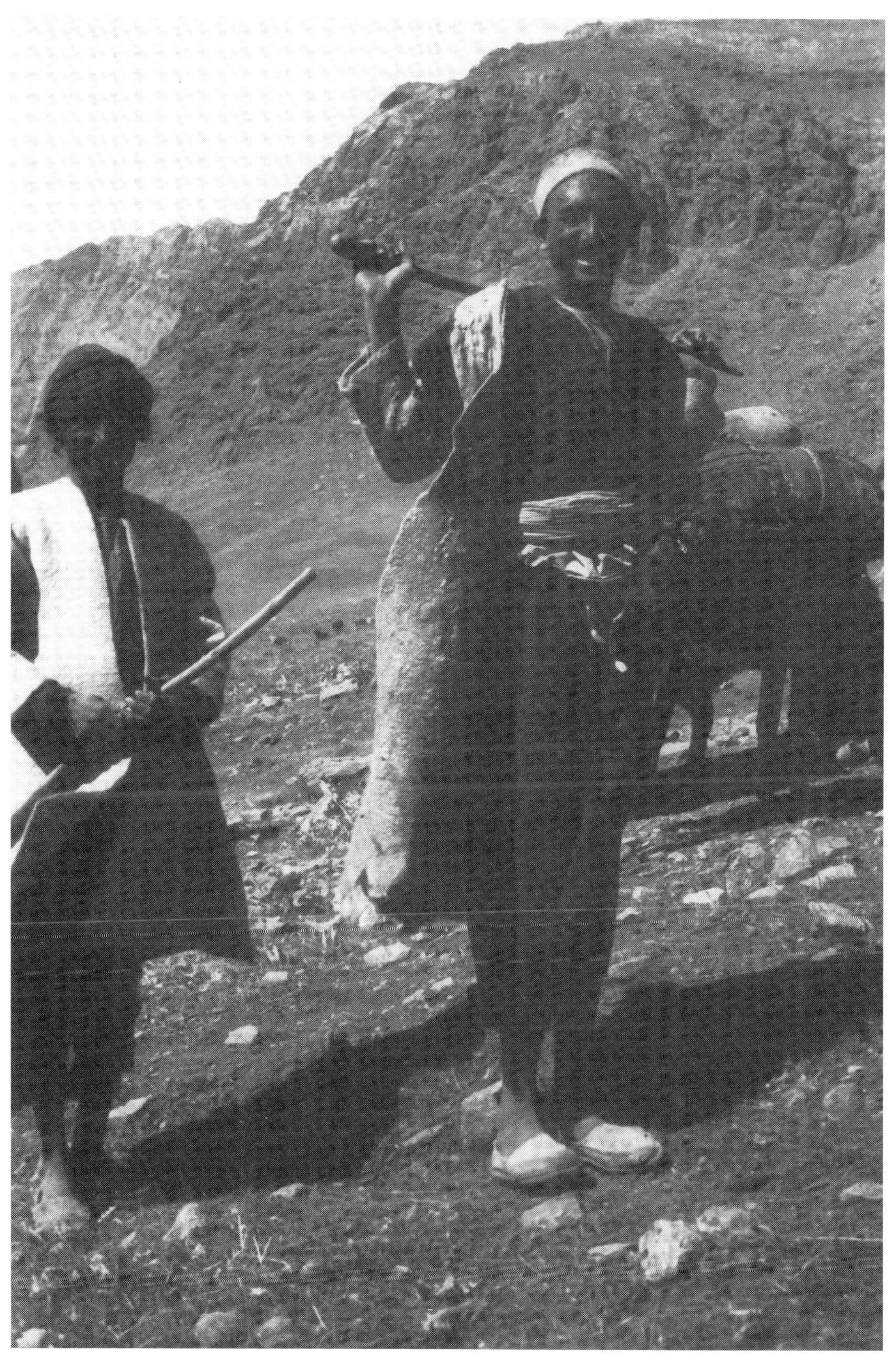

Lurs from Arjiné, Khava 1931

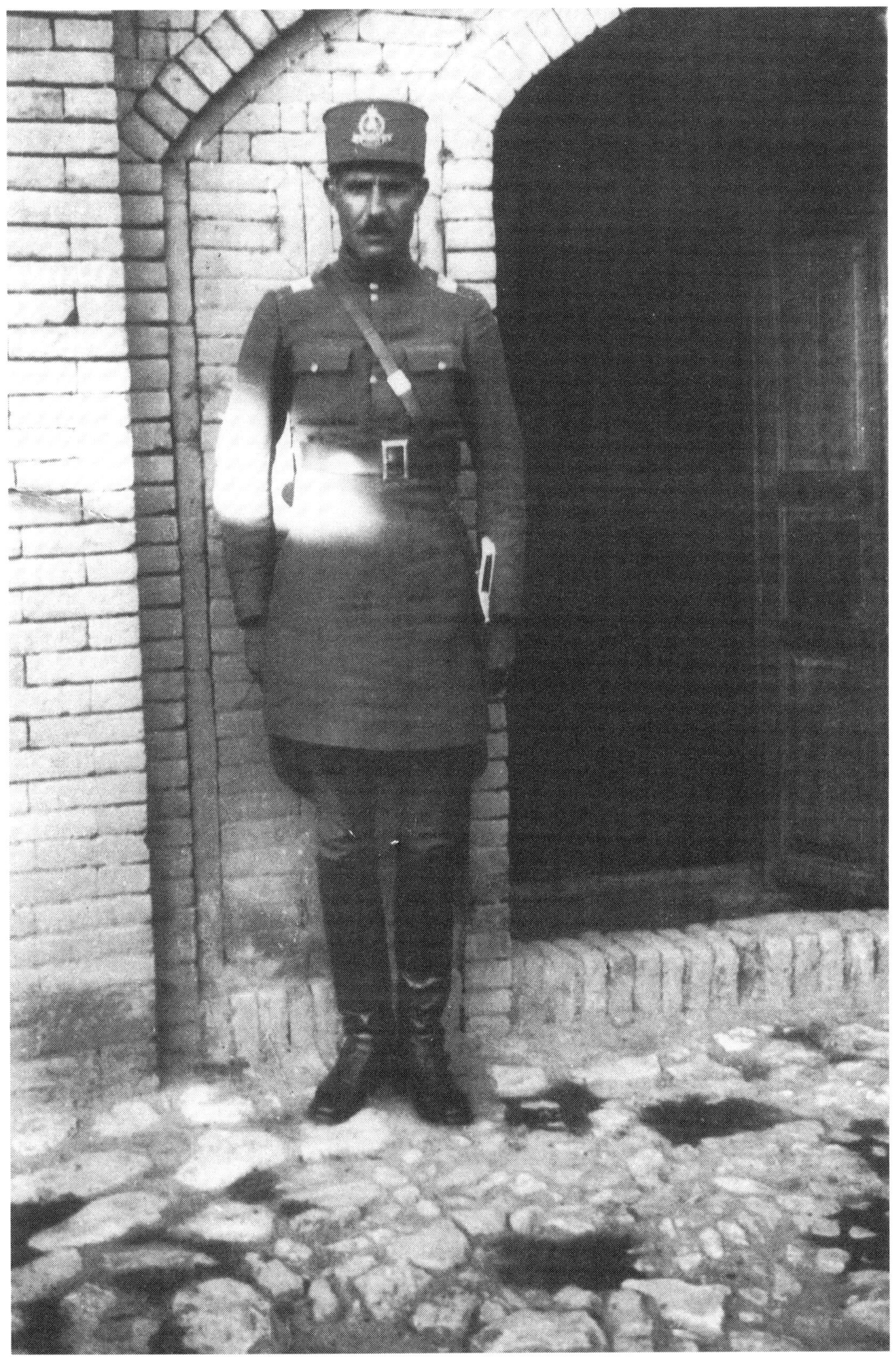

Commandant of Police, Luristan 1931. "He wanted to marry me."

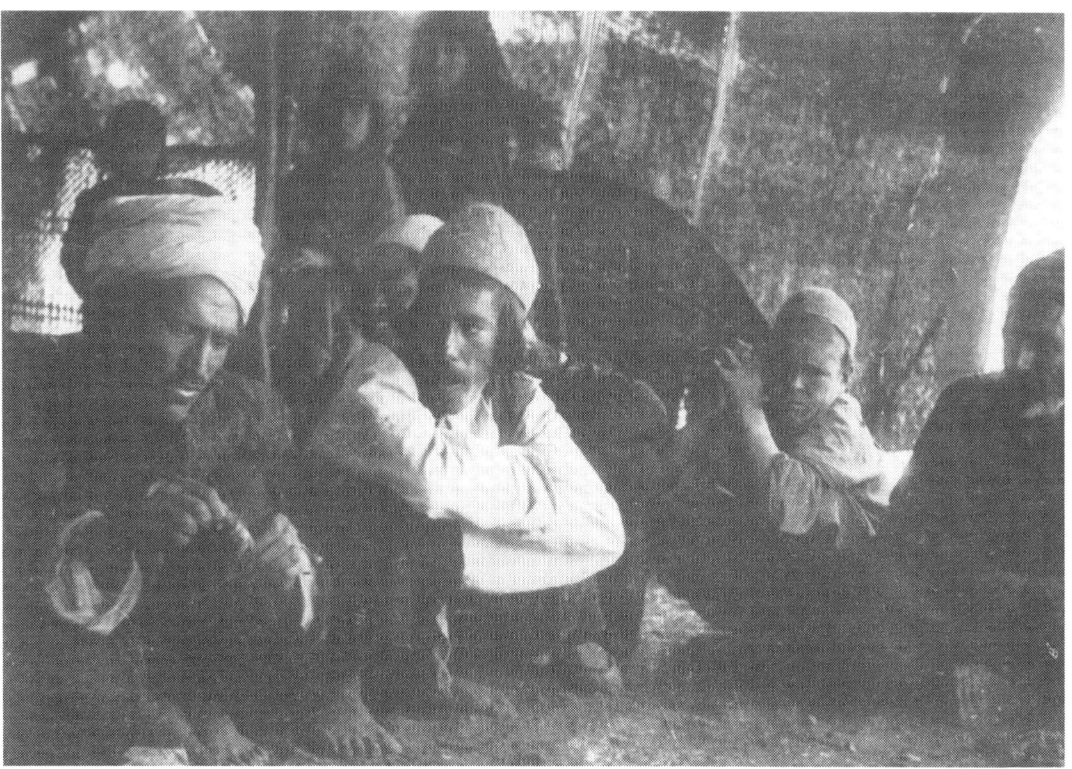

Tent interior near Alishtar 1931

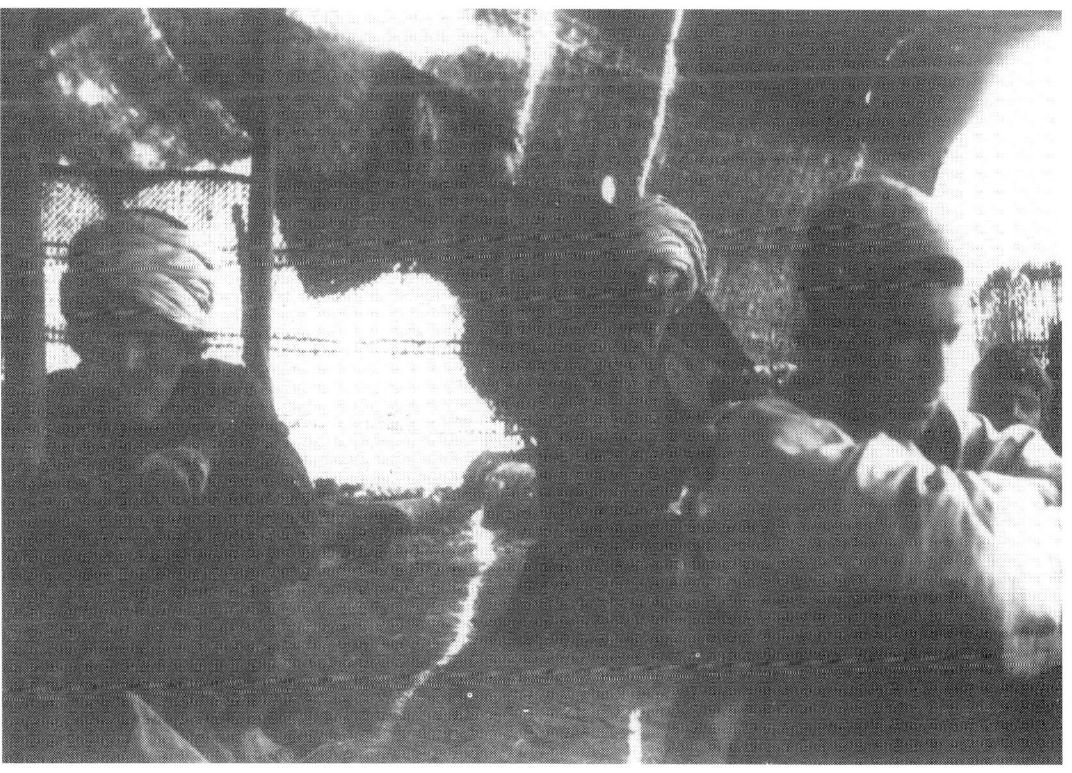

Tent interior, Deh Kush 1931

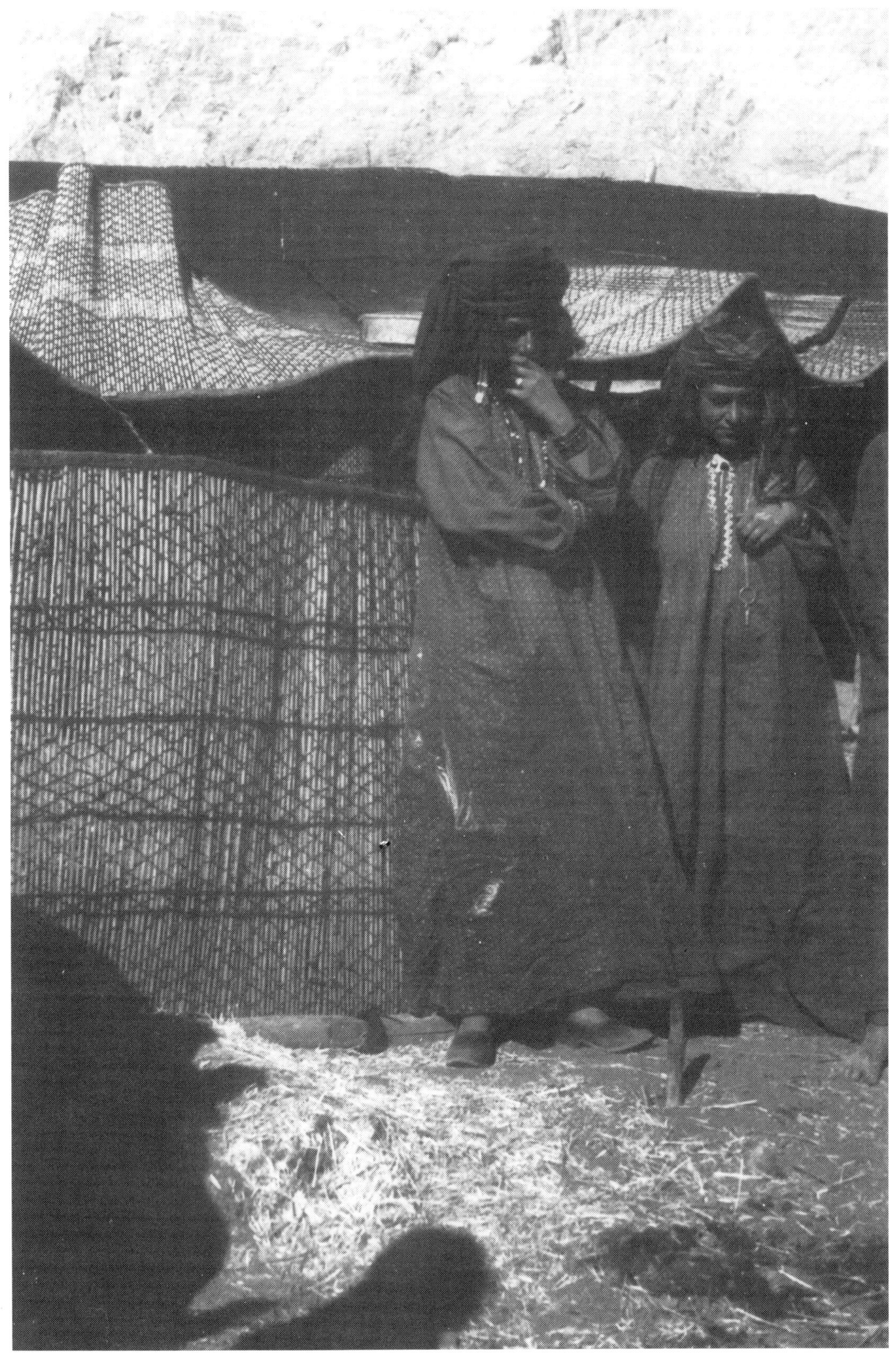

Alishtar Plain 1931

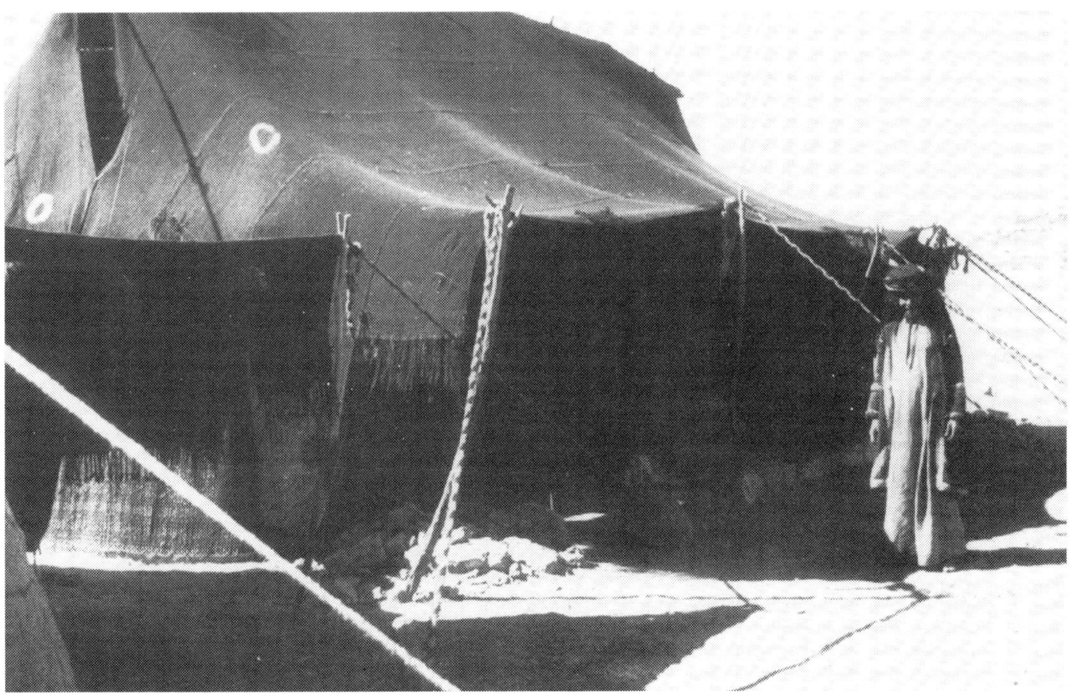

Tribeswoman, Dilfan 1931

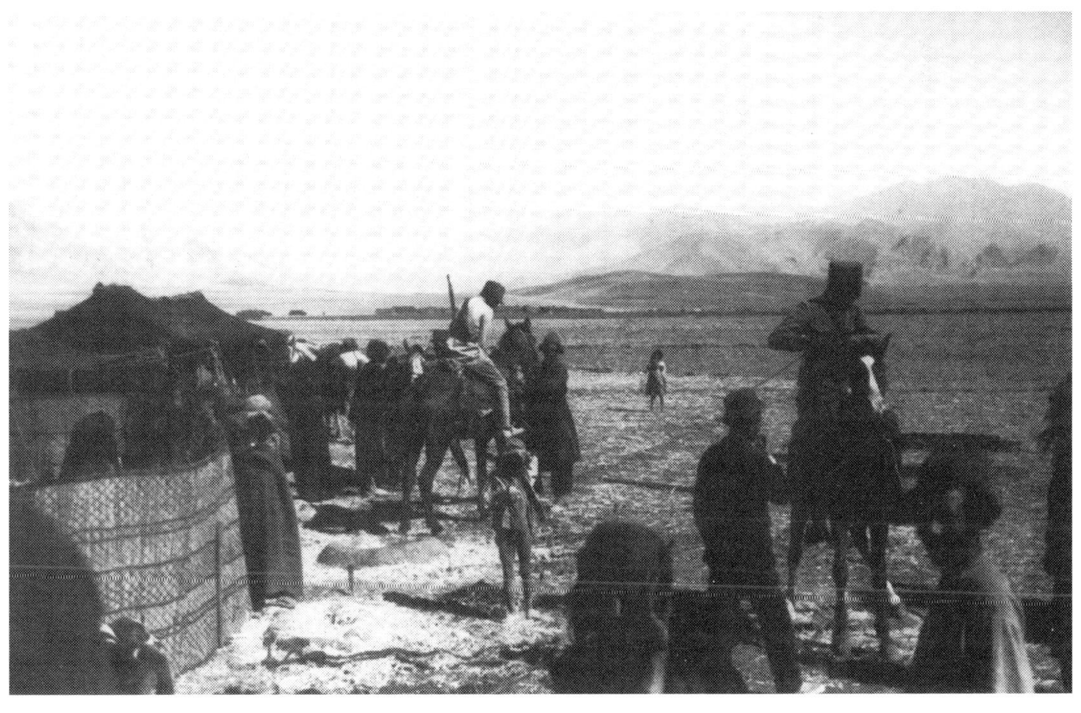

Police Escort, Gatchkah 1931

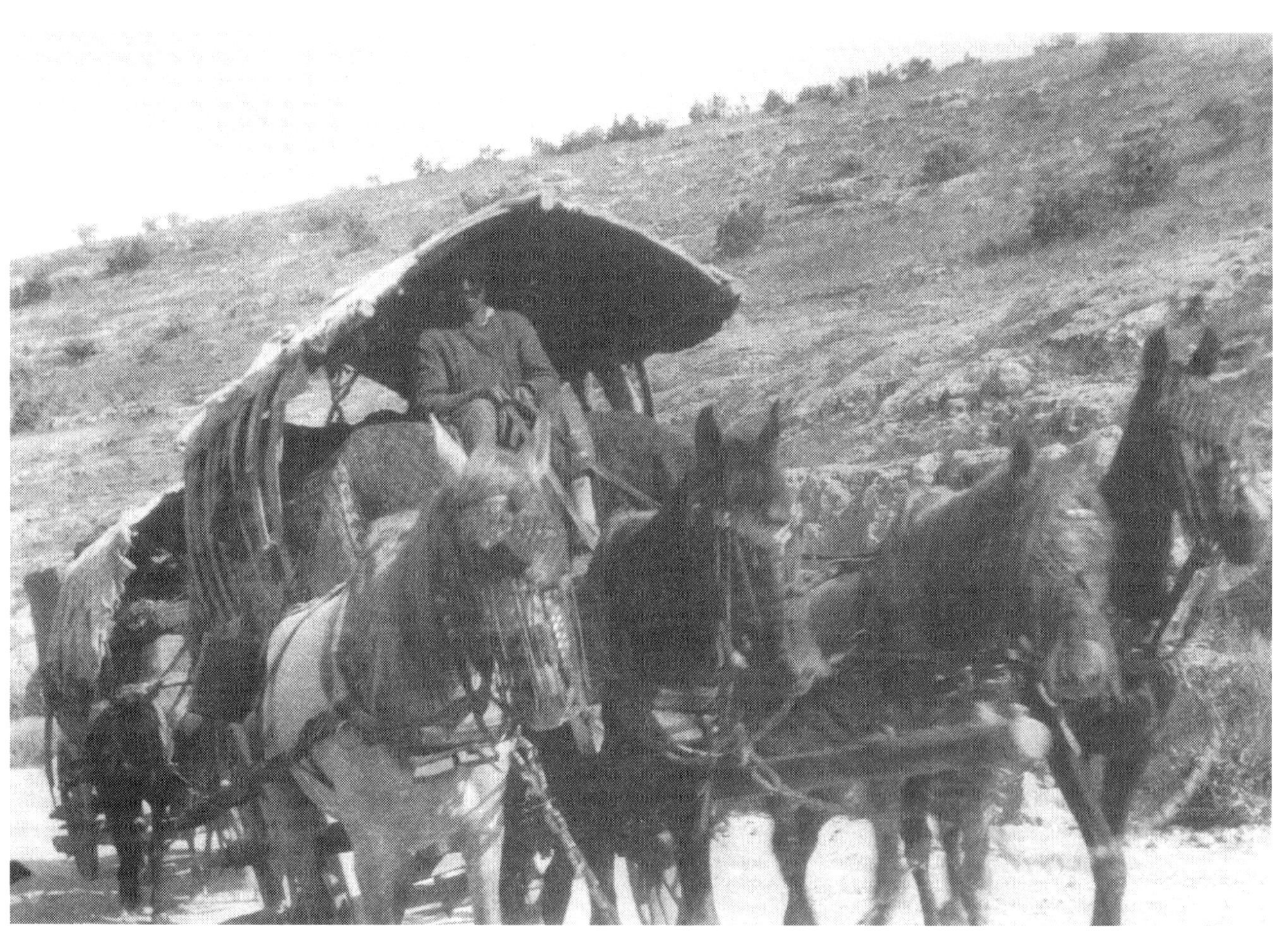

Road Cart, Kermanshah 1931

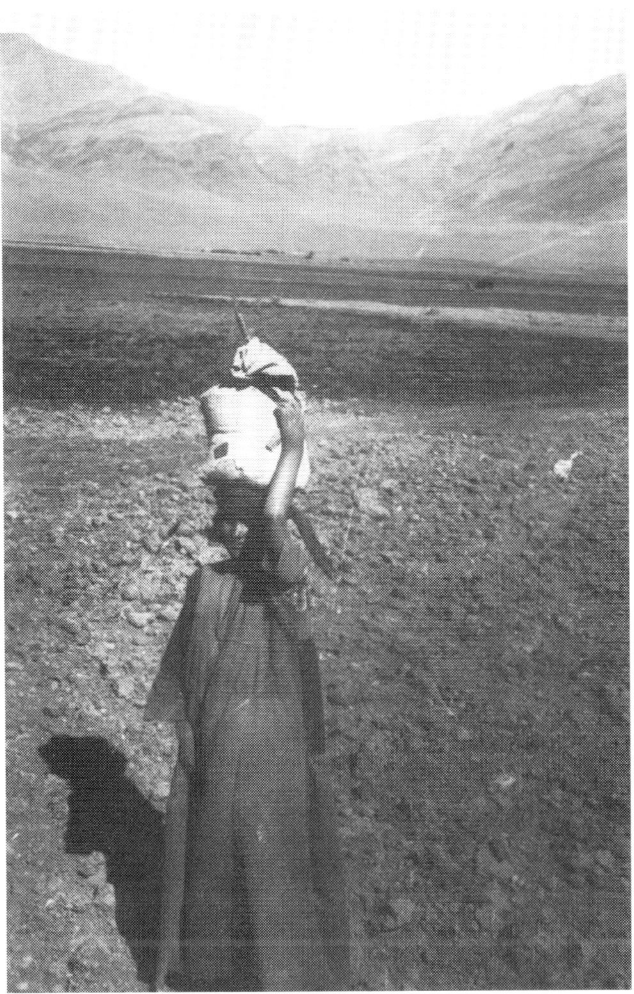

Woman at Qalʿa Kafrash 1931

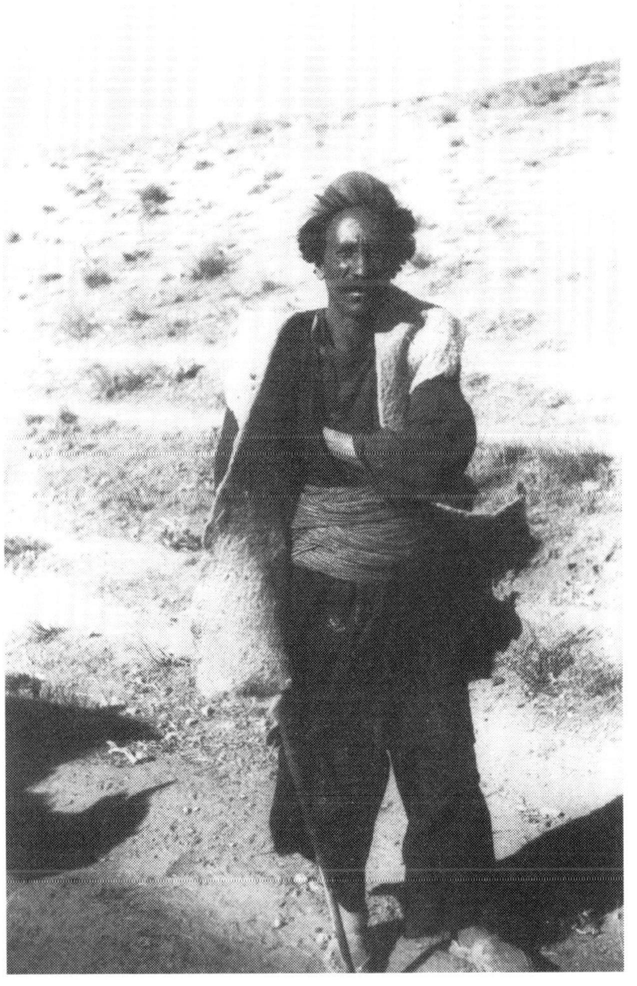

Lurish Tribesman 1931

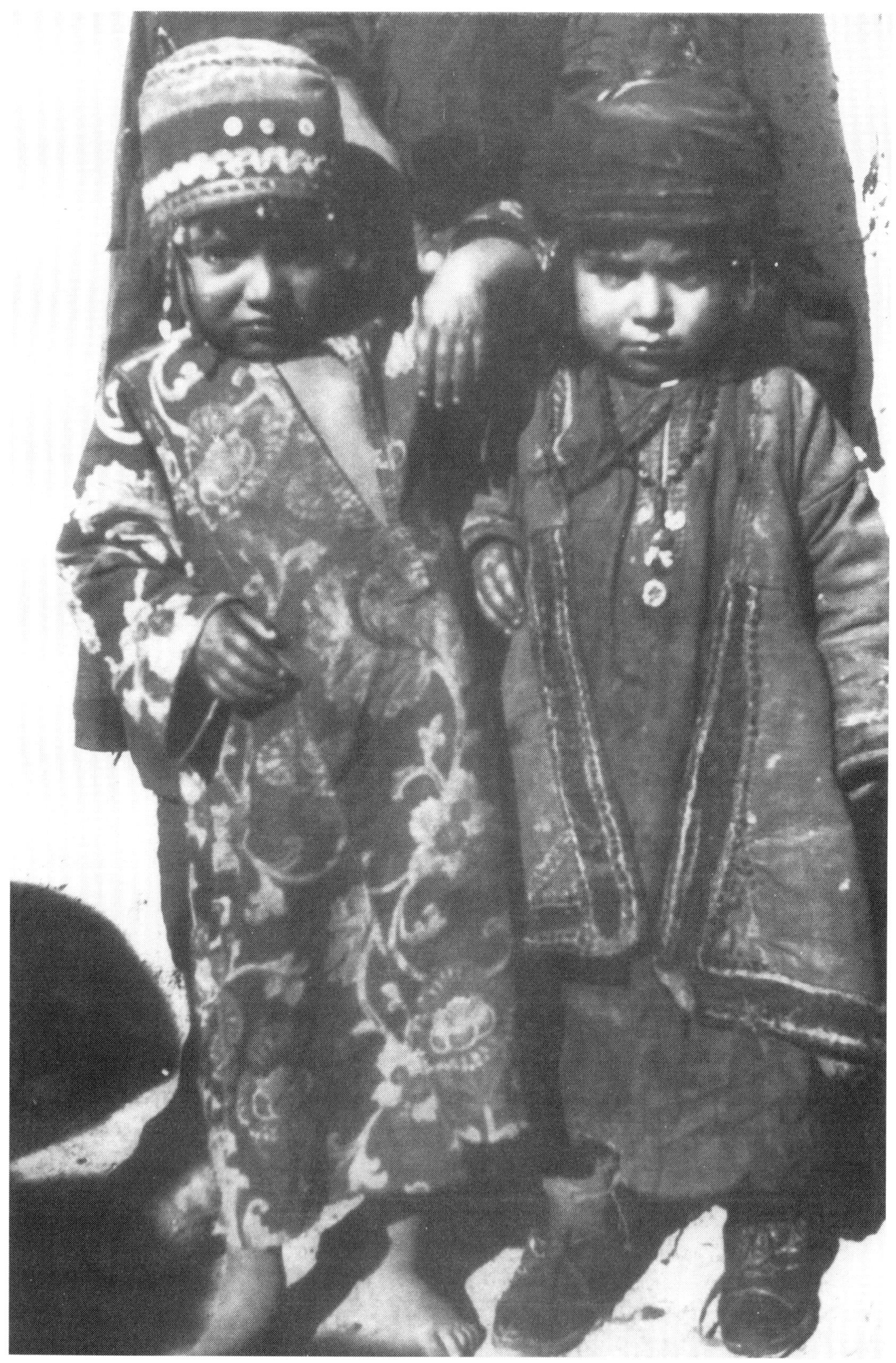

Children of Qal'a Kafrash 1931

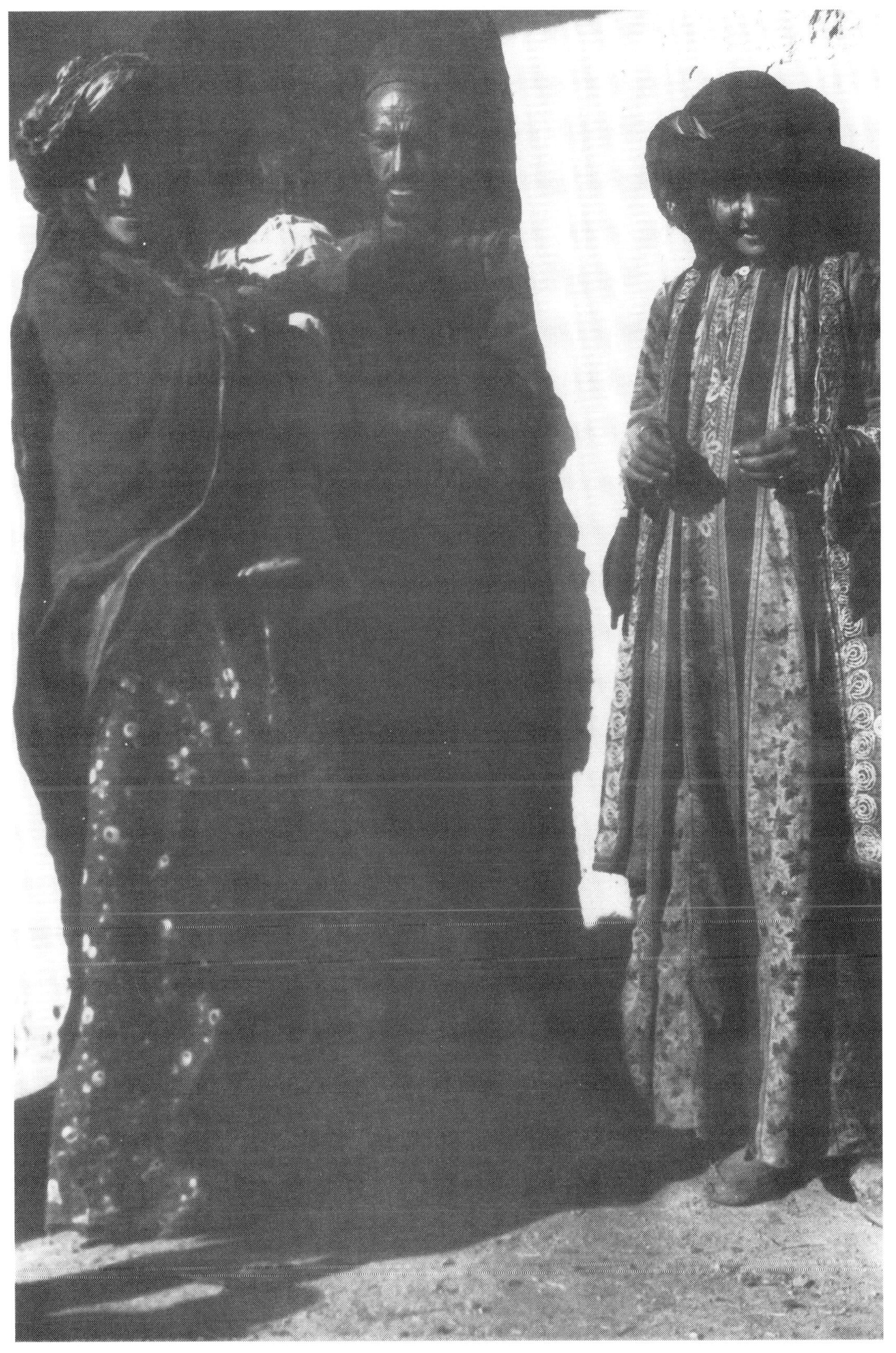

Women of Qal'a Kafrash 1931

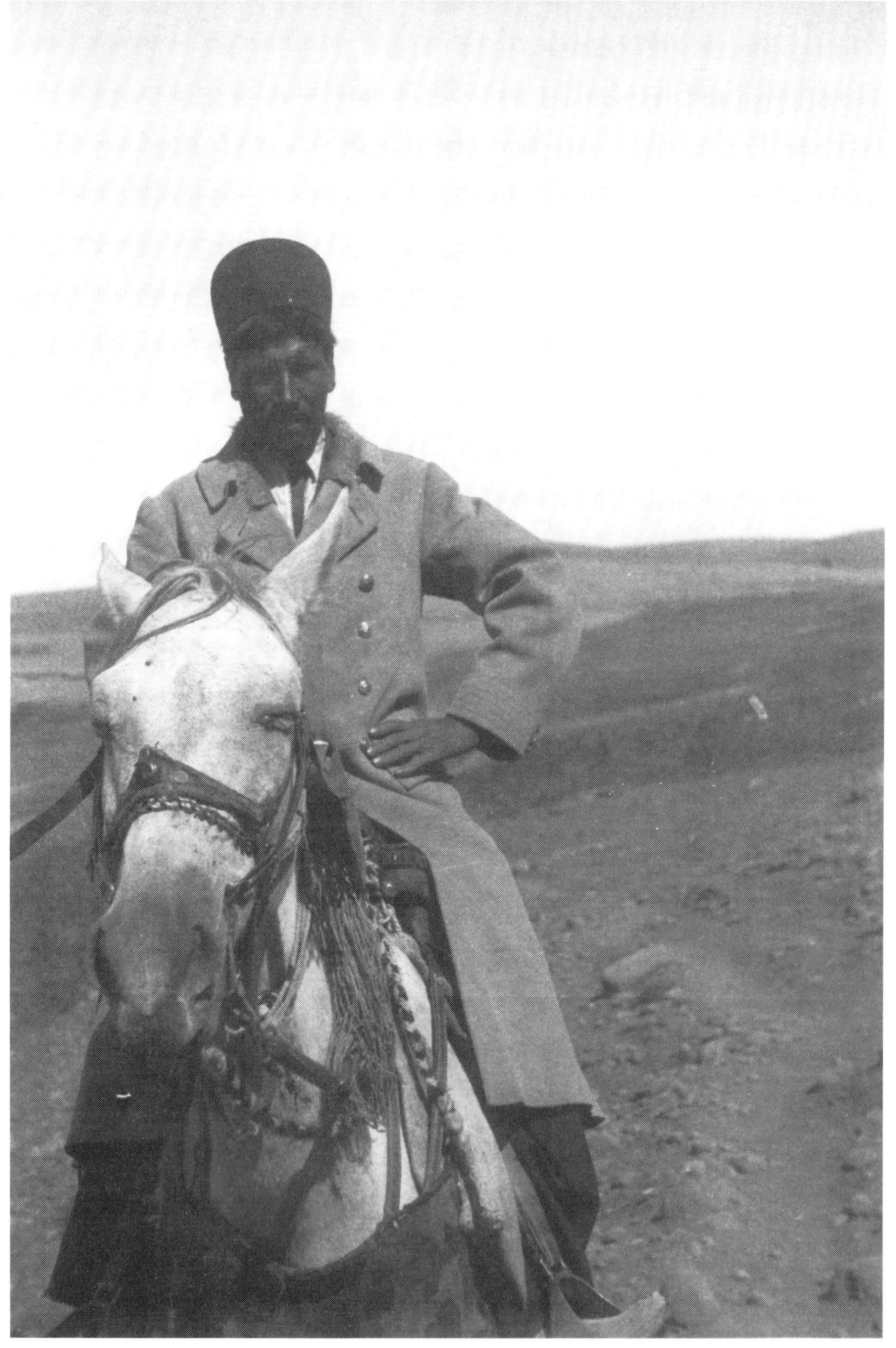

Keram Khan, a Kakavend Lur who acted as Freya's guide in October 1931

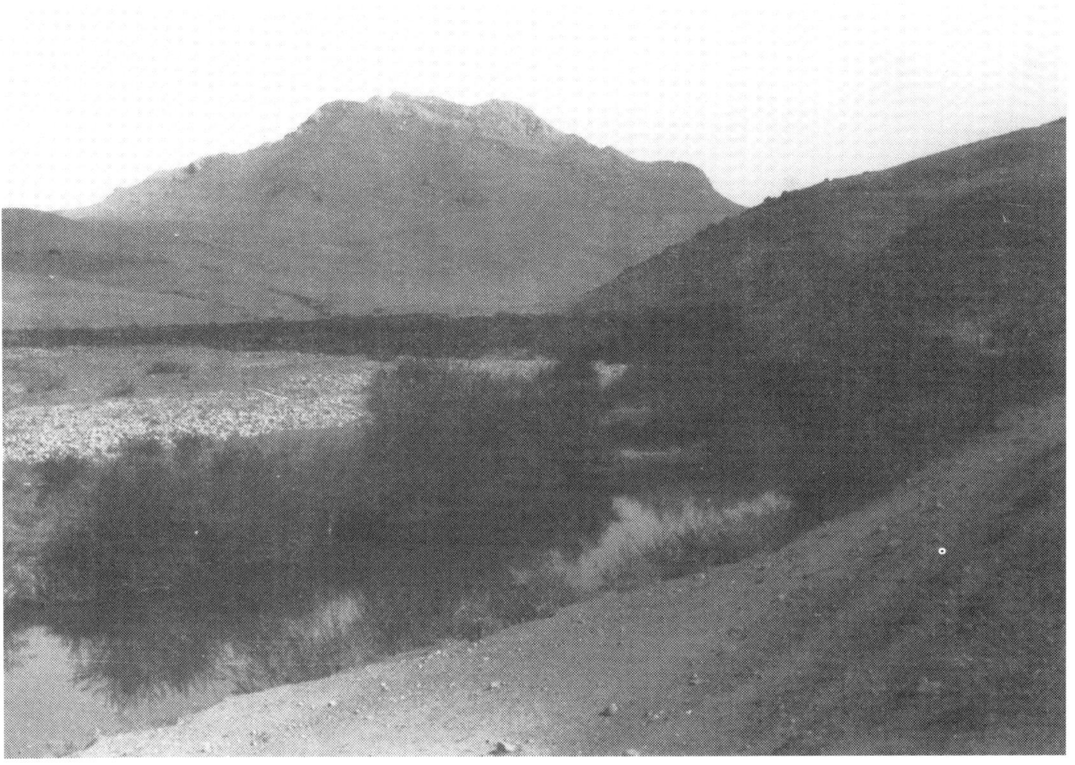

Chia Dizdan from Gizarud 1931

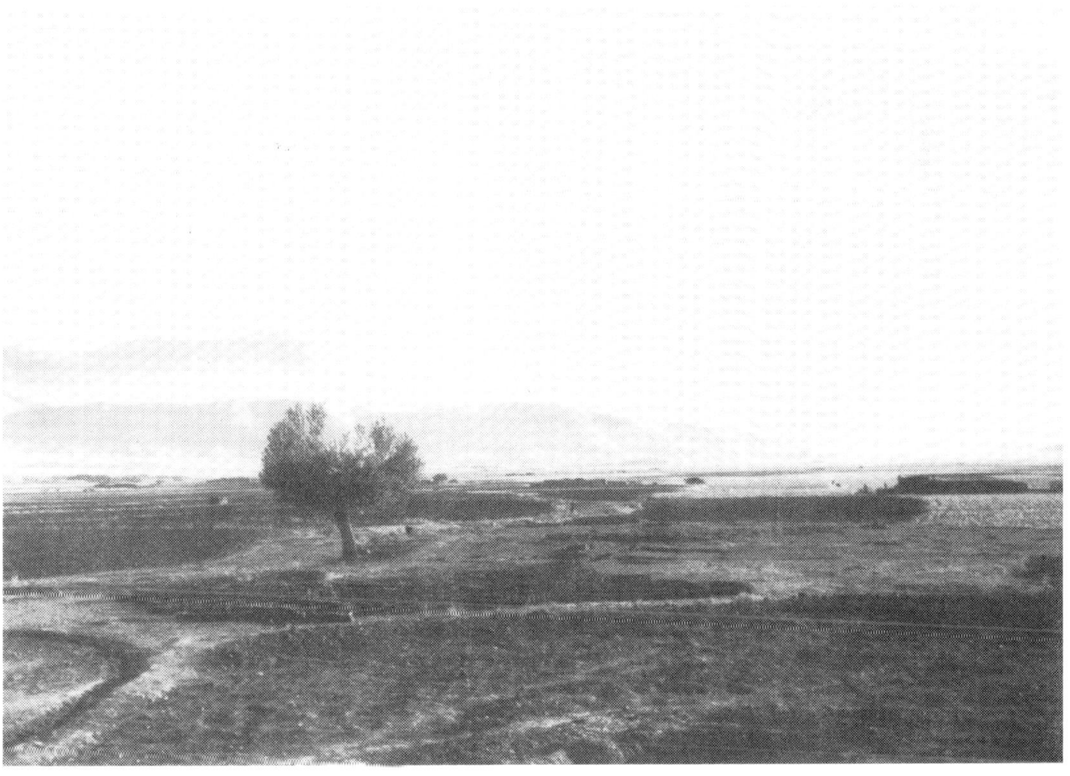

Nihavend Plain 1931

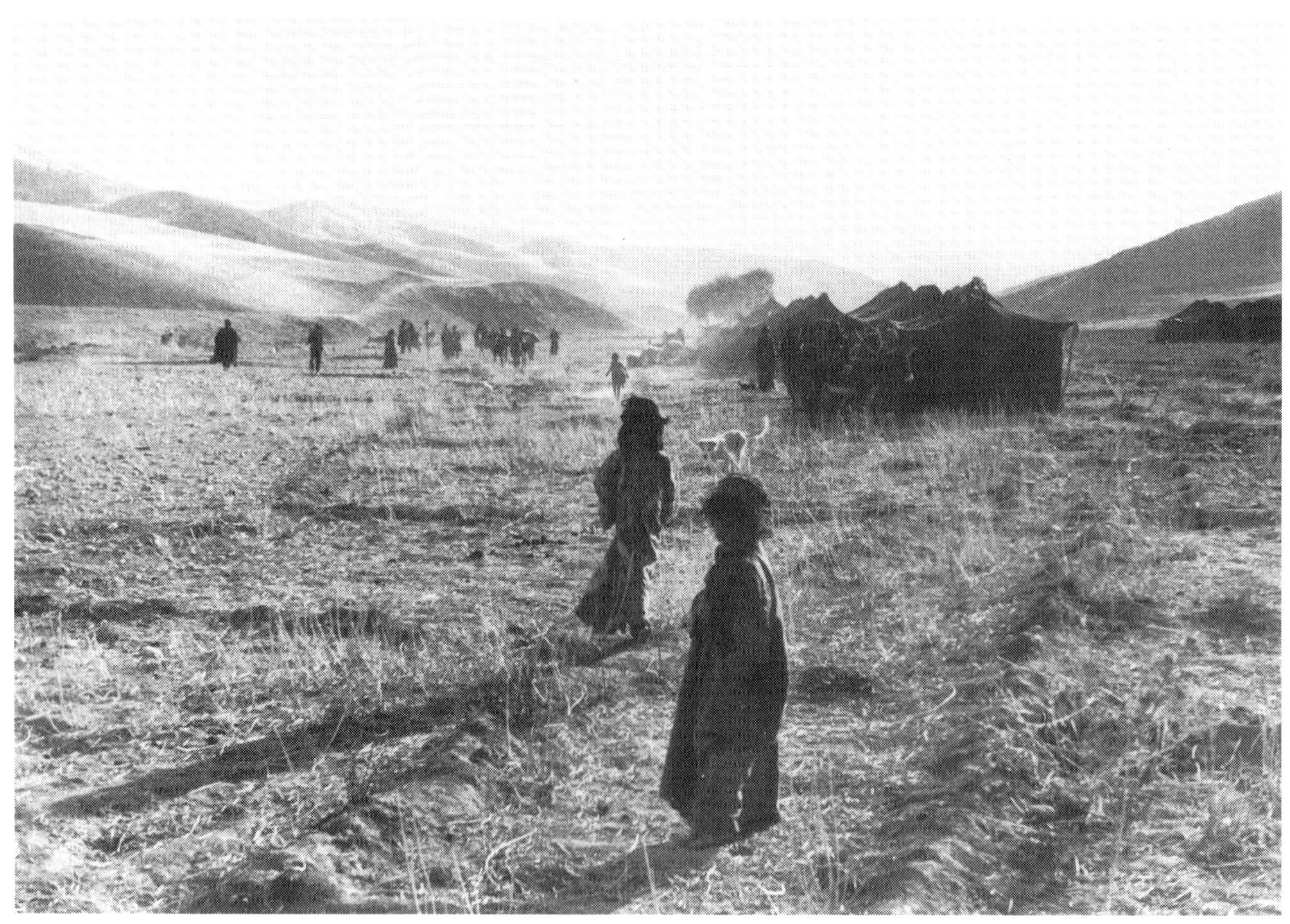

Luristan Camp, Dulistan 1931

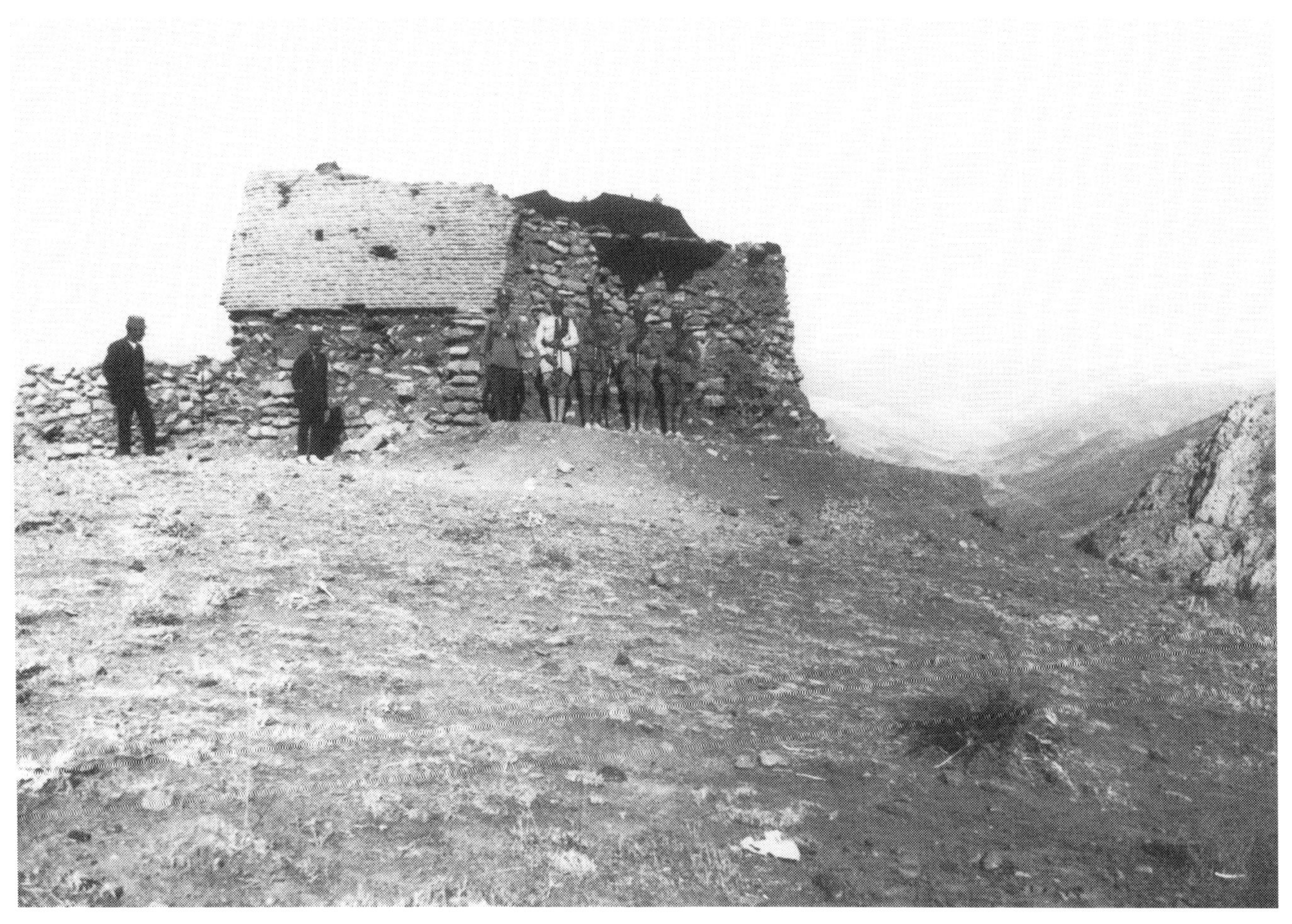

Police tower, Gatchkah Pass 1931

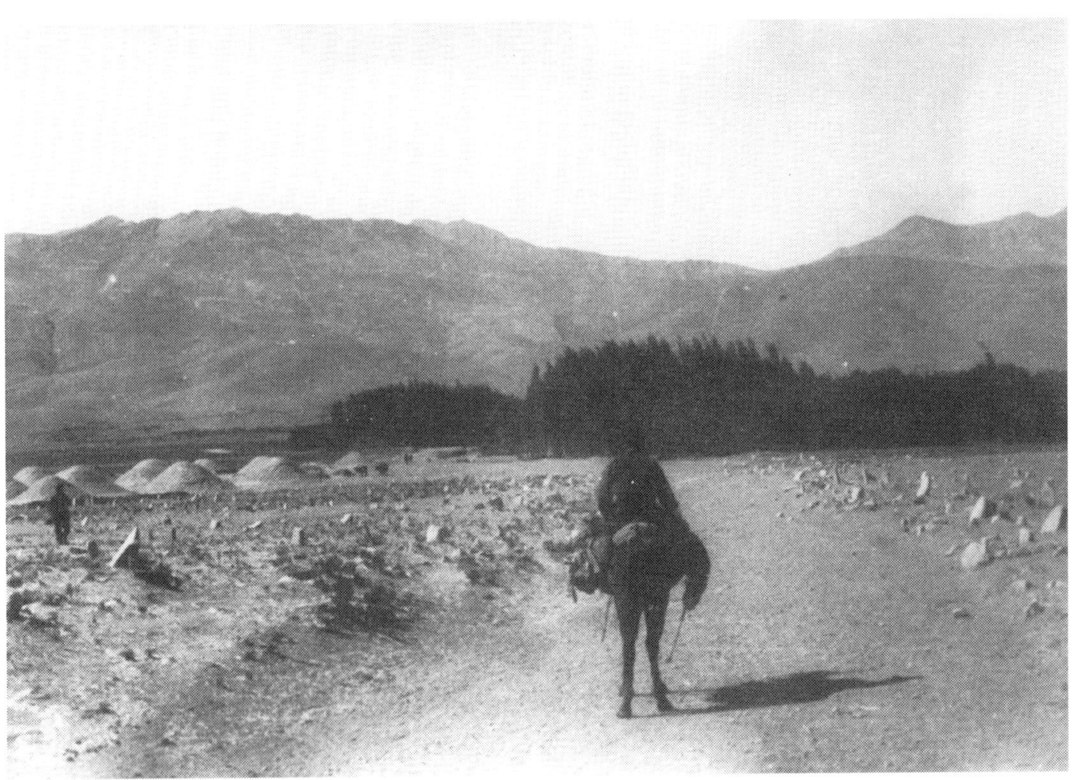

Track from Varazan to Khava 1931

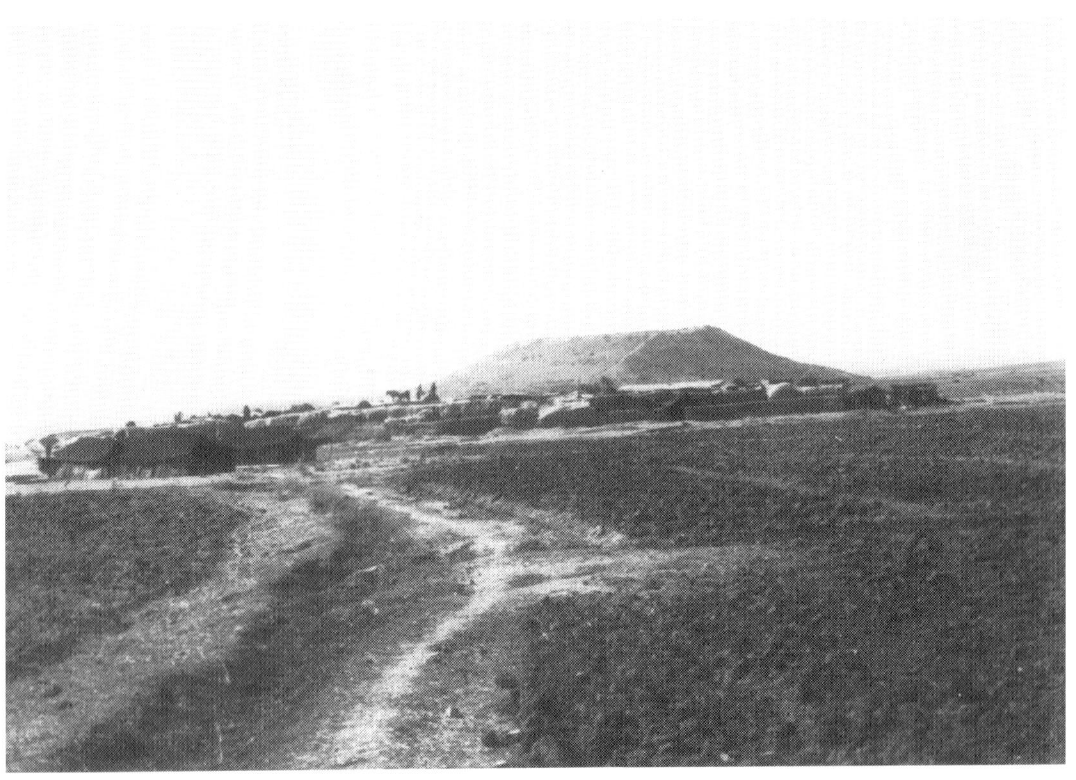

Mound of Qal'a Kafrash, Khava 1931

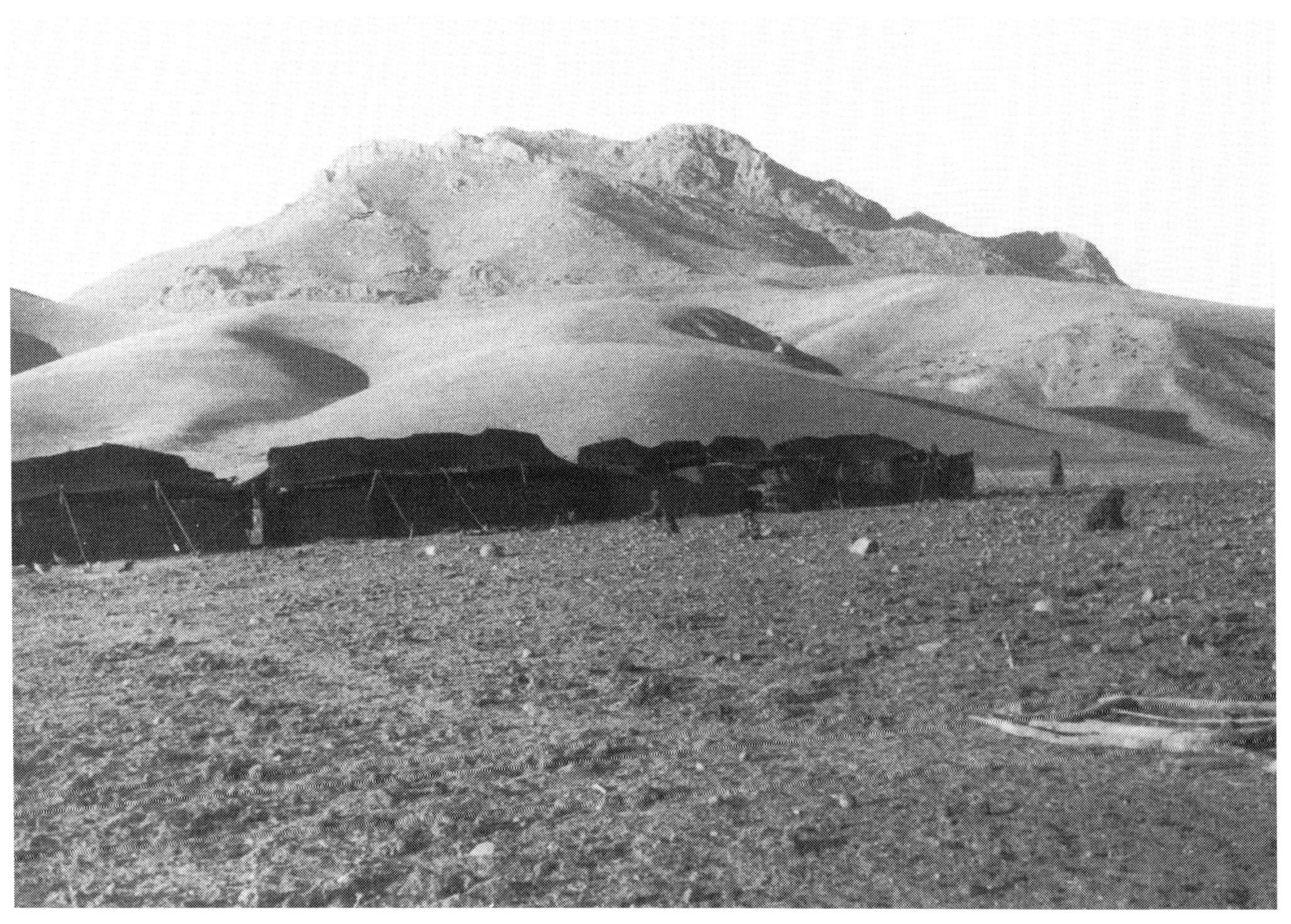

Camp at Chia Dozdan behind Tarazak 1931

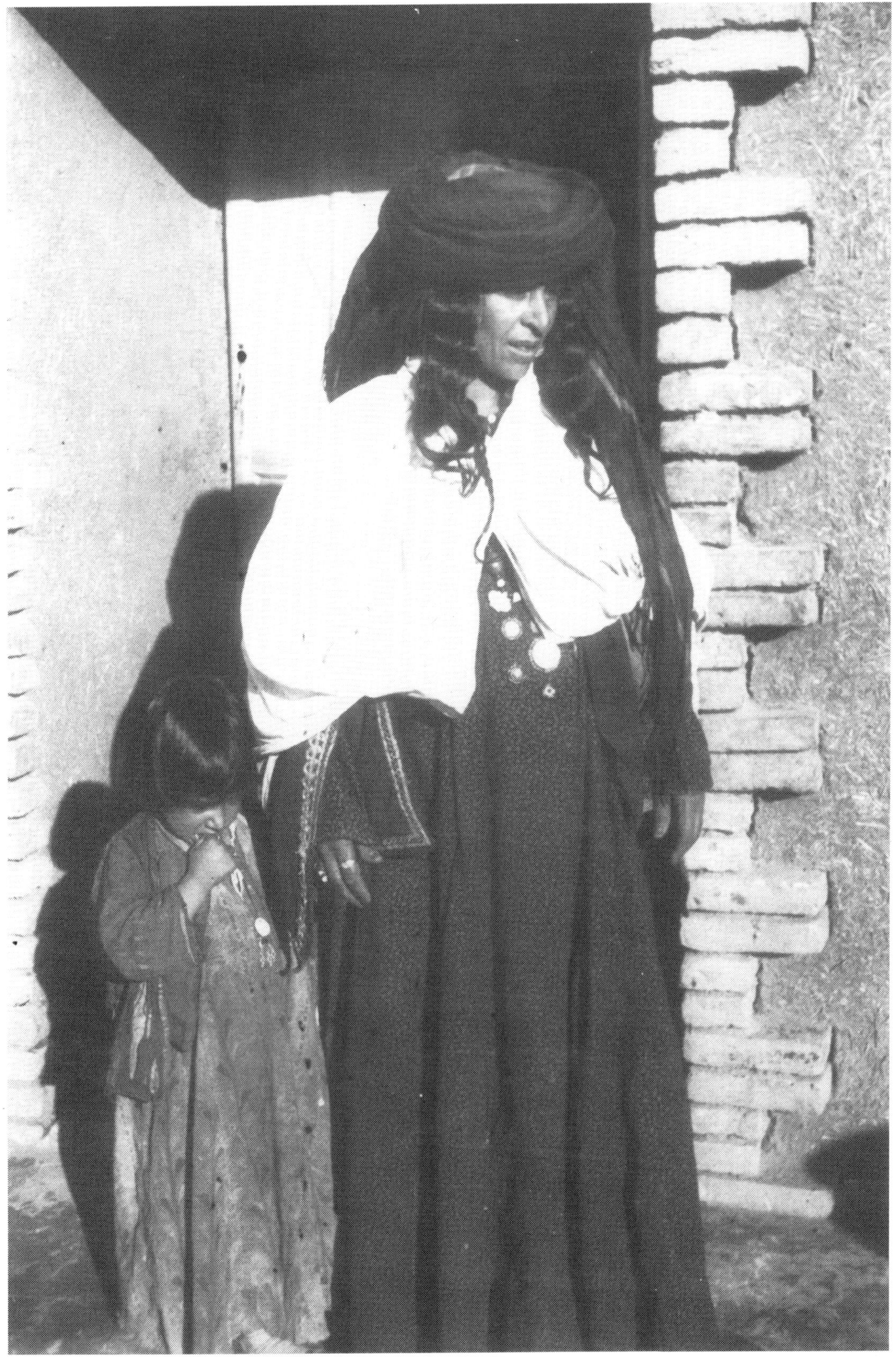

Woman at Alishtar 1931

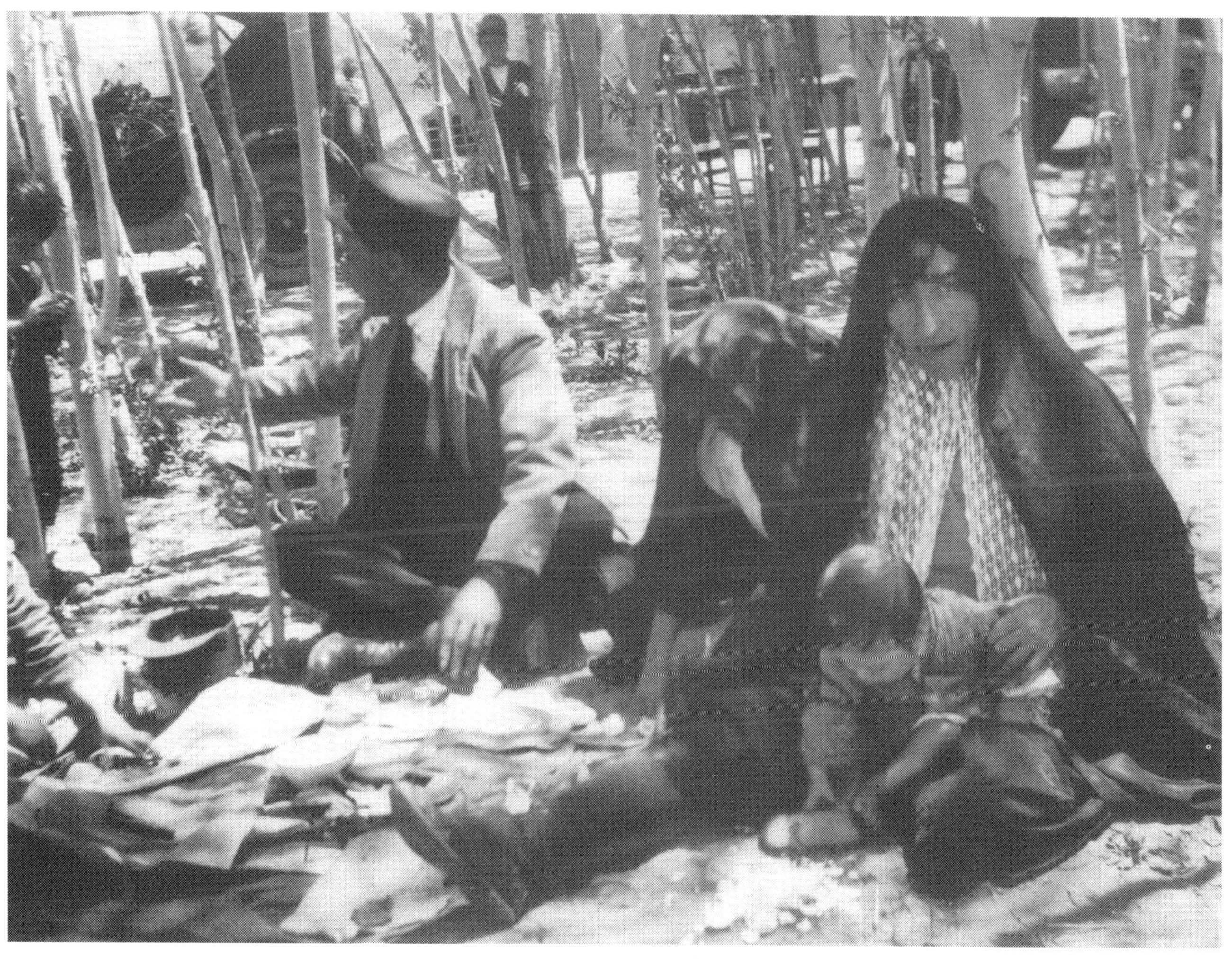

Roadside picnic, Kermanshah – Hamadan 1931

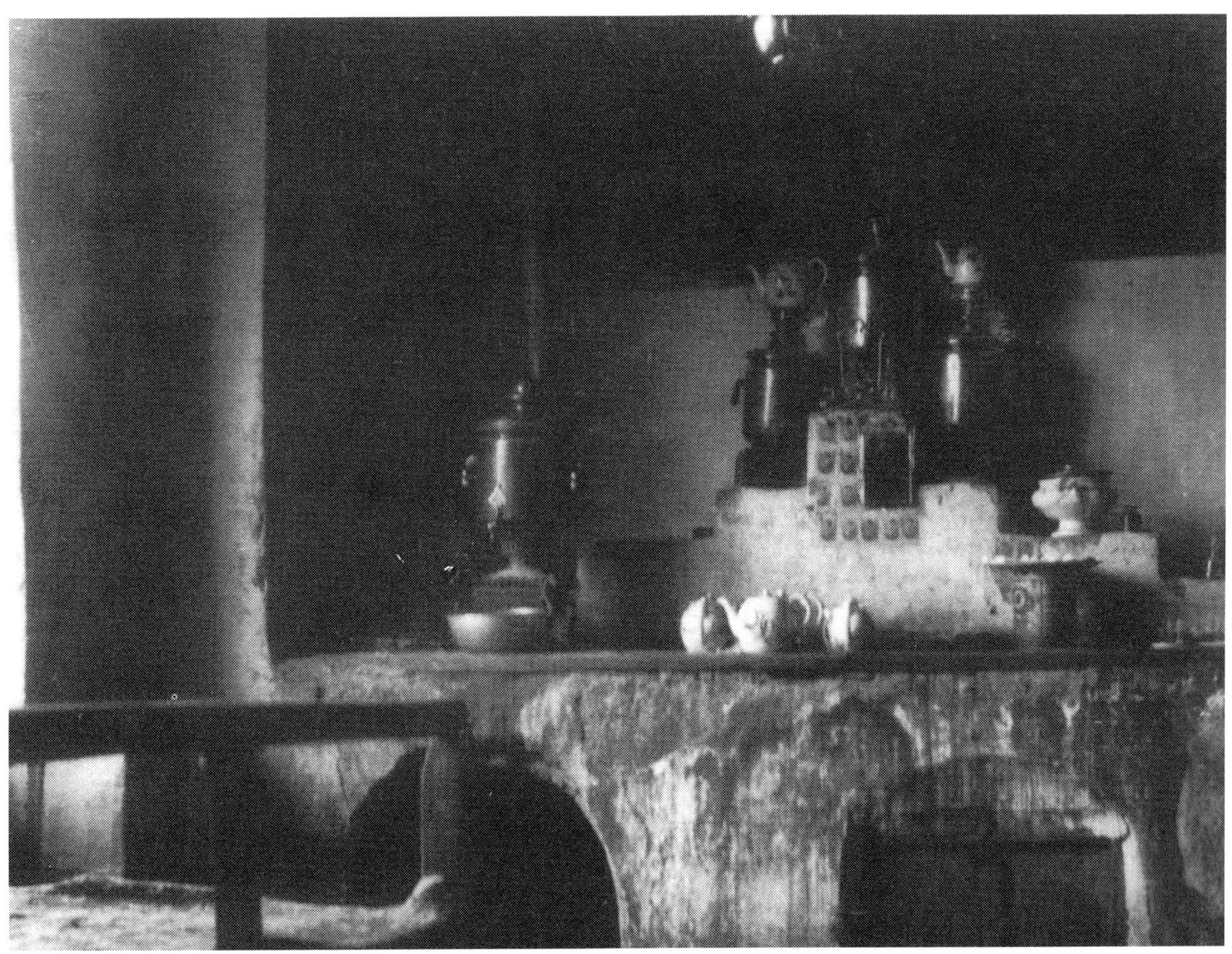

Chaikhana (tea house) Luristan 1931

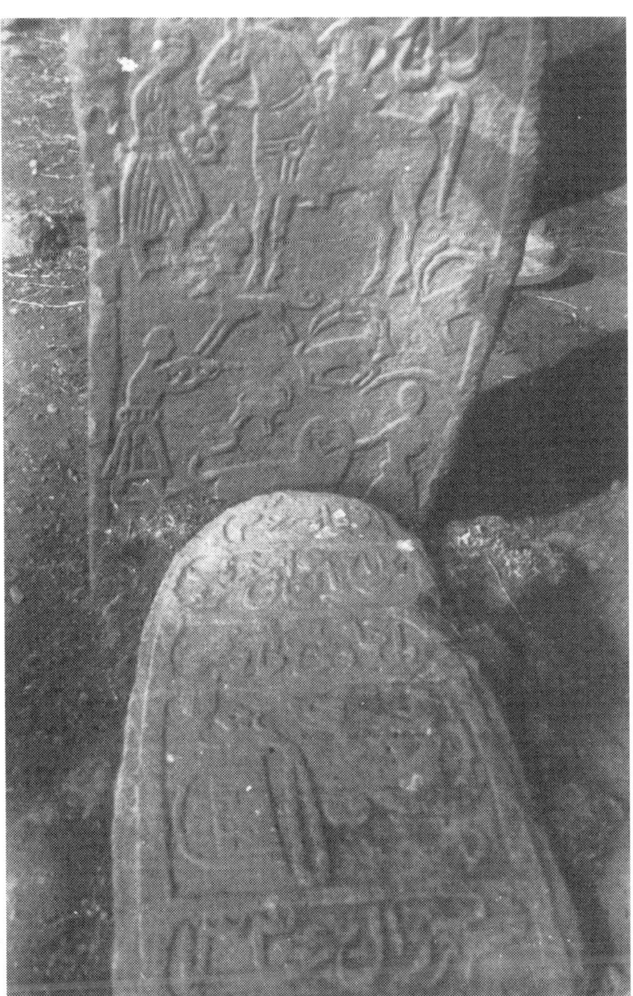

Modern tombstone, Alishtar 1931

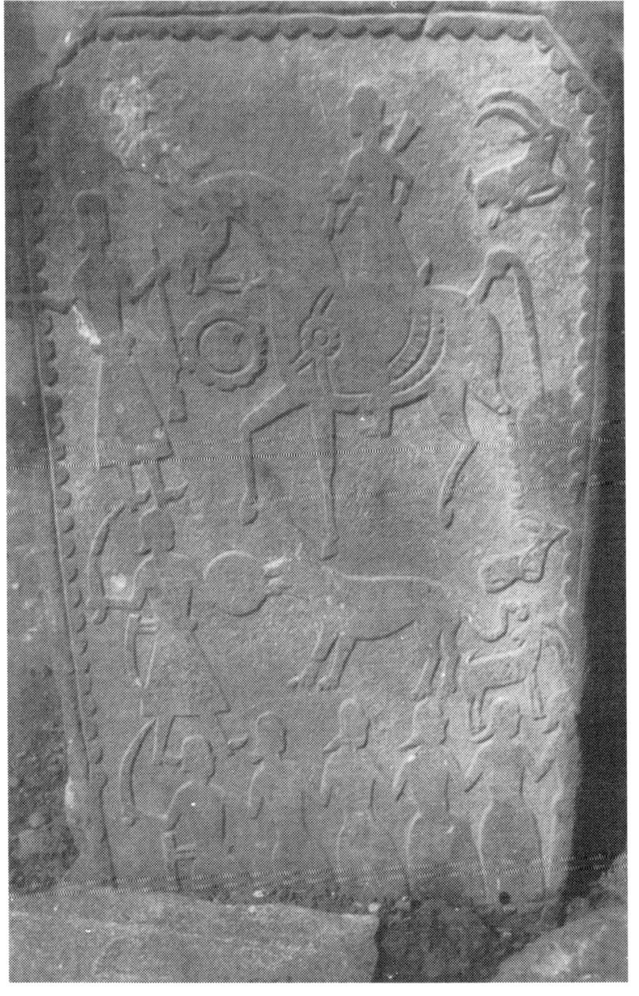

Modern tombstone, Alishtar 1931

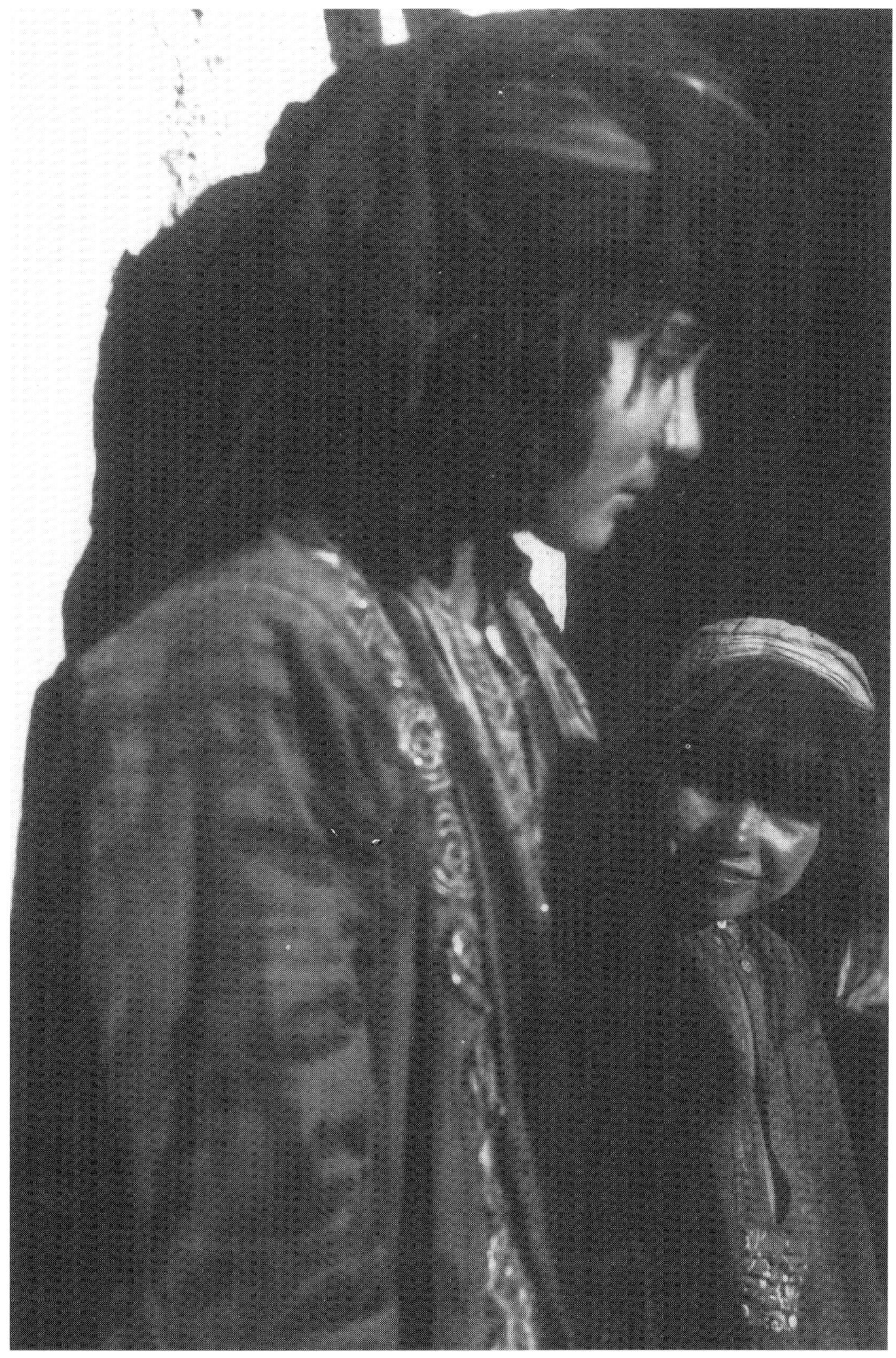

Bride at Qal'a Kafrash 1931

CENTRAL AND WESTERN PERSIA

After leaving Tehran in September 1931 Freya bought a seat in a taxi to Qum, Iran's religious capital, returning to Hamadan by way of Saveh, where she stopped to visit her former Farsi teacher. The teacher was out, but his nephews were friendly and took her to lunch in a garden full of pomegranates. "The carpet was spread; we sat and ate water melons and figs and pomegranates . . . They got out their opium pipes, and a brazier was brought and we were all as happy as can be." The next leg of her journey took ages, as the vehicle in which she had bought a seat kept breaking down. "You wouldn't believe so many things would be wrong with one car. The first breakdown always occurs just outside the town and is a sort of indispensable beginning of a Persian journey."

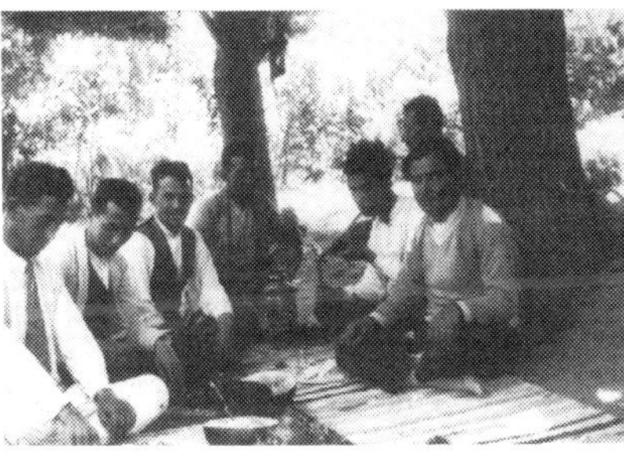

Picnic with opium
Saveh 1931

Freya was cheated of a projected visit to Isfahan, the most famous and beautiful of Persia's Islamic cities, by the Iraqi crisis of 1941. She finally got there in 1943 after a 1200-mile detour on the way from Delhi to Baghdad. She made two visits to Iran after the Second World War, in 1959 and 1969. In April 1959 she visited for the first time the ancient Persian capital of Persepolis. She was not overly impressed: "There is even now a mass-produced feeling about those rows and rows of Mede and Persian nobles walking beside one up every stairway and through every door," she told Jock Murray. As for the columns, whose capitals of leaves and flowers had been shredded-off "so that only little cabbagy bits remain", she thought they were probably more beautiful now than when they were new. To Sir Sidney Cockerell, former director of Fitzwilliam Museum at Cambridge, she adopted a more reverential tone: "The figures cut in stone relief, the Mede and Persian bodyguard, the bringers of tribute, move up the sides of the stairways so that one has the feeling of a crowd of ghosts, very silent now, but there."

From Persepolis she drove to Pasargadae to see the tomb of Cyrus. She found it to have been "done up with care and economy sadly combined, so that nothing remains to *communicate* with landscape . . ." Moving on to Shiraz she visited the tombs of Hafiz and Saadi, two of Persia's greatest poets. The tombs – like Cyrus's – had been somewhat municipalized "with electric lights and gravel and tidy flower beds filled with untidy charming flowers". A chorus of birds twittered around Saadi's tomb. She inspected the market and watched the Kashgai tribeswomen buying imported cottons from Japan, and was pleased to note that the double peaked felt cap worn by the Kashgai men since Achamenian times, was on sale. The Pahlavi cap she so abhorred was a thing of the past.

A week later she spent four steaming hot days as a guest of the Anglo-Iranian Oil Company at their refinery in Abadan. By now a fully-fledged celebrity, she received the VIP treatment. At Susa she was shown round the ancient city by Professor Guirshman, whom she had met at Nihavend in Luristan twenty-nine years before. He took her to lunch in the "fantastic castle of Susa" built by the French mission in the 1860s. Afterwards she inspected the great dam being built on the Susa river, and flew to Kharg island "filled with tombs of all ages dug into the coral". They saw the Karun river in "blinding sheets of light" and the long bridge built by Roman captives after the emperor Valerian's defeat by King Shapur in 260. The emperor died in captivity after suffering unspeakable tortures. In the late 1980s many of the places she photographed in this region of perennially contested frontiers – Kharg island, Dizful, the Karun river – would be battered in a war of even greater savagery.

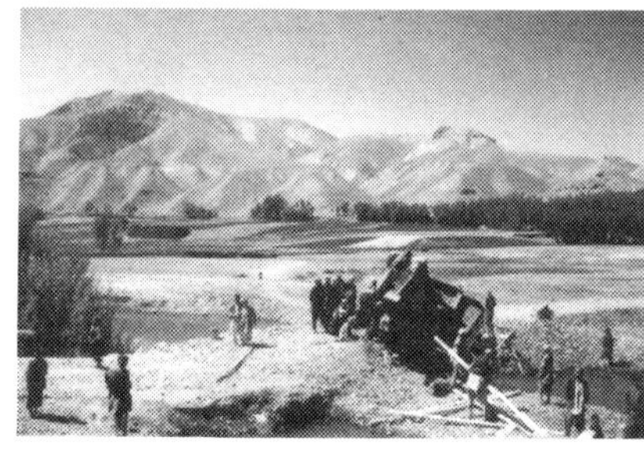

Hazards of the road
Persia 1931

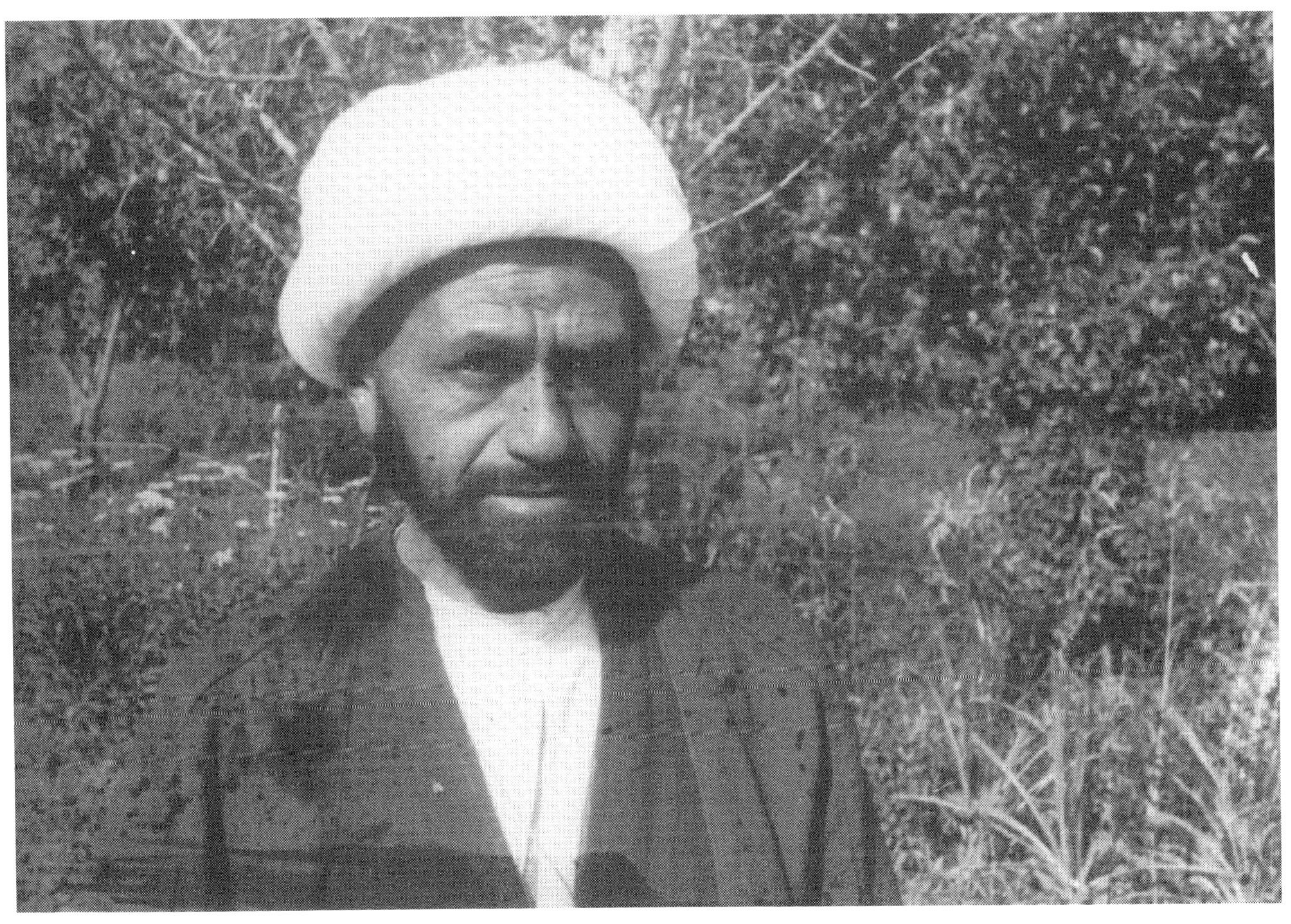

"My Mirza", Freya's Persian teacher, Hamadan 1930

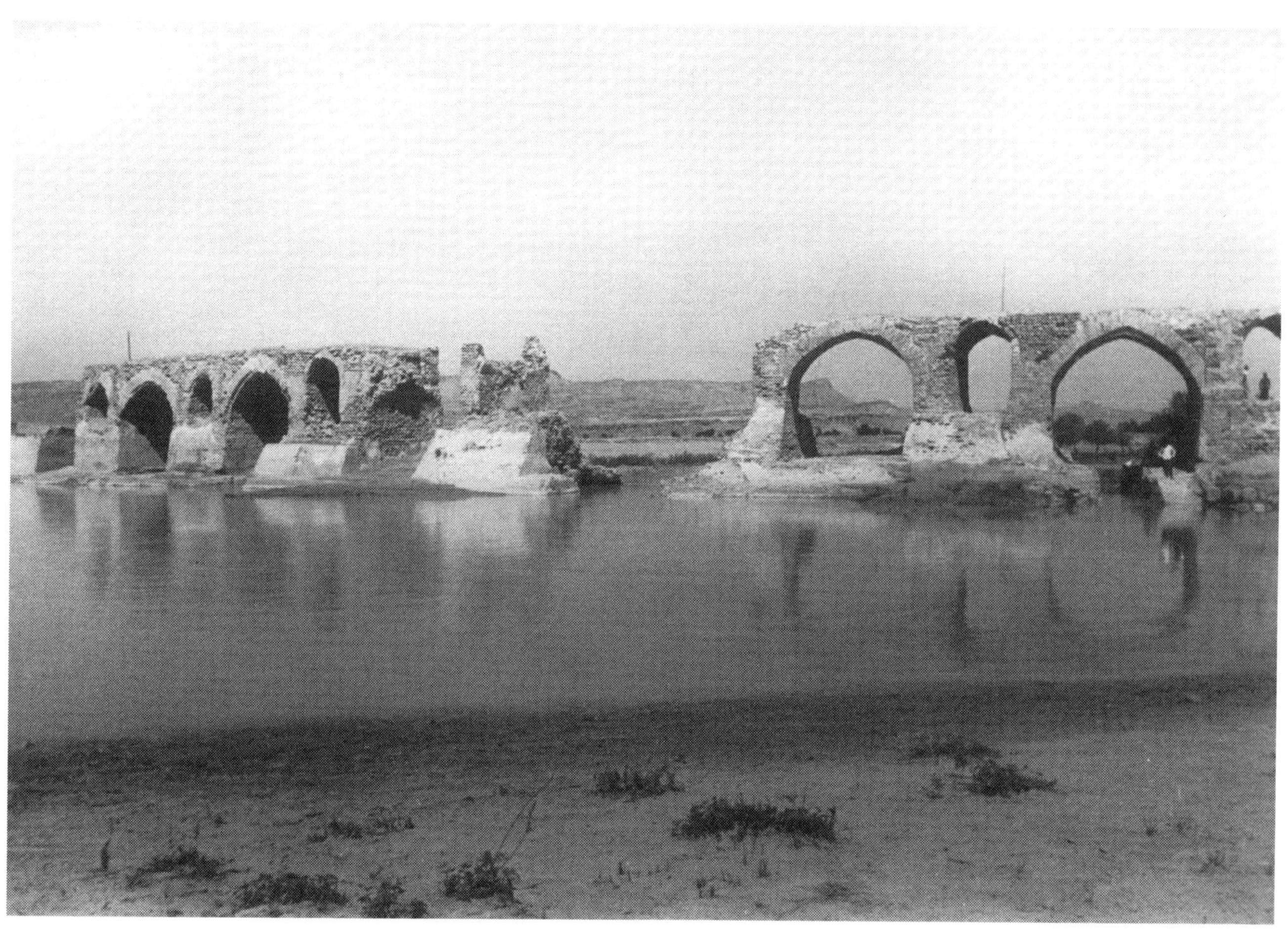

River Karun and bridge at Shuster 1959

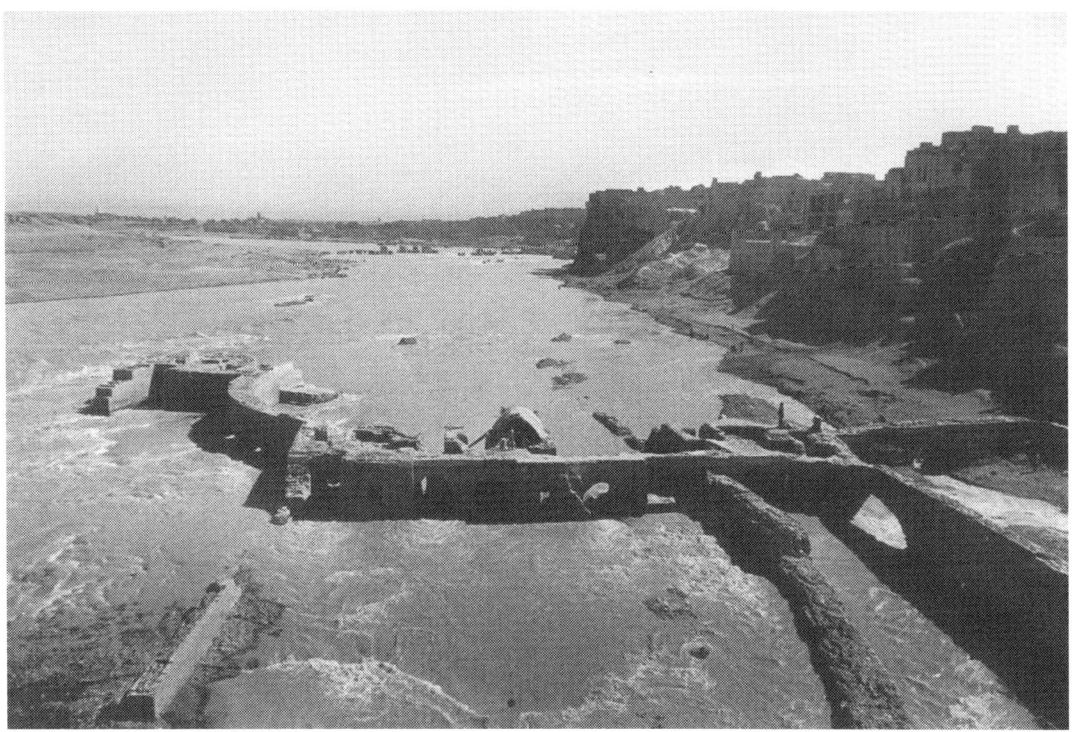

Dizful from bridge 1951

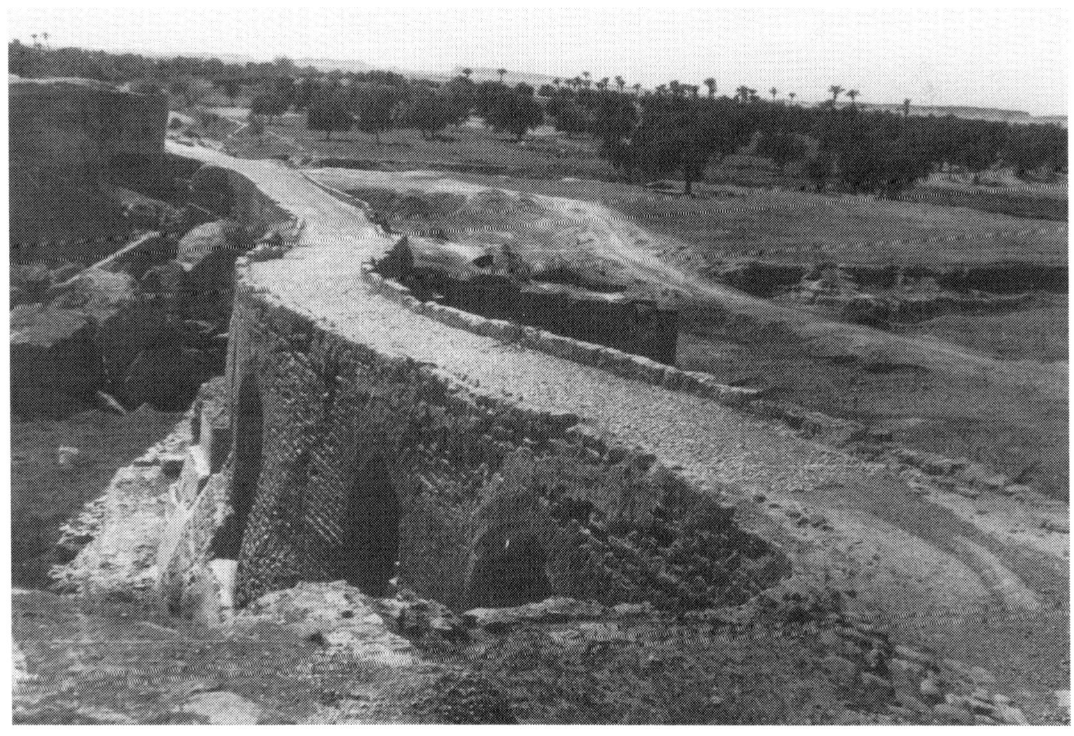

Bridge at Shuster 1959

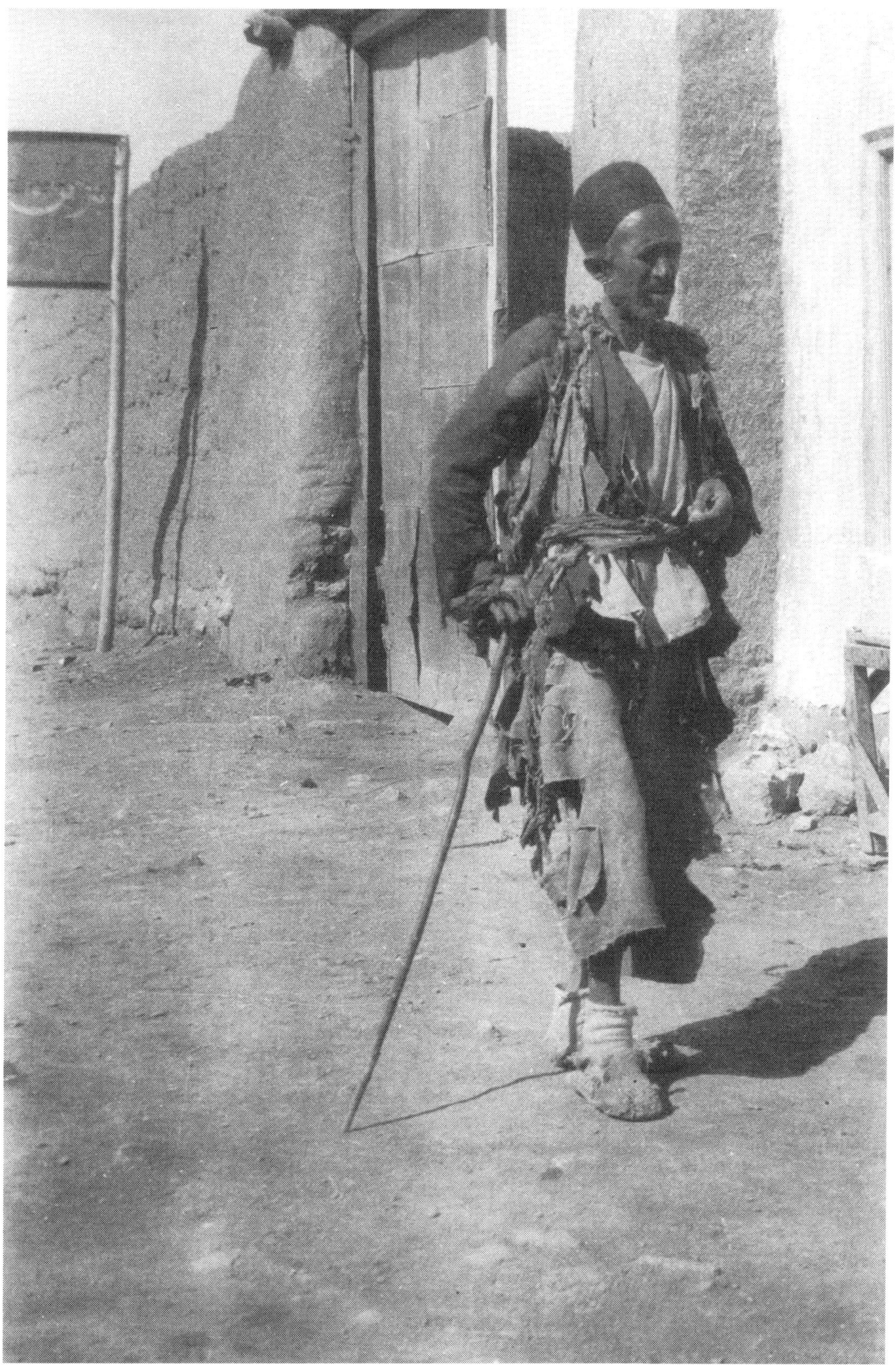

Beggar 1931

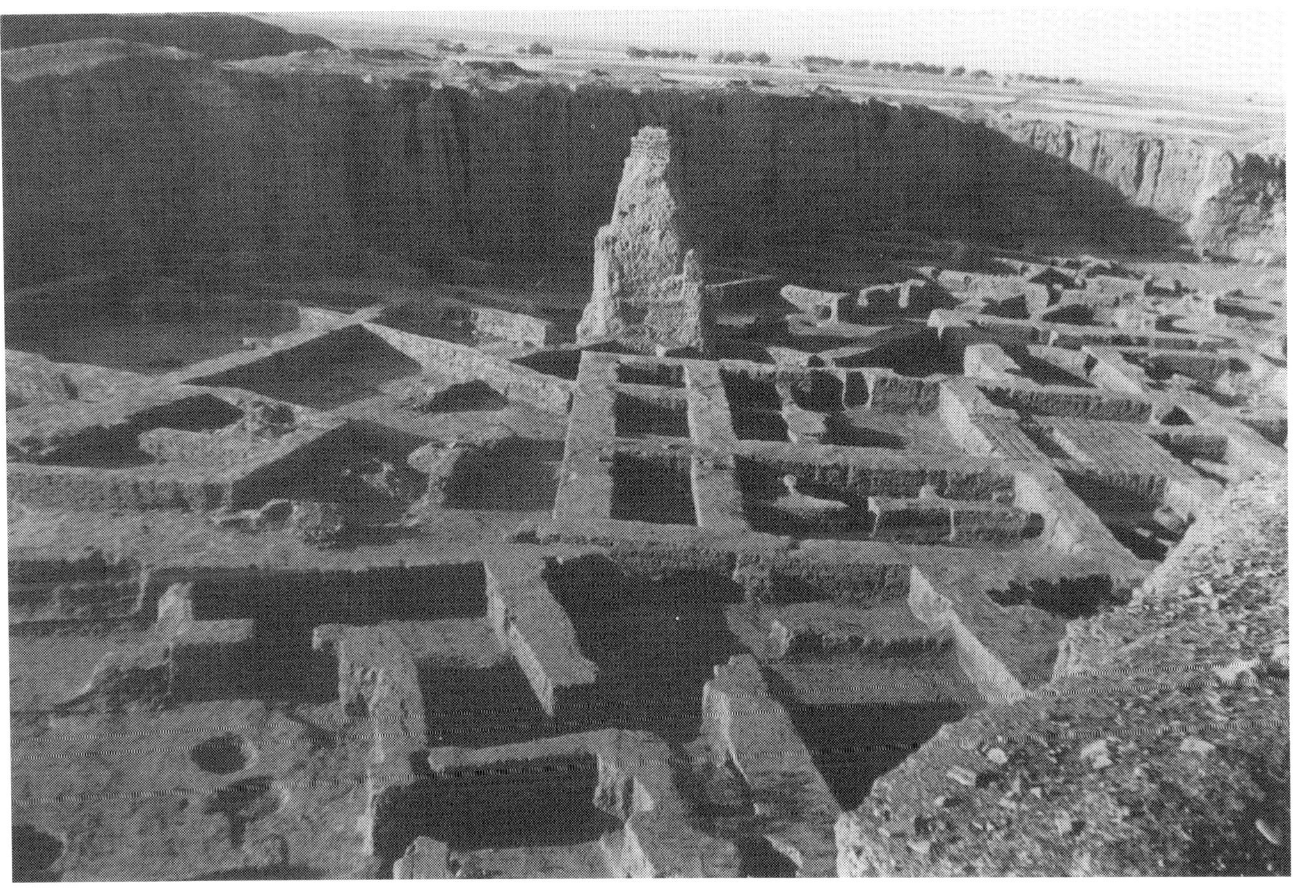

City of Susa, 11th Century

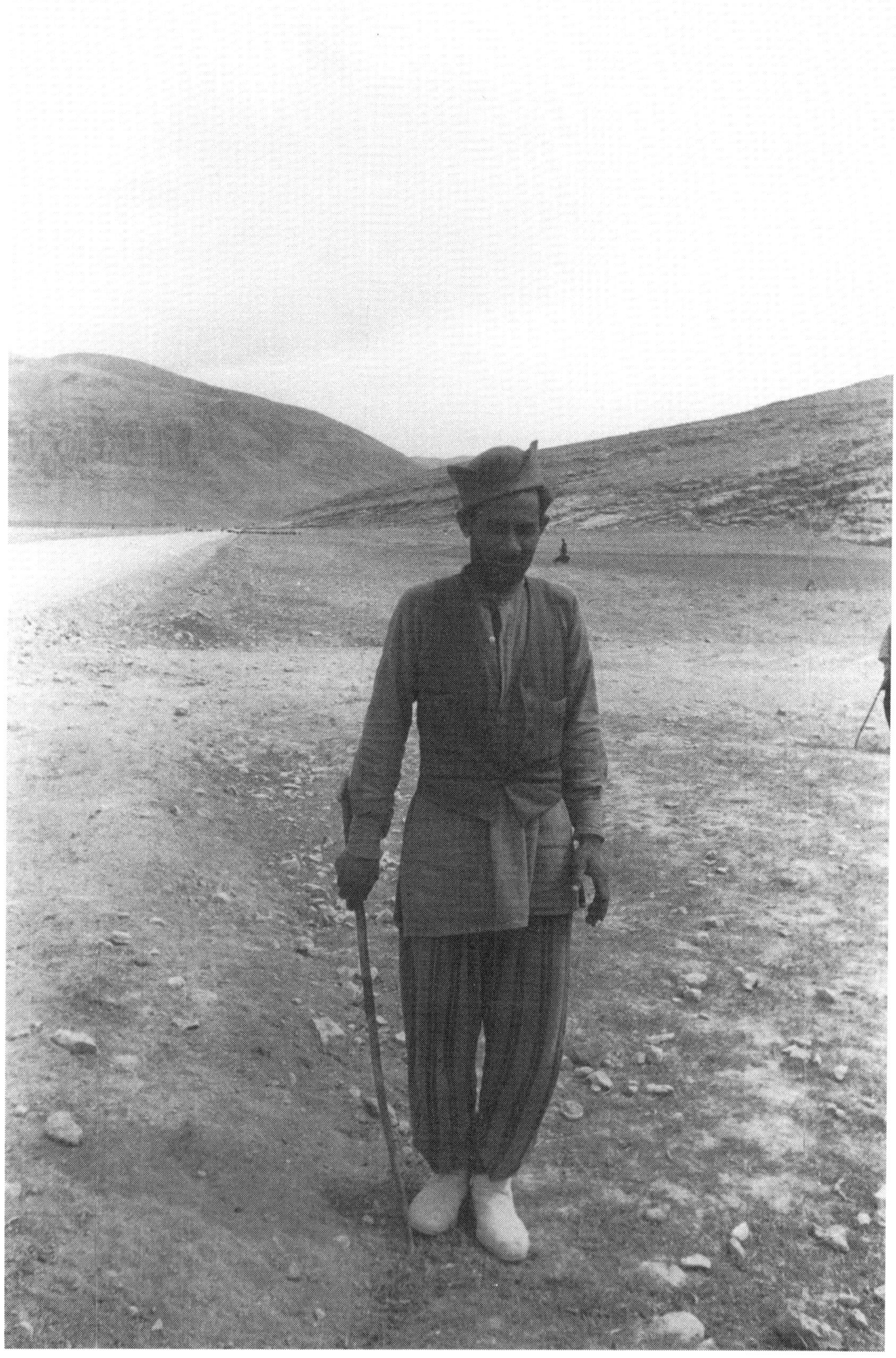

Kashgai tribesman wearing double-peaked felt hat 1959

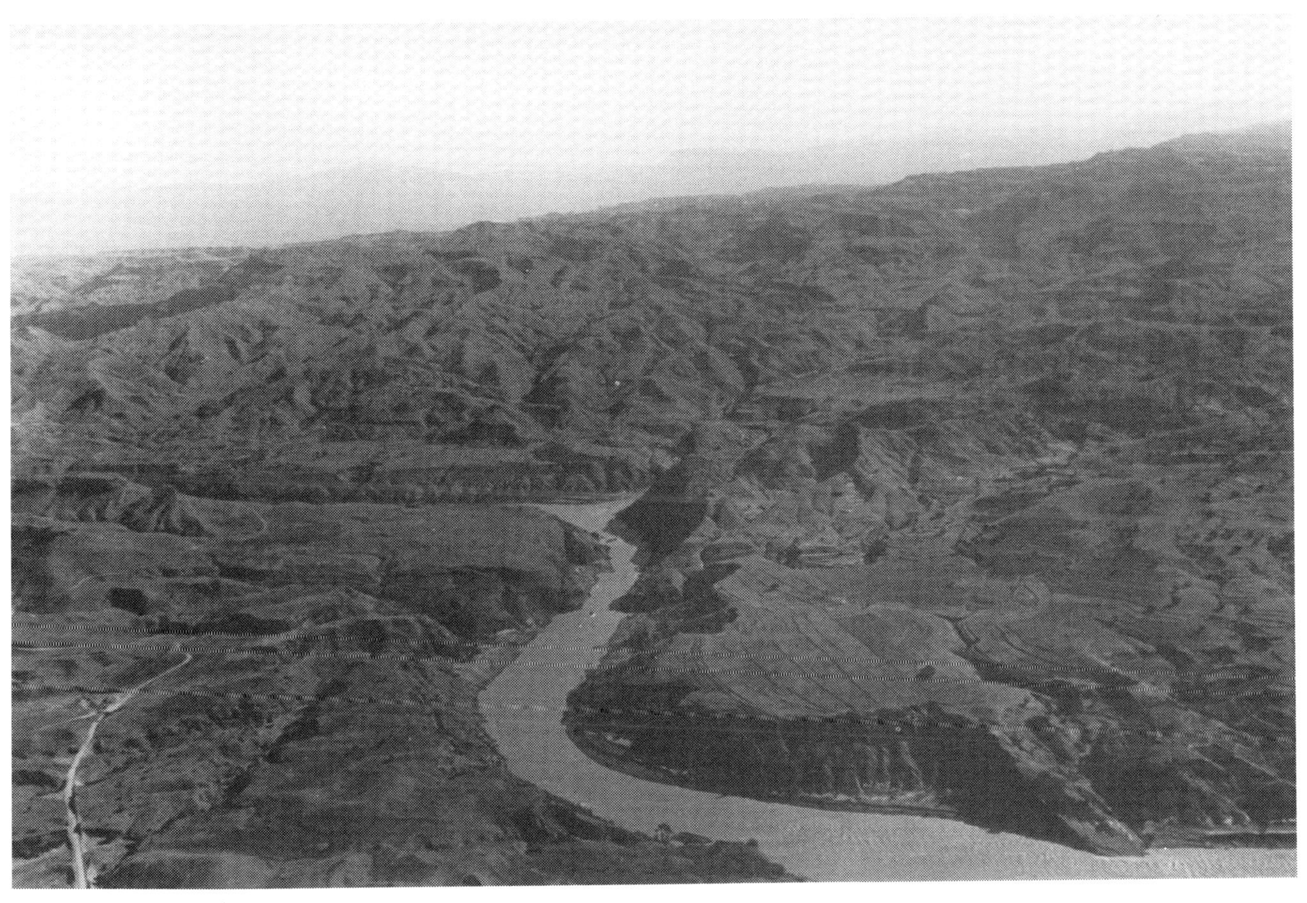

Karun River 1959. The area shown was due to be flooded by the construction of a dam.

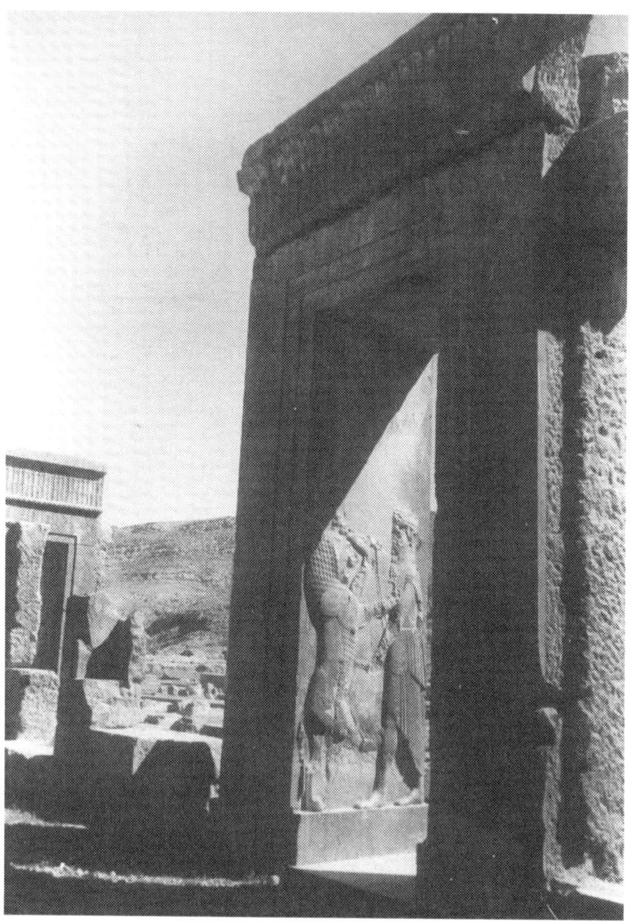

Persepolis 1959

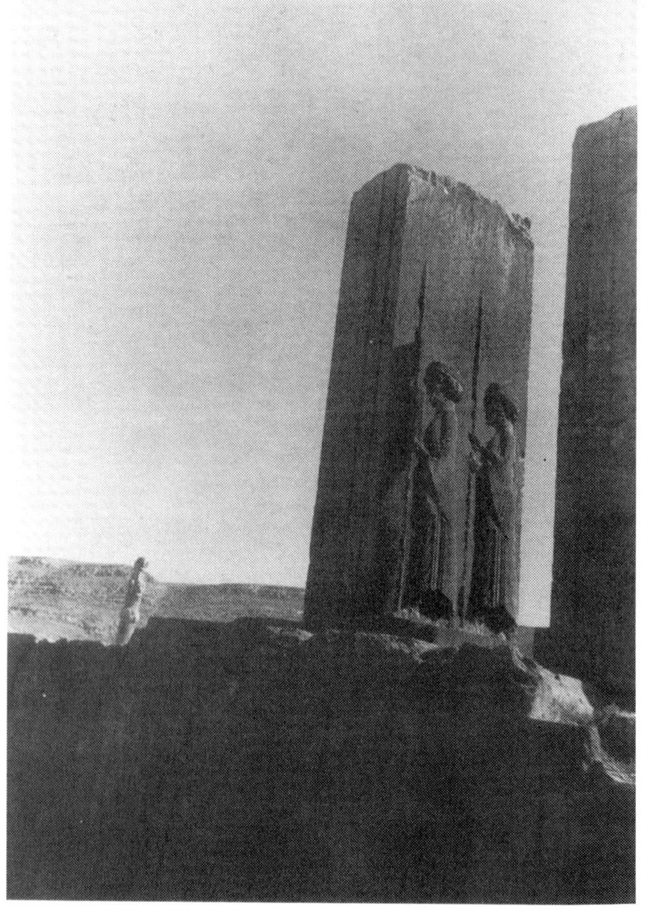

Persepolis 1959

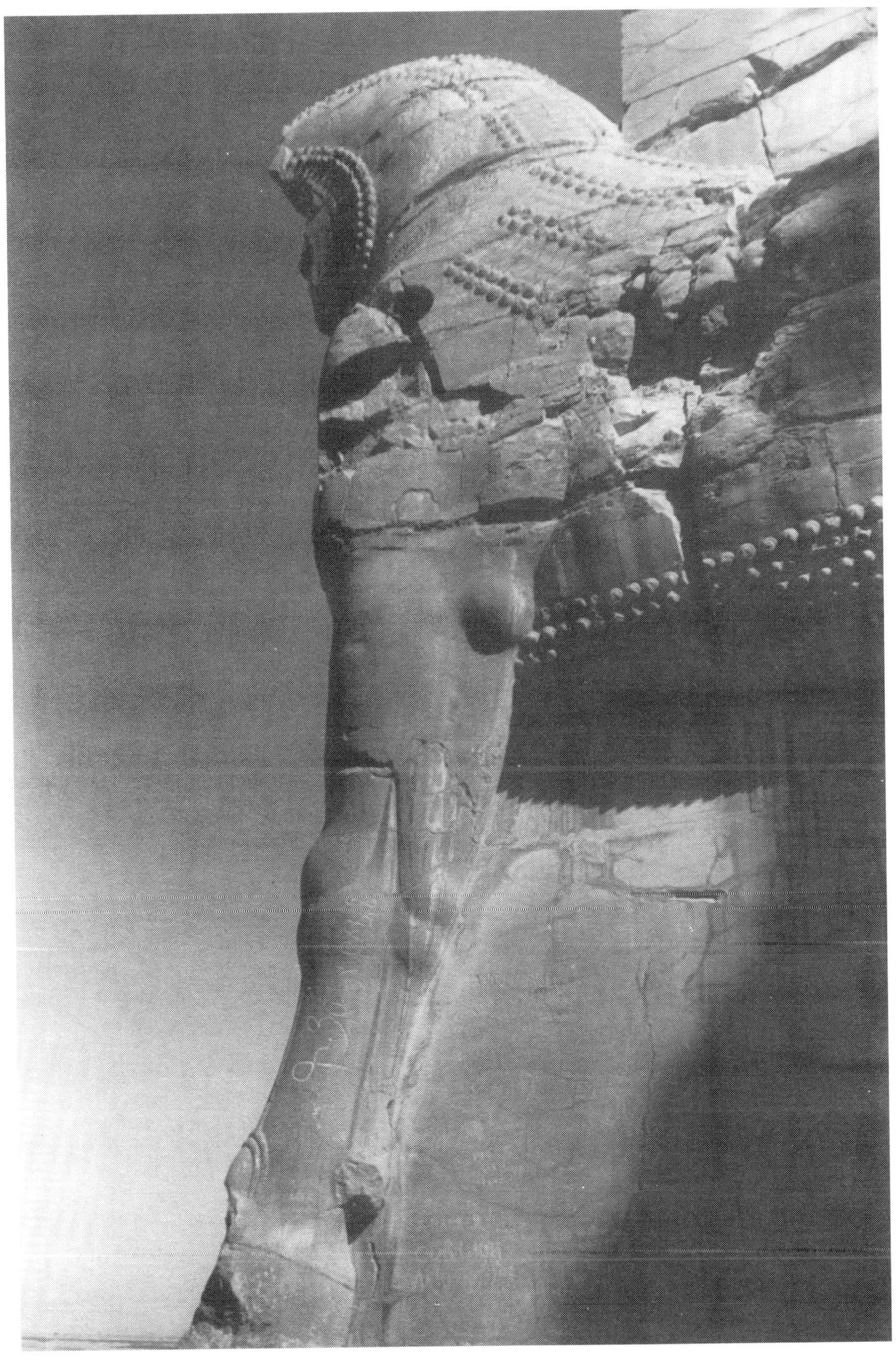

Sphinx gate, Persepolis 1959

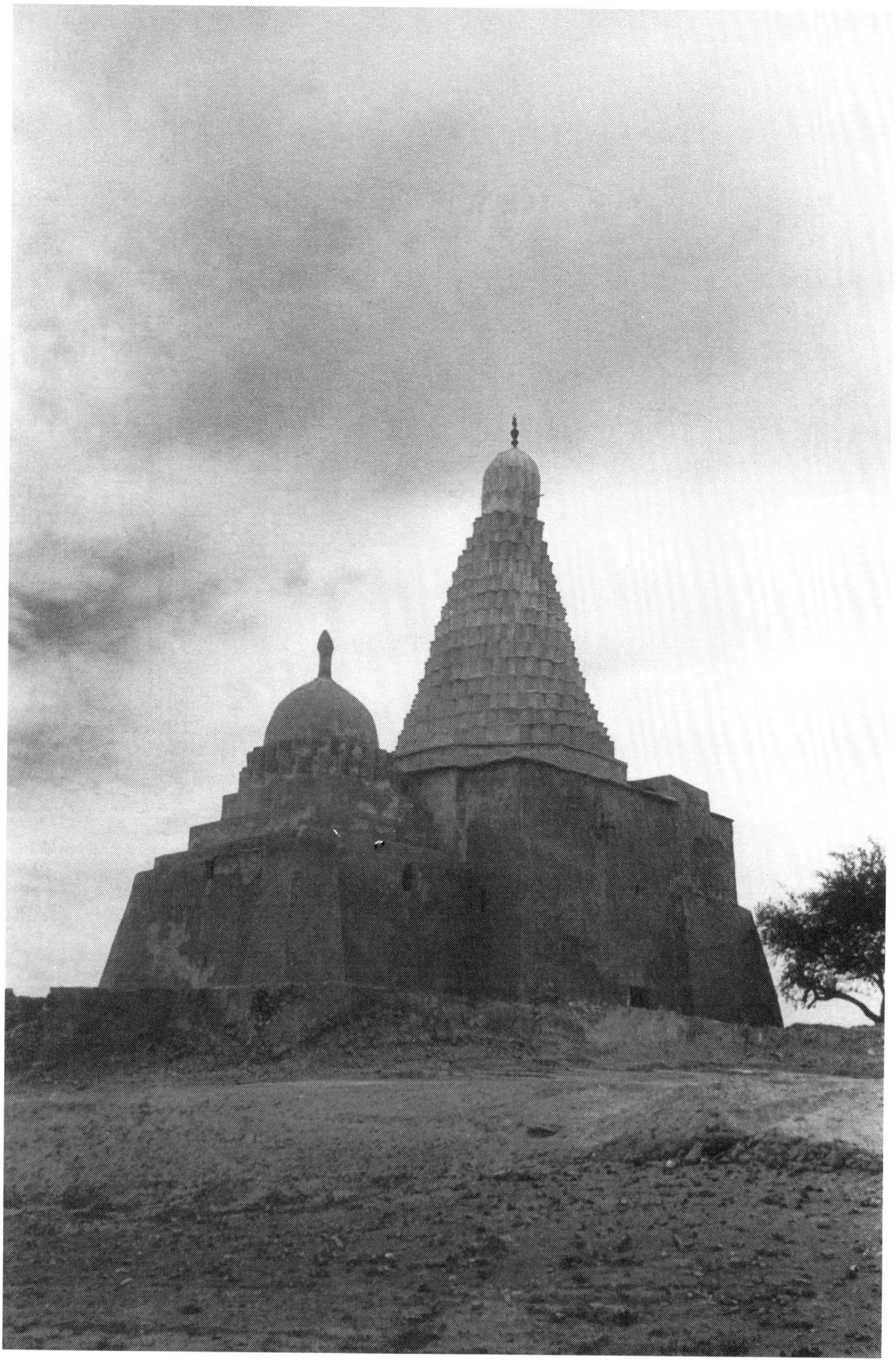

Kharg Island 1959: *Imamzadeh* on site of ancient fire temple.

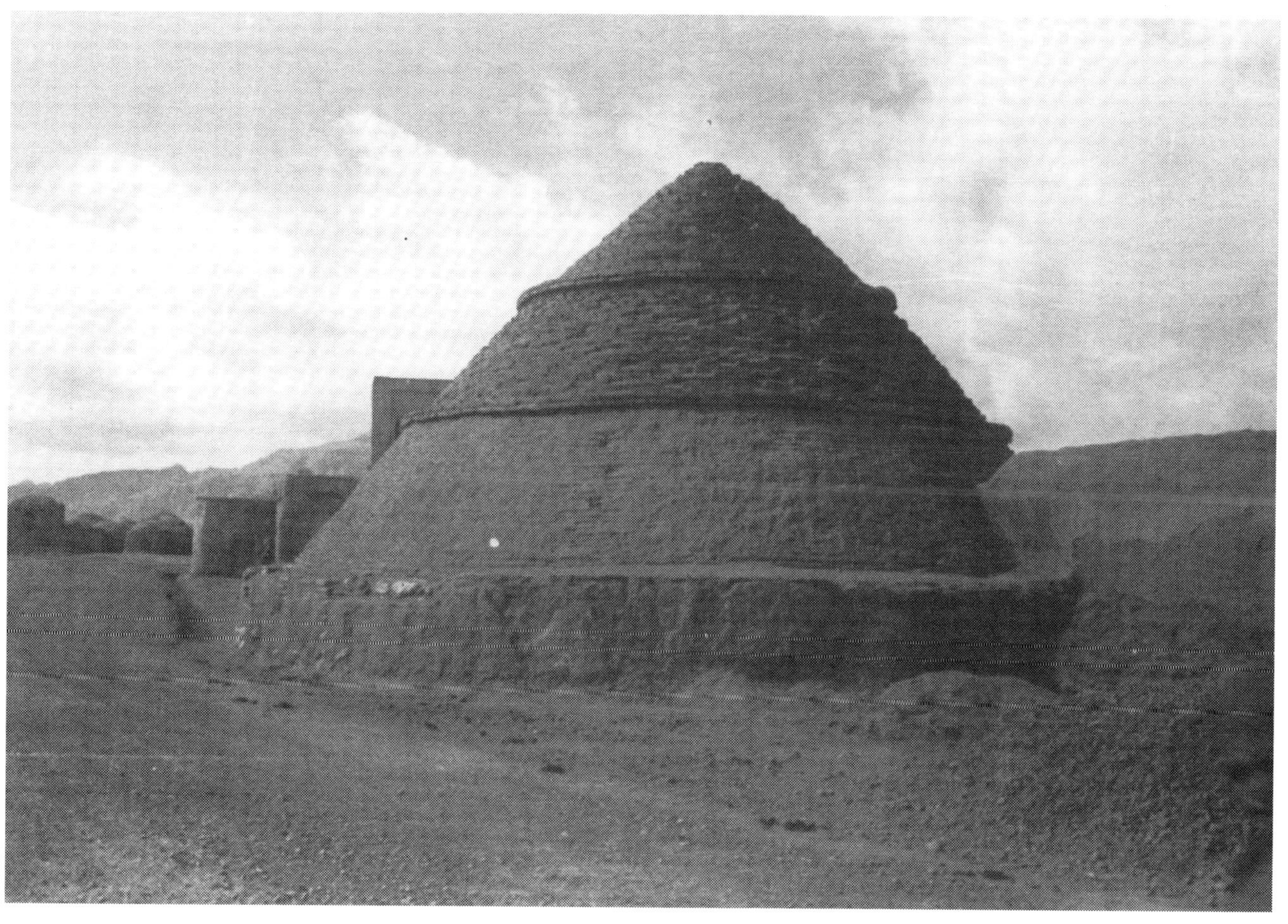

Icehouse on the way from Delhi to Tehran 1943

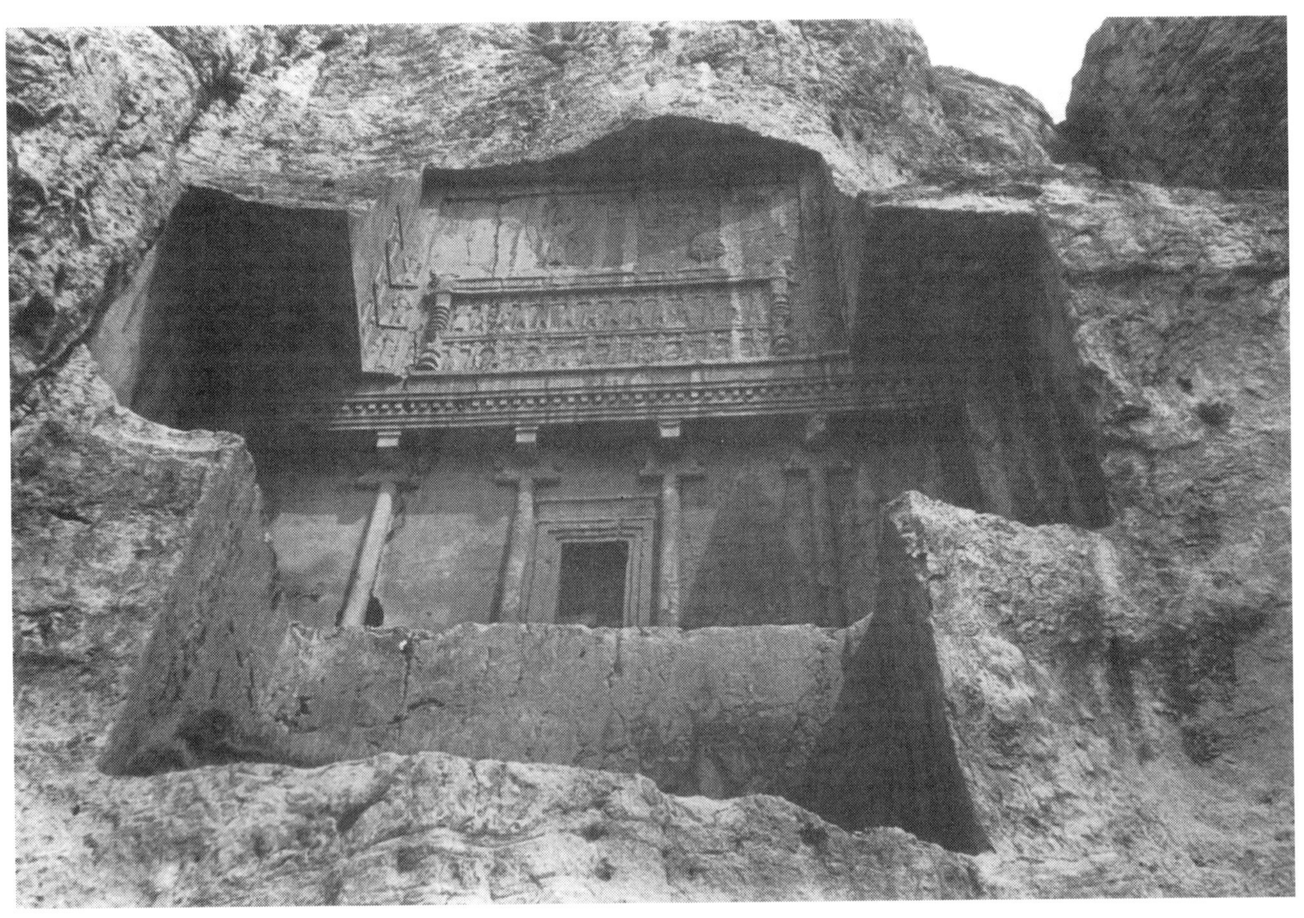

Naqshi-i-Rustum 1959

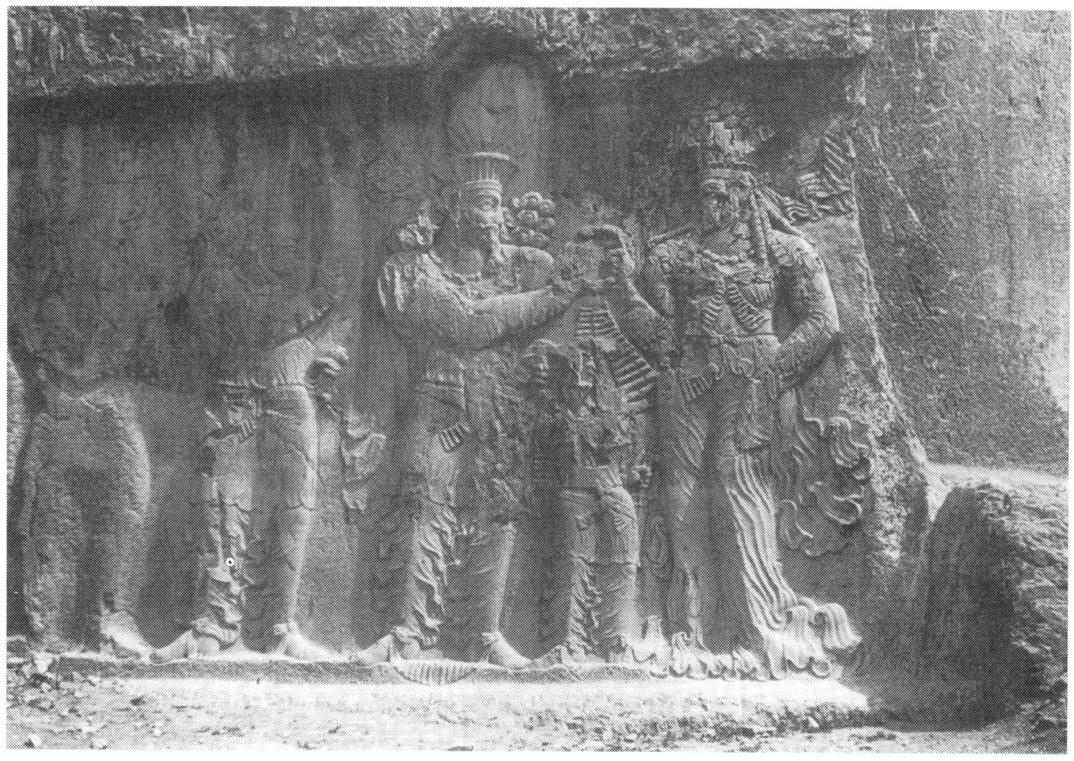

King Shapur and his Queen, Naqsh-i-Rustum 1959

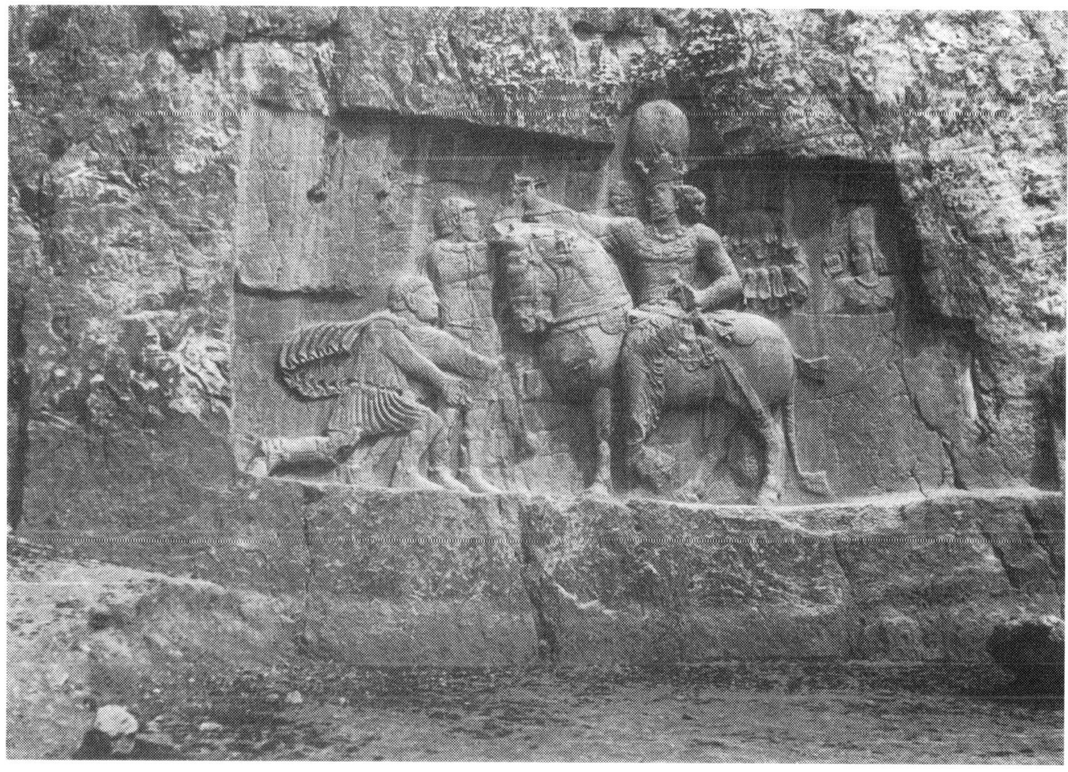

Valerian at the feet of Shapur, Naqsh-i-Rustum 1959

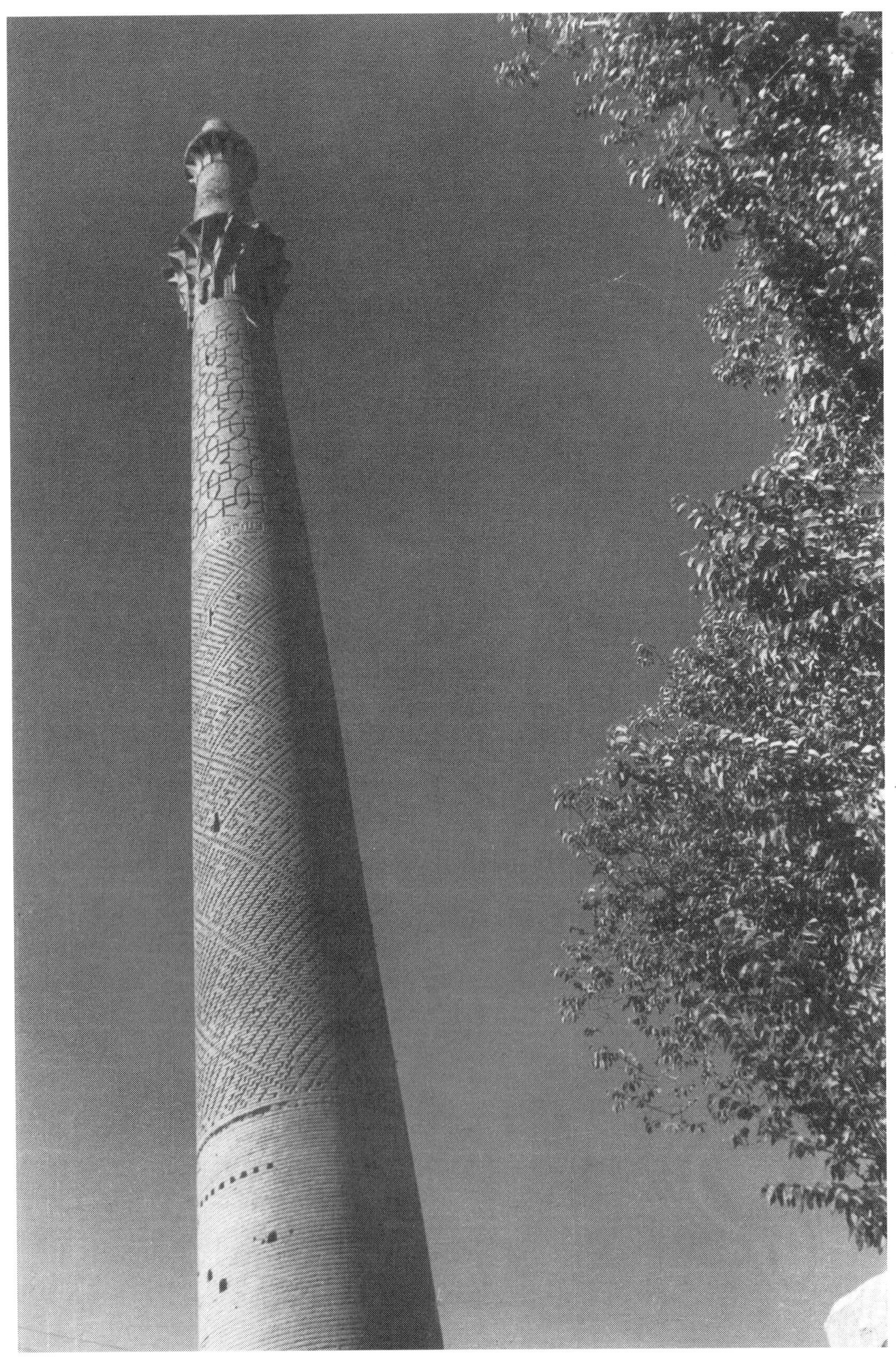

Minaret, Isfahan 1959

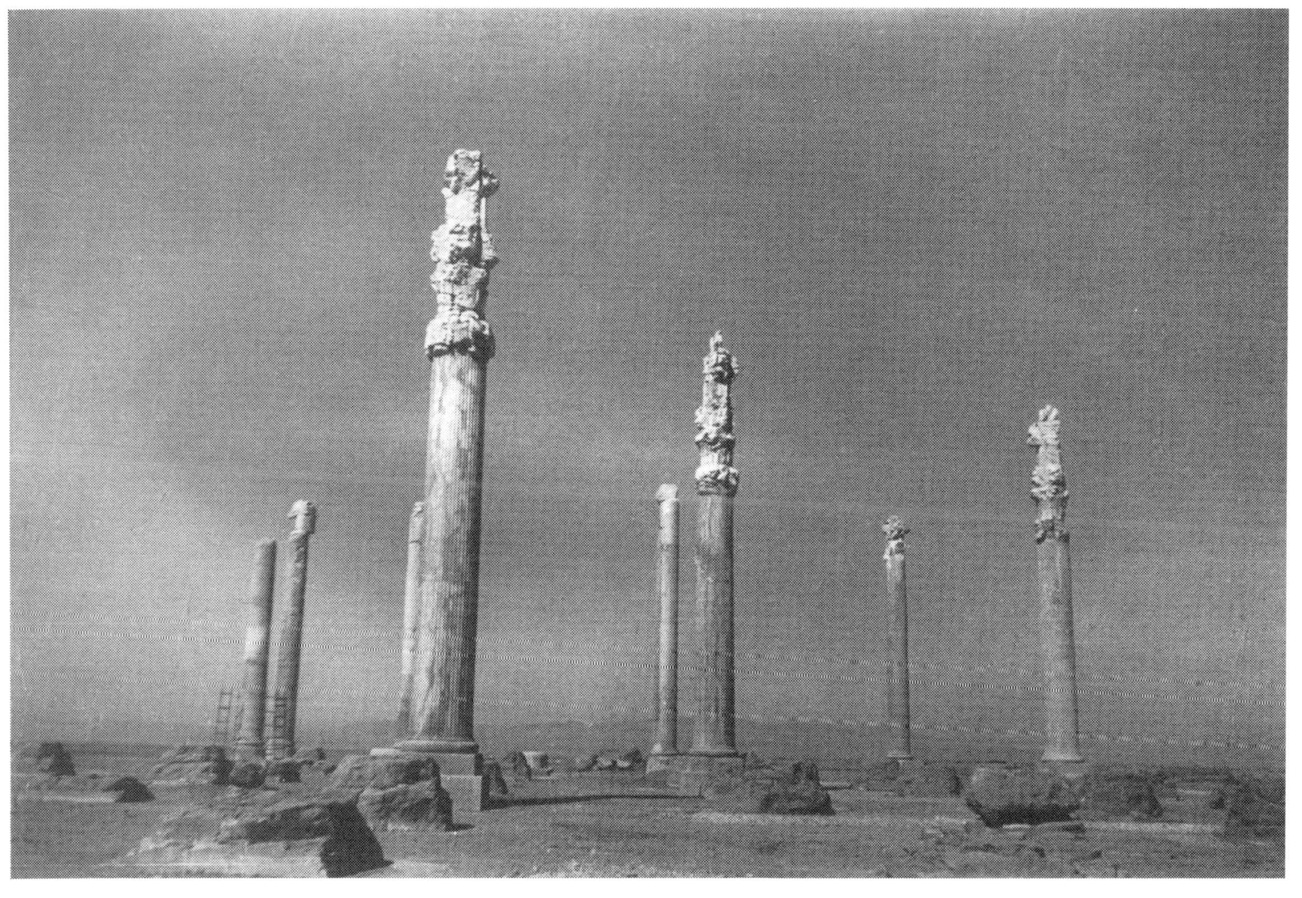

Persepolis 1959

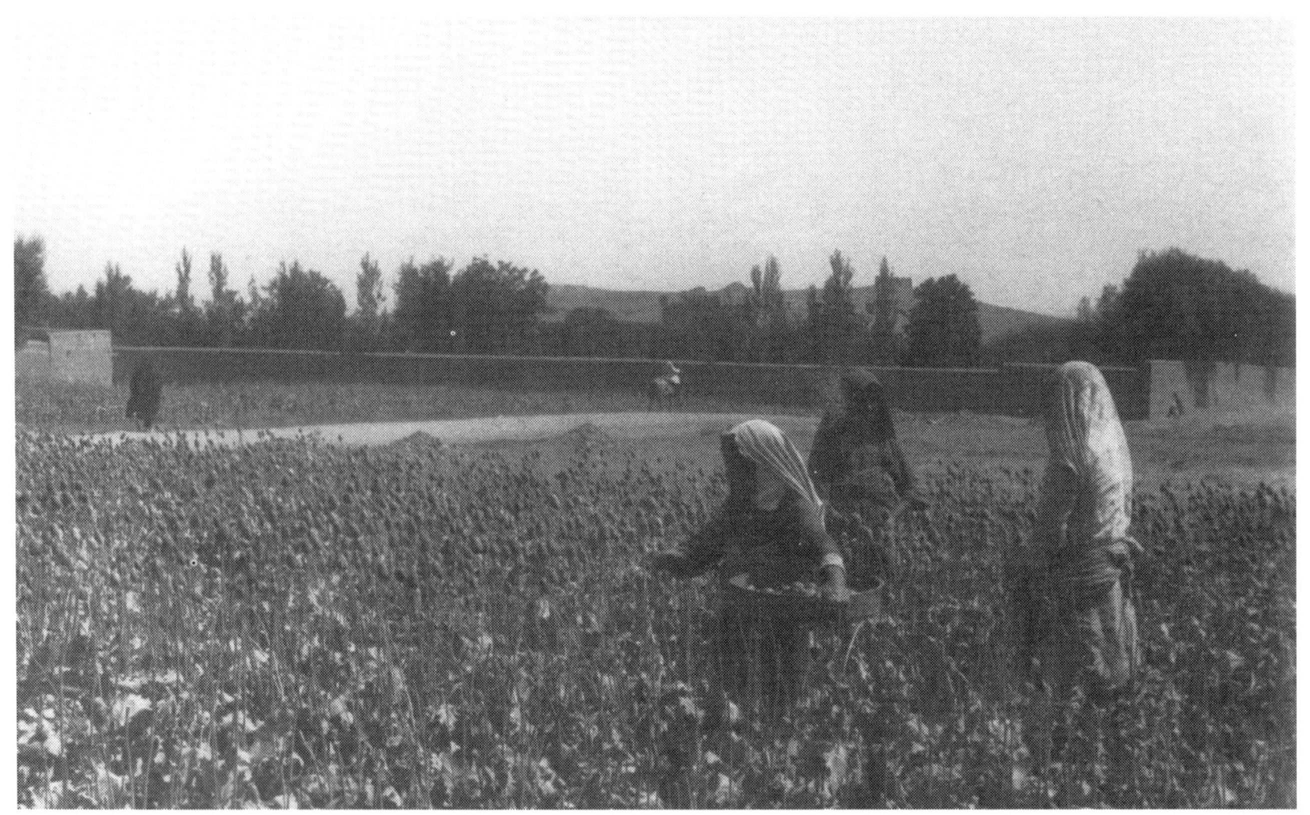

Opium harvest, Hamadan 1930

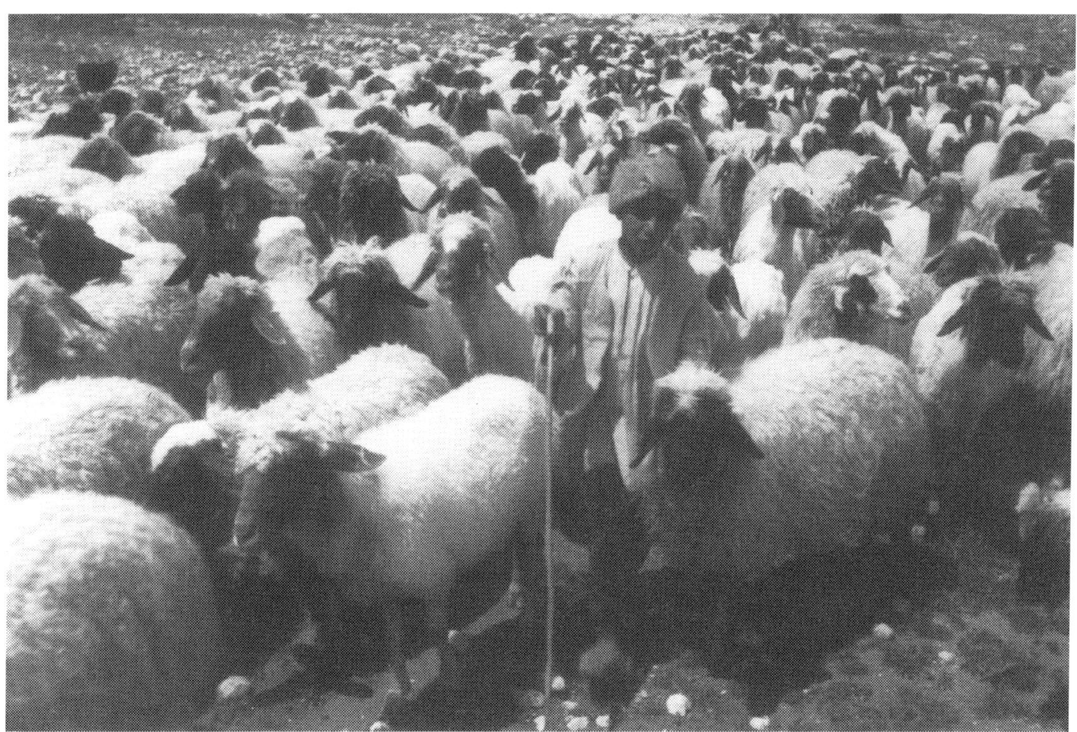

Shepherd photographed on way from Delhi to Tehran 1943

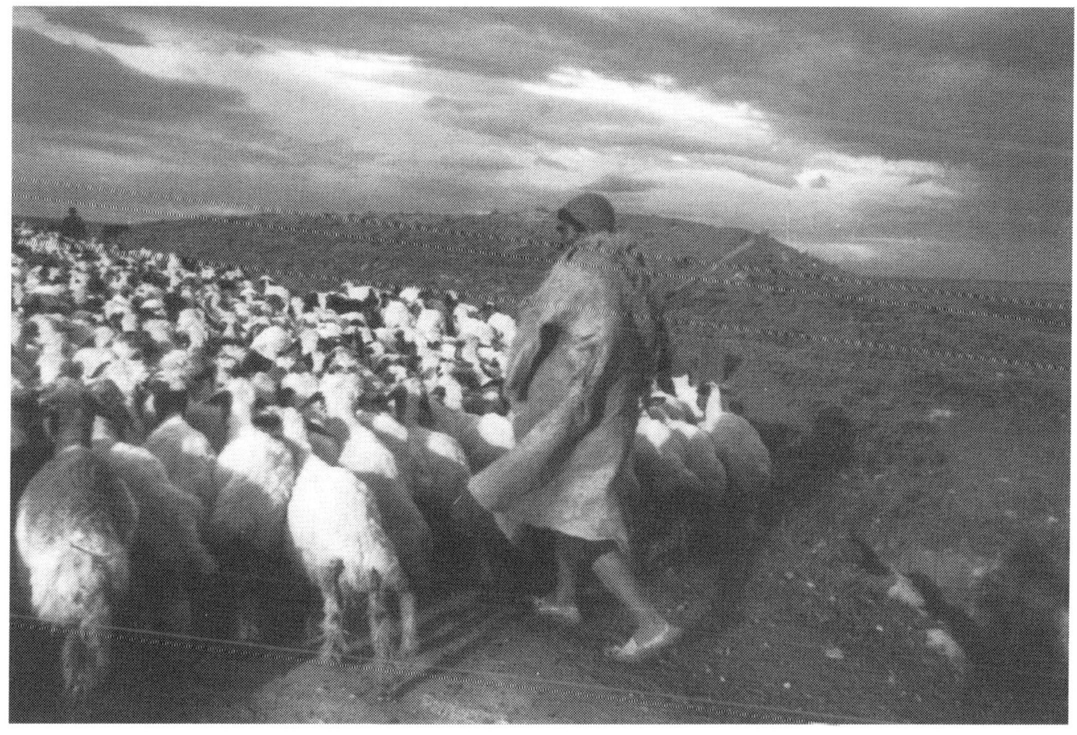

Shepherd photographed on way from Delhi to Tehran 1943

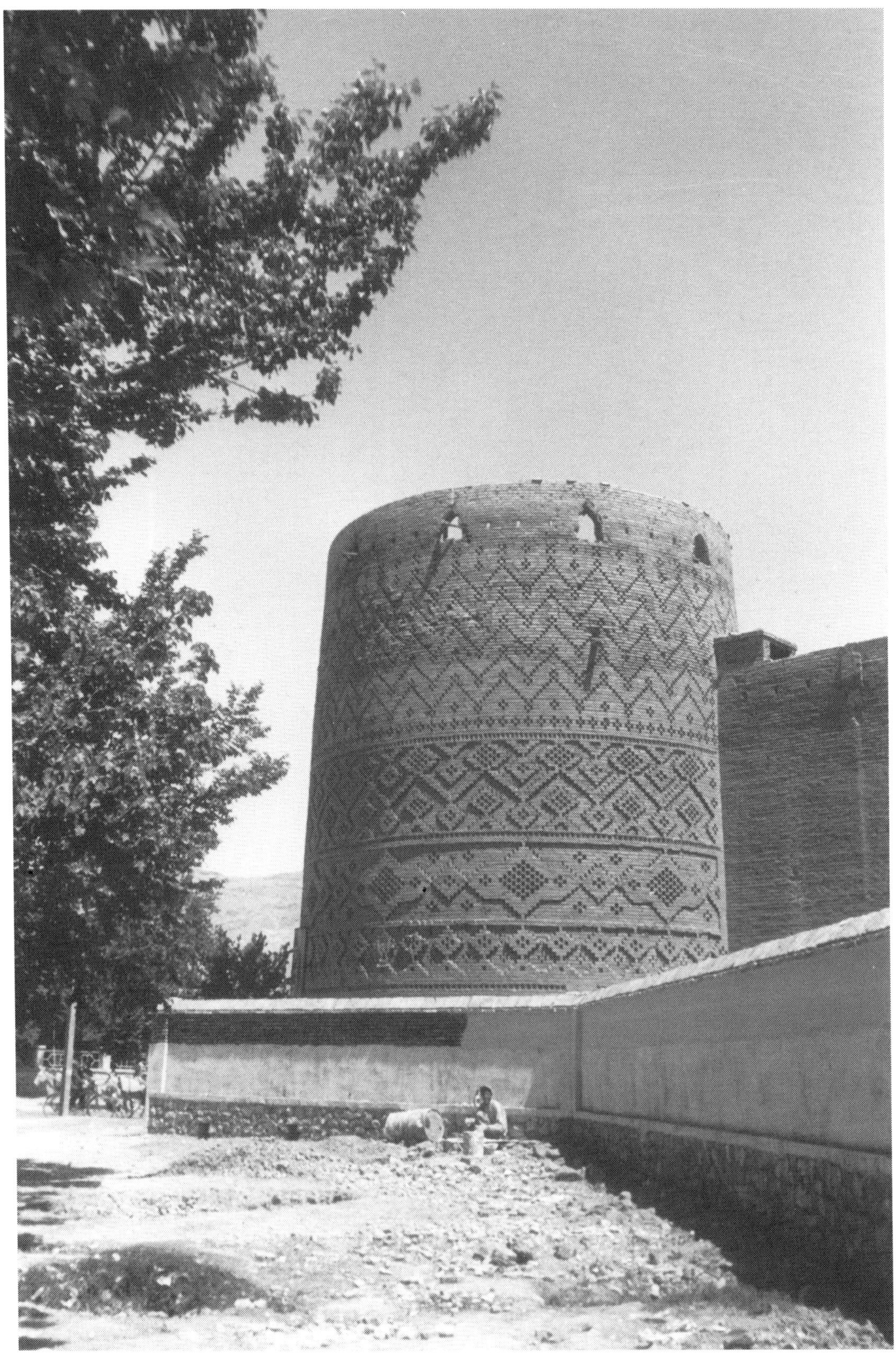

Shiraz tower 1959

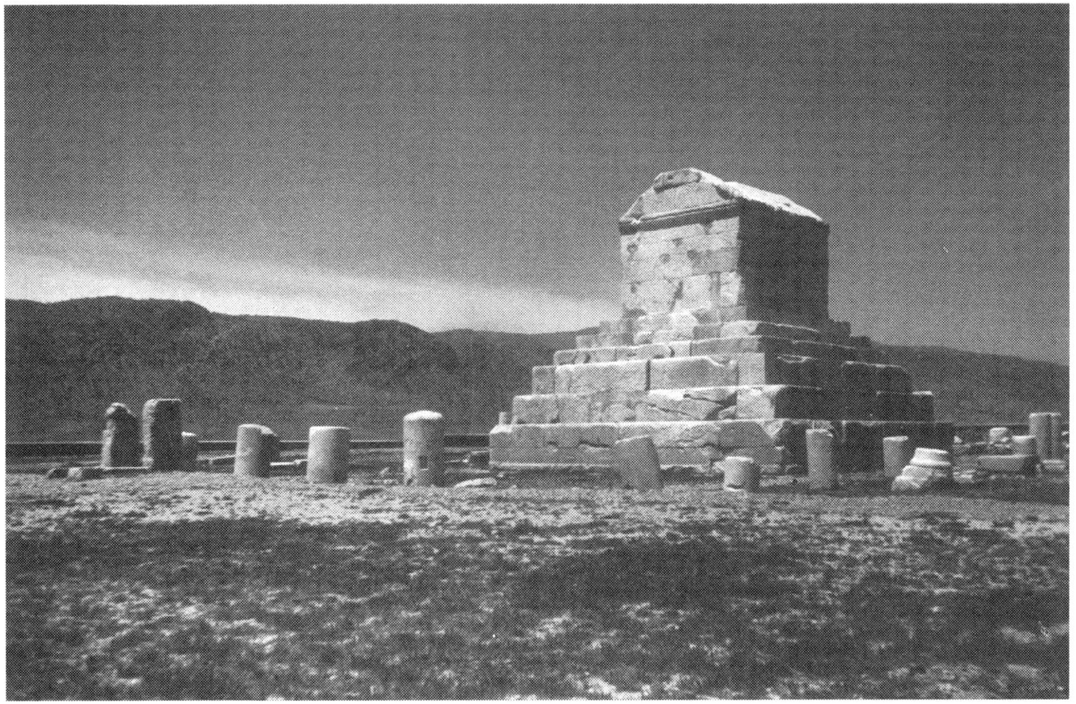

Pasargadae, Tomb of Cyrus 1959

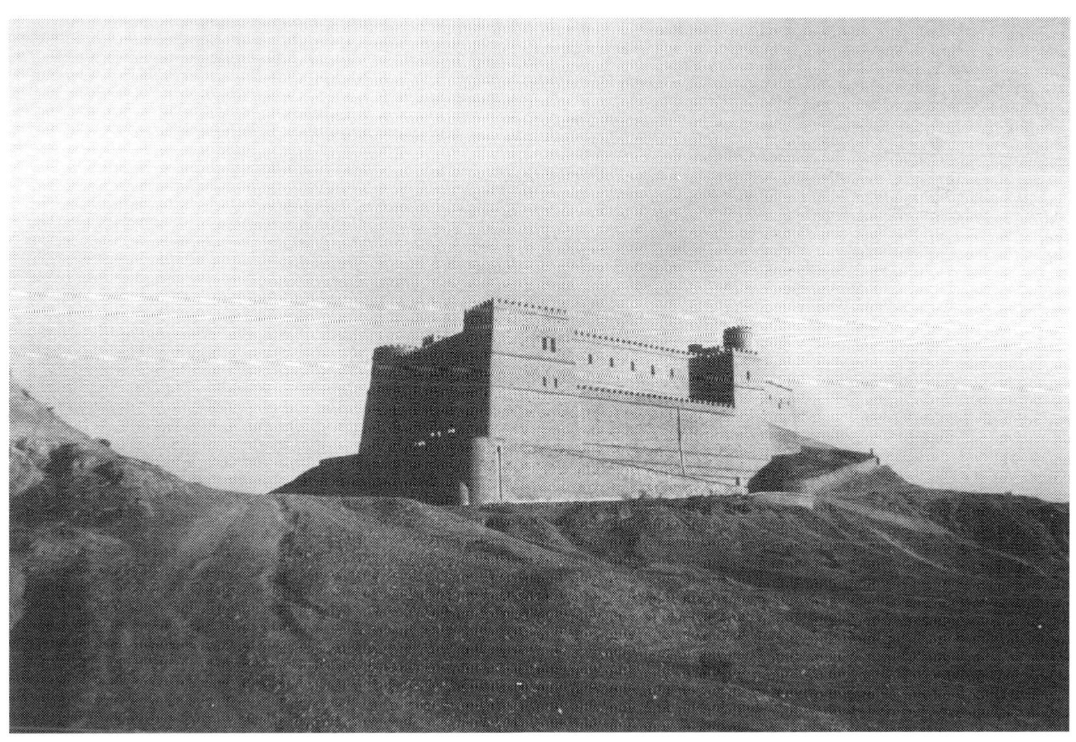

Castle built by French Mission, Susa 1959

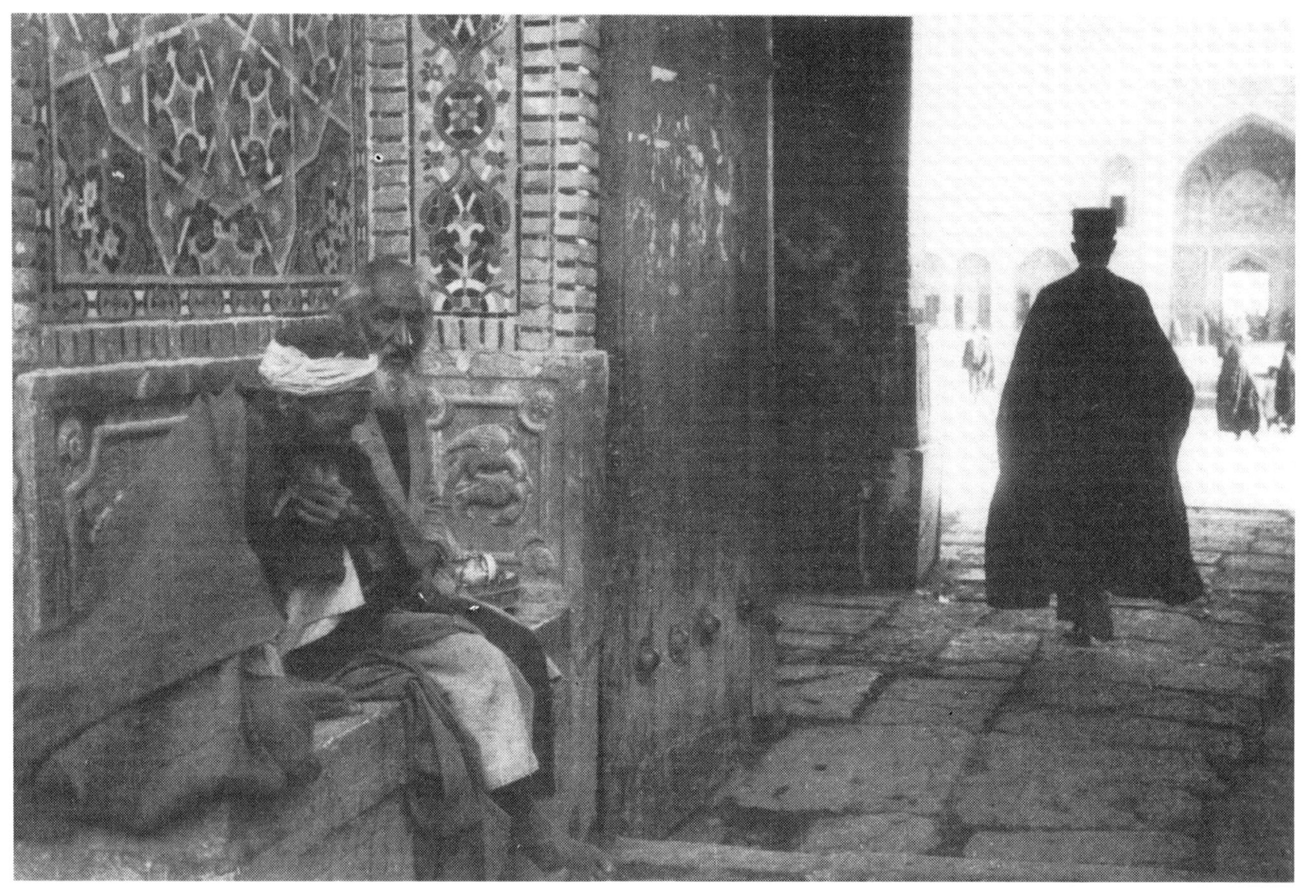

Beggars at Qum 1931

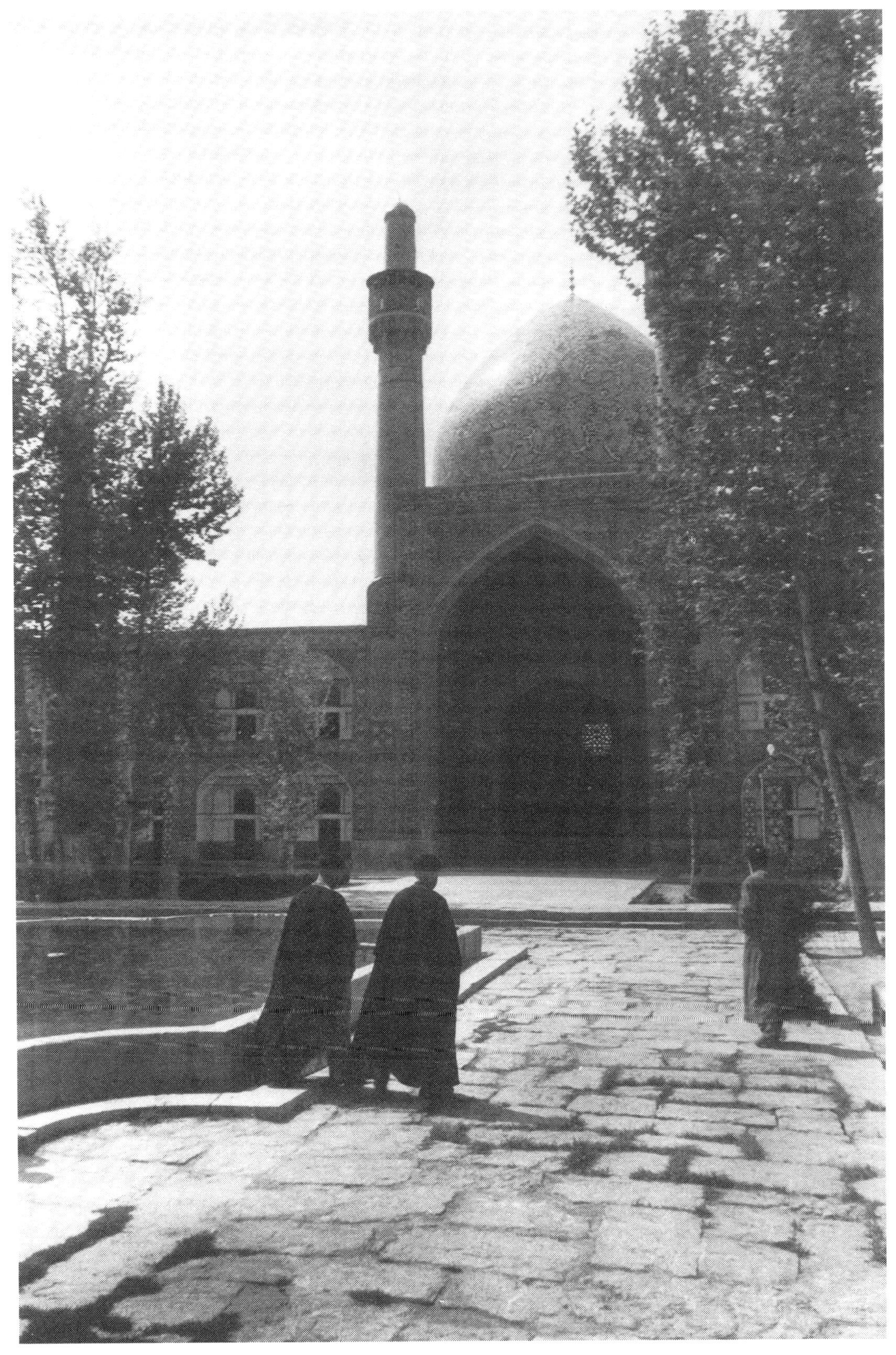

Madrasah, Isfahan 1959

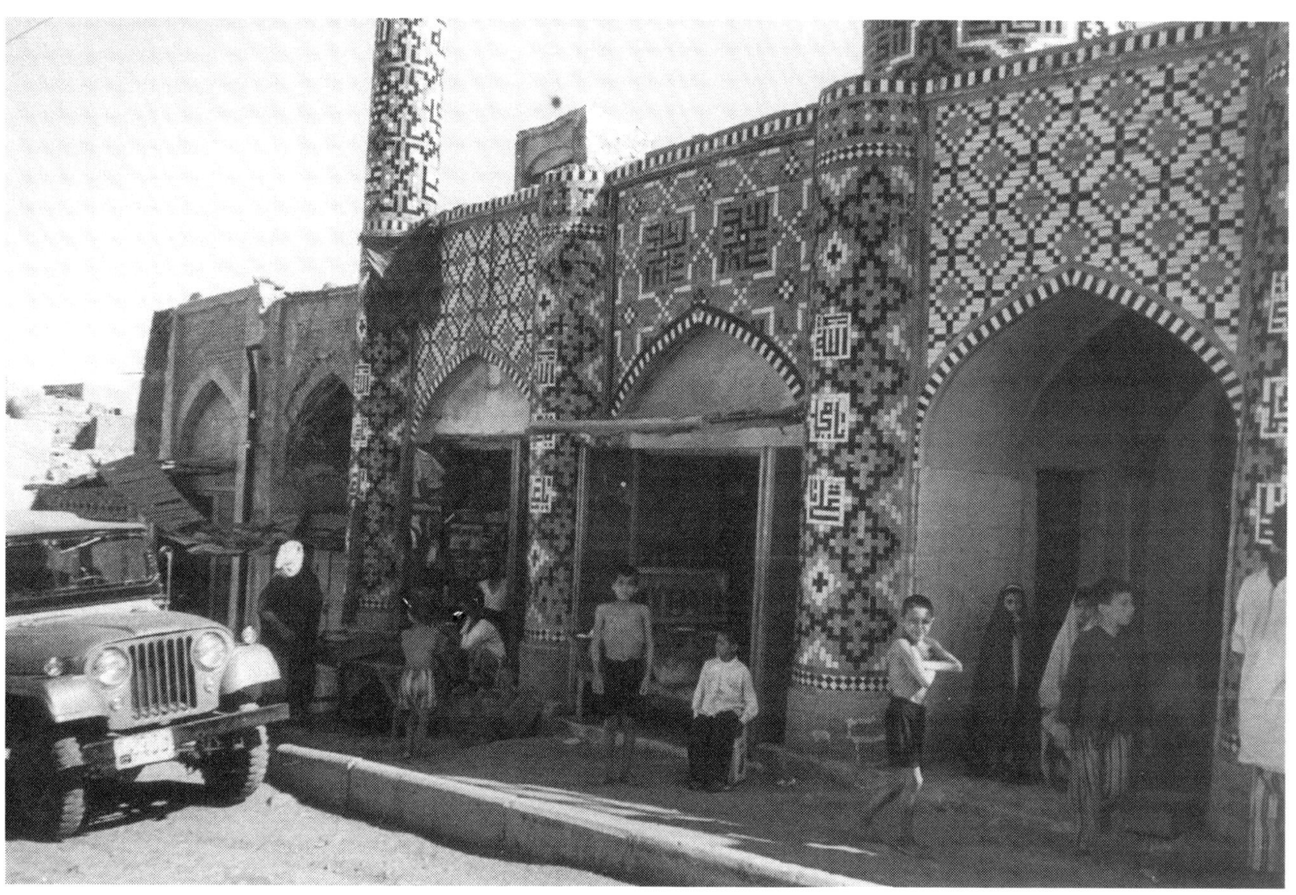

Shuster 1959

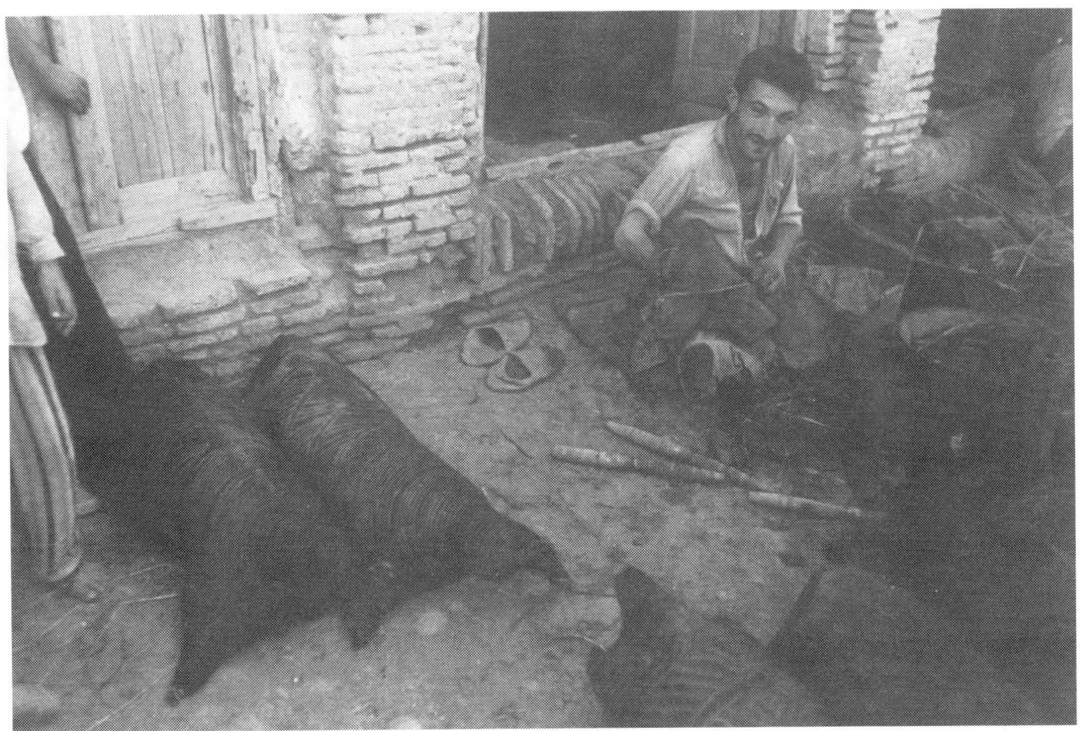

Making water-skins, Dizful 1959

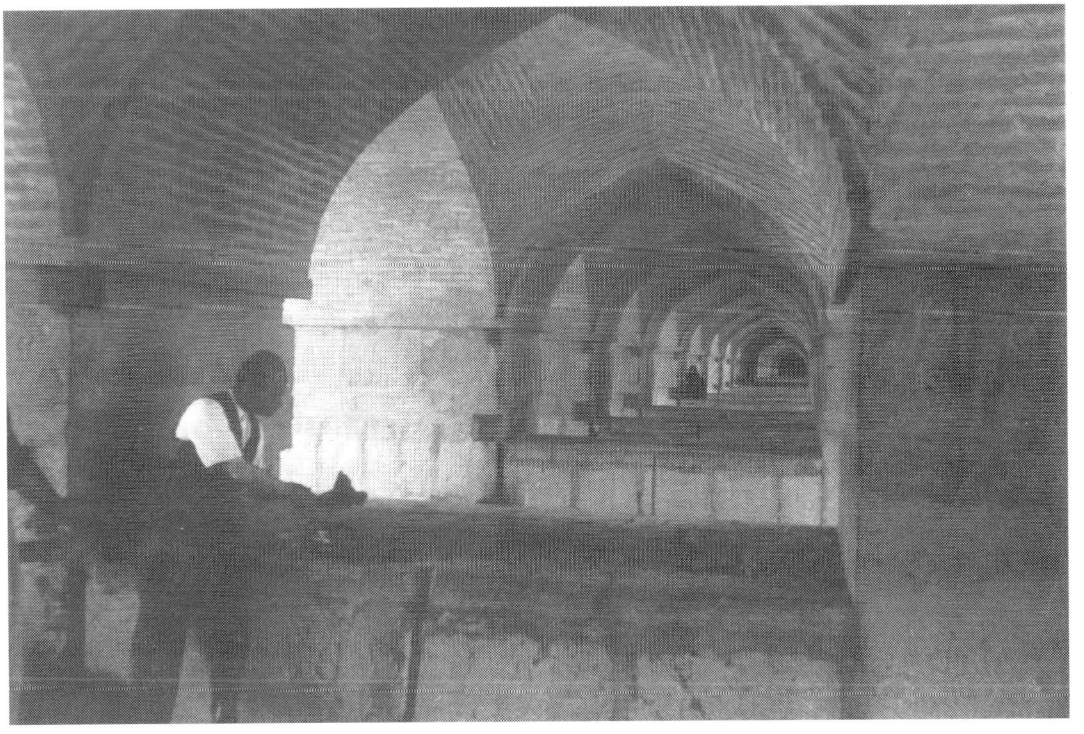

Isfahan 1959 "Under the Bridge"

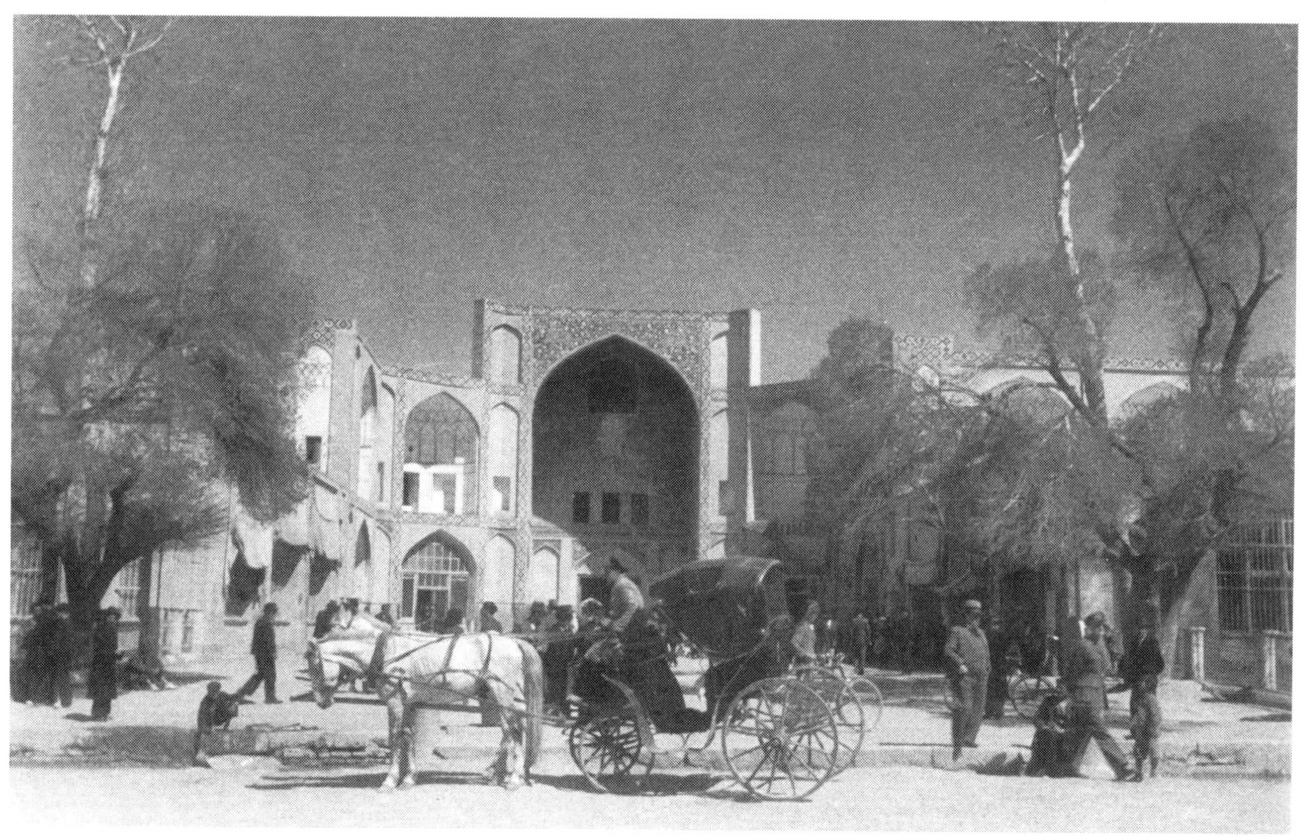

Isfahan 1943

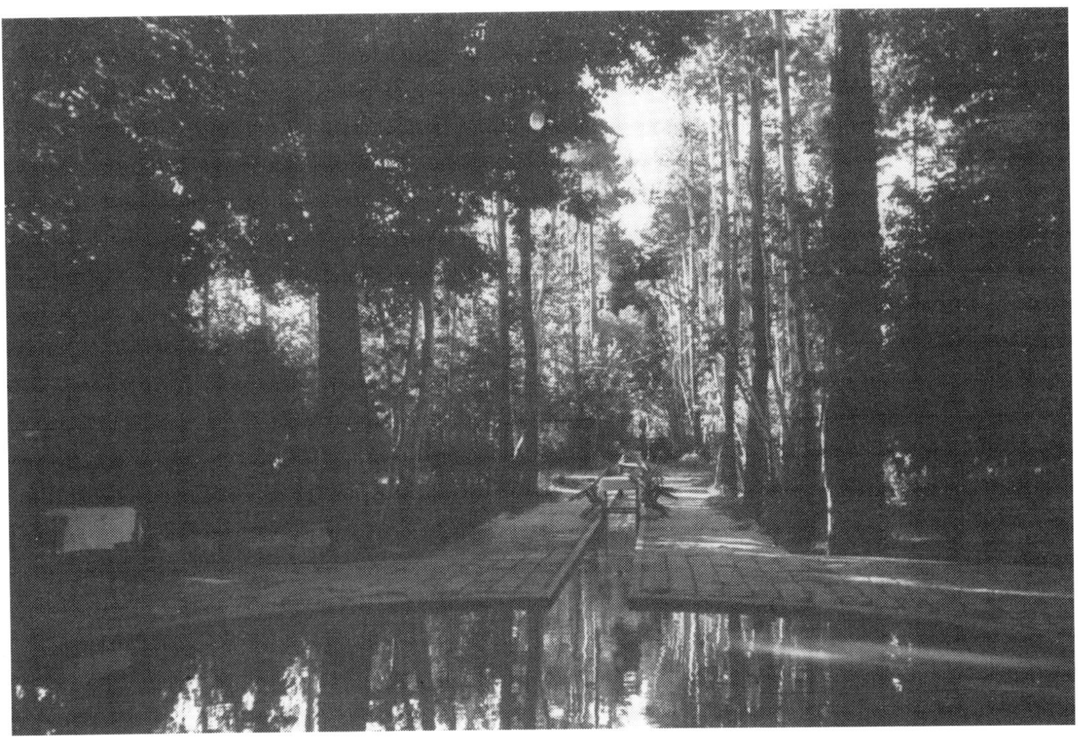

Shiraz 1959

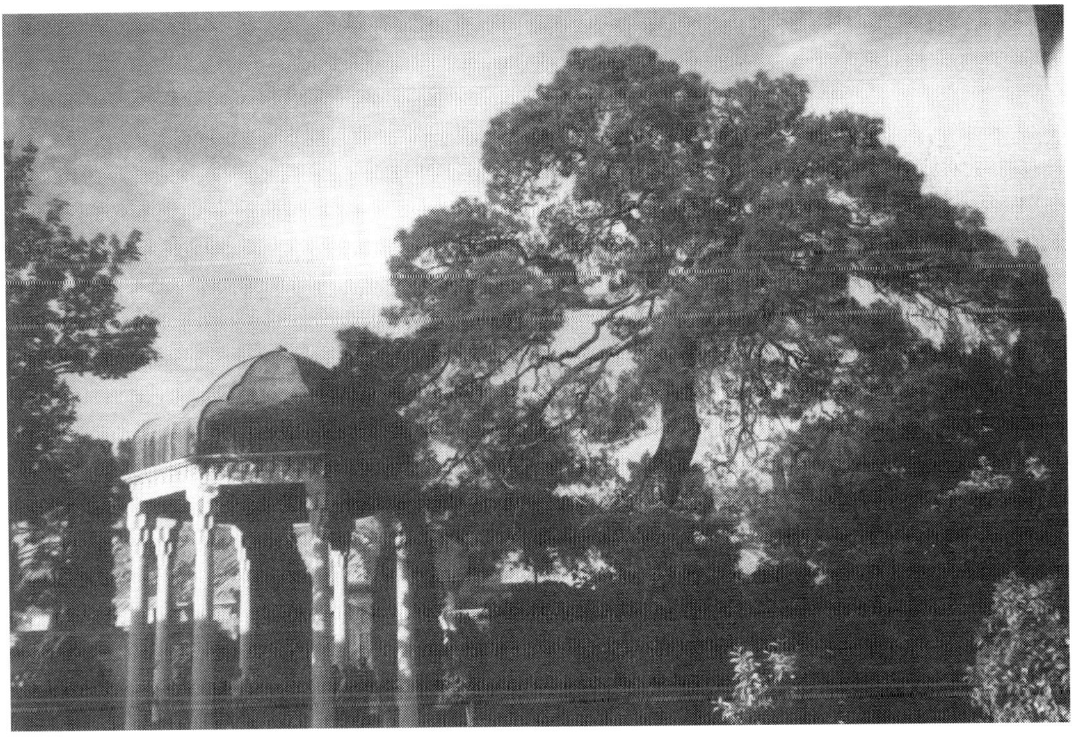

Tomb of Hafez, Shiraz 1959

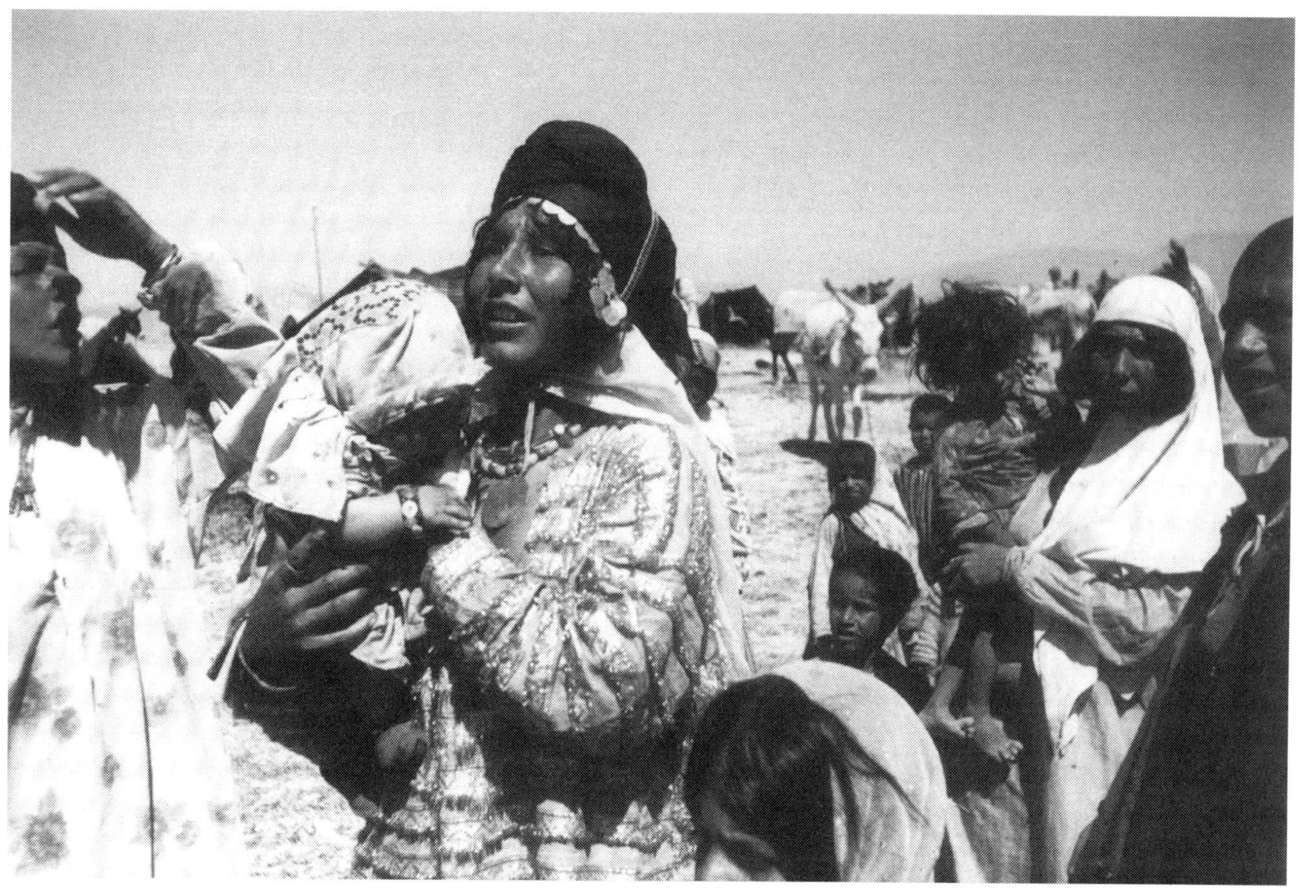

Kashgai tribeswoman, Persepolis 1959

CHRONOLOGY

1893	Born January 31st in Paris to Robert and Flora Stark.
1894	Sister Vera born.
1906	Loses part of her scalp in accident in Italian carpet factory.
1911	Enters Bedford College, London, boarding with Viva Jeyes. Meets Professor W. P. Ker who becomes her mentor. Robert Stark leaves his family and emigrates to Canada. Flora Stark remains in Italy.
1914	On the outbreak of war works briefly in the censorship department before volunteering as a nurse in G. M. Trevelyan's Italian ambulance unit.
1915	Serves in hospitals near Italian-Austrian front. Witnesses famous Italian retreat from Caporetto.
1921	Begins learning Arabic from her home at La Mortela near Genoa.
1923	Death of W. P. Ker while climbing with F.S. on Monte Rosa.
1926	Herbert Young, a friend of her father's, makes her his heir to the Casa Freia at Asolo, the Venetian hill town which becomes her home. Vera dies of septicaemia, following a miscarriage, leaving four young children.
1927	Enrols at the School of Oriental and African Studies in London to continue Arabic classes.
1927	December-March 1928. Spends winter in Broumana, near Beirut, improving Arabic.
1928	Visits Damascus. Expedition to Jebel Druze with Venetia Buddicom. Returns to Italy via Transjordan, Palestine and Egypt.
1929	Arrives in Baghdad.
1930–1	Visits Castles of the Assassins, and travels through Western Persia.
1932	*Baghdad Sketches* published by *Baghdad Times.*
1933	Travels in Persia earn the Royal Geographical Society's Back Memorial Grant.
1934	*Valleys of the Assassins* published to critical acclaim.
1935	First journey to the Hadhramaut in South Arabia (now Yemen).
1936	*The Southern Gates of Arabia* published.
1938	Wakefield Expedition to Hadhramaut with archaeologist Gertrude Caton Thompson.
1939	April-May: visits Crusader Castles in Syria. September: sent to Aden as assistant to Stewart Perowne in Government Information Department.
1940	February: travels to Sana'a, the Yemeni capital, to counter pro-Axis influence. June: Italy enters war - Sana'a remains neutral. September: transferred to Cairo. October: *Winter in Arabia* published. December: begins work recruiting Egyptians for anti-Axis "Brotherhood of Freedom".
1941	Divides time between Cairo and Baghdad, where she establishes Iraqi branch of the Brotherhood. May: endures siege of British Embassy by nationalist government of Rashid Ali al Gailani. Remains mostly in Baghdad till July 1942.
1942	April: visits Northern Iraq and Iraqi Kurdistan. July-October: on leave in Cyprus. Encouraged by Sir Sidney Cockerell begins work on first volume of autobiography *Traveller's Prelude.* November: Flora Stark dies in the USA. *Letter from Syria,* based on 1927-8 travels in Levant, published. Receives Founder's Gold Medal from Royal Geographic Society for travels in South Arabia.
1943	February-March: Visits Wavells in India. Drives back through Persia, selling government car at considerable profit in Tehran. October-June 1944: tours USA to defend British policy of restricting Jewish immigration into Palestine.
1944	August-January 1945: stays in England, writing *East is West.*

1945	February: flies to India to work with Lady Wavell in mustering support for Empire among Indian women. May 3rd VE Day. July: returns to Casa Freia in Asolo. Works for Ministry of Information setting up reading centres in Italy under auspices of Allied Military Government.
1947	October: marries Stewart Perowne.
1948	February: joins Perowne in Barbados, where he was Deputy Governor. July: returns to Italy and remains in Europe apart from visit to West Indies in December-March 1949. *Perseus in the Wind,* essays, published.
1950	March: joins Perowne in Libya where he has been appointed Adviser to new government of King Idris. *Traveller's Prelude* published. Visits Greece.
1951	March: returns to Asolo, deciding marriage is over. Honorary Degree from Glasgow University. *Beyond Euphrates* (autobiography vol. II), published.
1952	Marriage dissolved. Autumn: travels in Greece and Turkey.
1953	June: awarded CBE in Coronation Honours. *Coast of Incense* (autobiography vol. III) published.
1954	March-August: travels in Syria, Turkey and Greece. *Ionia: A Quest* published.
1956	May-July: visits "lost" Byzantine cities in Northern Syria and Southern Turkey. *The Lycian Shore* published.
1957	Autumn: visits Turkey, Mosul and Baghdad.
1958	July-August: visits Northern and Central Turkey. *Alexander's Path* published.
1959	Visits Iran, Greece, Lebanon and Kenya. *Riding to the Tigris* published.
1960	Visits Tunisia, Greece and Turkey
1961	Visits Cambodia, China, India, Turkey, Lebanon and Egypt. *Dust in the Lion's Paw* (autobiography vol. IV) published.
1962	Visits central Turkey.
1963	Visits Istanbul. *The Journey's Echo* - an anthology, published.
1964	Begins building Montoria, new house outside Asolo.
1966	Sells Casa Freia to Asolo municipality. Visits Greece and Turkey. *Rome on the Euphrates* published.
1967	September: visits Afghanistan, Samarkand, Bukhara and Tashkent.
1968	Visits Afghanistan and Greece. *The Zodiac Arch*, anthology, published.
1970	November: visits Nepal. *The Minaret of Djam* published.
1972	Becomes Dame of the British Empire in New Year's Honours.
1973	Sells Montoria, moves to flat in Asolo. Visits Kashmir.
1975	Visits Bodrum and Istanbul in Turkey.
1976	March: visits Sana'a, North Yemen and Southern Turkey. Stays with Queen Mother in Castle of Mey. *A Peak in Darien*, essays, published.
1977	To Syria with BBC television crew for journey down the Euphrates on specially constructed raft.
1984	Revisits Nepal with BBC television crew.
1985	Receives Freedom of the City of Asolo.
1993	31 January: celebrates 100th birthday.
1993	9 May: dies at her home in Asolo.

All of Freya Stark's books are published by John Murray with the exception of eight volumes of letters edited by Lucy and Caroline Moorehead, published by Michael Russell between 1974 and 1982. A book of photographs of South Arabia, *Seen in the Hadhramaut*, appeared in 1938. *Over the Rim of the World*, a selection of letters edited by Caroline Moorehead, published by Murrays in association with Michael Russell, appeared in 1988. Books about Freya Stark include *A Tower in the Wall* by Alexander Maitland (Blackwood 1982), *Traveller Through Time* by Malise Ruthven (Viking 1986), *Freya Stark* by Caroline Moorehead (Penguin 1986) and *Freya Stark – a biography* by Molly Izzard (Hodder & Stoughton 1993).